VICTIMS OF JUSTICE

REVISITED

VICTIMS OF JUSTICE

REVISITED

Thomas Frisbie
and
Randy Garrett

NORTHWESTERN UNIVERSITY PRESS
EVANSTON, ILLINOIS

Northwestern University Press
Evanston, Illinois 60208-4170

Printed in the United States of America

10   9   8   7   6   5   4   3   2   1

ISBN 0-8101-2236-7

Library of Congress Cataloging-in-Publication Data

Frisbie, Thomas.
    Victims of justice revisited / Thomas Frisbie and Randy Garrett.
    p. cm.
    Includes index.
    ISBN 0-8101-2236-7 (trade paper : alk. paper)
    1. Murder—Illinois—Naperville—Case studies. 2. Trials
(Murder)—Illinois—Naperville—Case studies. 3. Nicarico, Jeanine.
4. Cruz, Rolando—Trials, litigation, etc. 5. Hernandez, Alejandro
(Alex Hernandez)—Trials, litigation, etc. 6. Buckley, Stephen,
1963– —Trials, litigation, etc. 7. Dugan, Brian, 1956– —Trials,
litigation, etc. I. Garrett, Randy. II. Title.
HV6534.N17F75 2004
364.152′3′0977324—dc22

                                                         2004020385

CONTENTS

PHOTOGRAPHS

AUTHORS' NOTE

OUR INVOLVEMENT IN THIS CASE started in separate ways.

Thomas Frisbie, a reporter for the *Chicago Sun-Times*, was assigned to the case by assistant city editor Dick Mitchell in 1986. It turned out to be an assignment that was to last many years.

Randy Garrett, as this book will describe, became interested in the case during the first trial. He saw it as a modern mystery and felt it was a case he would like to write a book about. Eventually, a *Chicago Tribune* columnist called him "the leading lay expert on the case."

In researching this book, we were assisted by a great number of people. We wish especially to thank John Sam, Mary Brigid Kenney, Edward Cisowski, and the late James Teal, whose determination to stand up for the truth even at high personal cost helped bring this story to light.

We also wish to thank Roger and Karen Schnorr and Michael and Sheree Ackerman for their help and to extend our sympathy to them and the other victims in this story, including Thomas and Patricia Nicarico.

Many lawyers helped us greatly in our research. Our thanks go to them all, especially Gary Johnson, Michael Metnick, Jeffrey Urdangen, Lawrence Marshall, John Hanlon, Joseph Birkett, Jed Stone, Terry Gillespie, Frank Wesolowski, Terry Ekl, Nan Nolan, Tom Breen, Matthew Kennelly, Marlene Kamish, Jeffrey Winick, Scott Turow, Tom Laz, William J. Kunkle Jr., Carol Anfinson, Jane Raley, Brian Telander, Jeremy Margolis, Patrick Tuite, Thomas

McCulloch, Sara Bartosz, G. Flint Taylor, Ronald Sadowski, Cliff Lund, Darren Watts, Daniel Collins, James Sotos, John Kinsella, Anne S. "Andi" Kenney, Tim Gabrielsen, Thomas F. Sullivan Jr., Thomas P. Sullivan, and Susan Valentine.

Some people who helped us asked that we not use their names. Nevertheless, we wish to acknowledge our debt to those associates of Brian Dugan, surviving victims of Brian Dugan, DuPage County employees, jurors, and law enforcement authorities whose willingness to share information was immensely valuable.

Several journalists who did an excellent job covering the case shared their insights with us. We especially wish to thank Rob Warden, Antone "Tripp" Baltz III, Eric Zorn, Dan Rozek, Janet Petsche, Hal Dardick, Steve Warmbir, Ted Gregory, Chana Bernstein, Michael Briggs, Andrew Herrmann, Jay Foot, and Char Bercaw.

Several people who provided us information have passed away since we started this project. Nevertheless, we would like to acknowledge our indebtedness to Bruce Bartimes, John and Marilyn Buckley, Patty Levi, and Melvin Lewis.

Our thanks also for the invaluable help of Thomas Atchison, James Barry, the Reverend Richard Bennett, Mark Benson, Richard Besler, J. D. Bowers, Brad Bowman, Locke Bowman, Carol Brusatori, Michael Buckley, Norma Buckley, Jane Buikstra, Michael Callahan, Bill Clutter, Pat Colander, John J. Conway, Bob Covelli, Dora Cruz, Dan Davis, John Eierman, Judge Thomas Fitzgerald, Gayle Franzen, Ellen Frisbie, Felicity Frisbie, Margaret Frisbie, Patrick Frisbie, Paul Frisbie, Margery Frisbie, Richard Frisbie, Teresa Frisbie, Gary Garretson, Philip Gilman, John Gorajczyk, Larry Green, Judith Halper, Charles Hamm, David Hamm, Haydee Hernandez, Nic Howell, Adonna Jerman, Louis Jerman, T. J.

Johnson, Kelly Kennedy, Joe King, Richard Klicki, Edward Kowal, Cynthia Kraft, Bernice Larson, Ron Logeman, Owen Lovejoy, Annmarie Mahany, Anne Malone, Michael Malone, Marty Mannion, David Masenheimer, Kris Mason, Veronica McBurse, Sue McKenna, Ronald Mehling, Marilyn Meyer, John Millner, Marianne Narro, James and Burlene Nickel, Joe Pavia, Gary Peterlin, Steve Quast, John Rea, Wilfredo Rios, Jon Ripsky, Jim Ritter, Francis Rodrigue, Dan Rozek, Nila Simane, Klyde Snodgrass, Marilyn Stadler, Nancy Suero, Eloise Suk, Wanda Mowery-Thompson, Dr. Robert A. Thorud, Craig Tobin, Russell Tuttle, Michael Uvenile, Anton Valukas, Nancy Van Pelt, Katie Volness, Timothy White, and Dr. Benjamin Yocke.

We wish to acknowledge our debt to our agent for the first edition of this volume, Jane Dystel; our first editor, Stephen S. Power; and the editor of this revised and much expanded edition, Susan Betz.

The quotations in this book are for the most part taken from official records or from tape-recorded interviews. In some cases, the quotations have been edited to fix grammatical errors or to omit extraneous references. The dialogue that is not taken from official records is reconstructed based on the memory of one or more participants.

The quotations at the beginnings of the fourth, fifth, and eleventh chapters are taken from *In Spite of Innocence* by Michael L. Radelet and Hugo A. Bedau.

CAST OF CHARACTERS

MELISSA ACKERMAN. Seven-year-old girl from Somonauk, Illinois, murdered in 1985.

CAROL ANFINSON. DuPage County public defender for Stephen Buckley.

JOSEPH BIRKETT. DuPage County state's attorney, 1996–present.

TOM BREEN. Lawyer for Rolando Cruz.

STEPHEN BUCKLEY. Defendant charged in 1984 with the murder of Jeanine Nicarico.

ARTHUR BURRELL. Witness testifying against Rolando Cruz and Alejandro Hernandez.

MICHAEL CALLAHAN. Juror at the 1985 trial.

EDWARD CISOWSKI. Illinois State Police commander. Investigated Brian Dugan's admissions.

BILL CLUTTER. Legal investigator for Alejandro Hernandez.

ROLANDO CRUZ. Defendant charged in 1984 with the murder of Jeanine Nicarico.

ERNIE DIBENEDETTO. Lawyer for Robert Winkler.

RICHARD DORIA. DuPage County sheriff.

BRIAN DUGAN. Murder suspect; later confessed to multiple crimes.

JOHN EIERMAN. Legal investigator for Rolando Cruz.

TERRY EKL. Lawyer for Tom Knight.

J. MICHAEL FITZSIMMONS. DuPage County state's attorney, 1976–84.

TIMOTHY GABRIELSEN. Illinois appellate public defender for Rolando Cruz.

TERRY GILLESPIE. Lawyer for Dennis Kurzawa.

JOHN HANLON. Illinois appellate public defender for Rolando Cruz.

JAMES D. HEIPLE. Illinois Supreme Court justice, 1990–2000.

ALEJANDRO "ALEX" HERNANDEZ. Defendant charged in 1984 with the murder of Jeanine Nicarico.

GARY JOHNSON. Lawyer for Stephen Buckley.

WILLIAM A. KELLY. Illinois Fifteenth Circuit judge, presided at DuPage Seven trial.

MATTHEW KENNELLY. Lawyer for Rolando Cruz.

MARY BRIGID KENNEY. Illinois assistant attorney general who resigned.

ROBERT KILANDER. First assistant DuPage County state's attorney, 1984–91.

PATRICK KING. Assistant DuPage County state's attorney, later assistant U.S. attorney.

JOHN KINSELLA. Helped prosecute 1995 trial. First assistant DuPage County state's attorney, 1996–2003.

TOM KNIGHT. Chief DuPage County criminal prosecutor.

EDWARD KOWAL. DuPage County circuit judge at 1985 and 1990 trials.

WILLIAM J. KUNKLE JR. Special state's attorney in DuPage Seven case.

DENNIS KURZAWA. DuPage County sheriff's detective. Testified about "vision" statement.

JOSEPH LARAIA. Lawyer for James Montesano.

TOM LAZ. Public defender for Rolando Cruz.

CLIFF LUND. Lawyer for Stephen Buckley.

GEORGE LYNCH. Lawyer for James Montesano.

TERENCE MADSEN. Illinois assistant attorney general.

ARMINDO "PENGUINO" MARQUEZ. Witness testifying against Alejandro Hernandez.

LAWRENCE MARSHALL. Lawyer for Rolando Cruz.

THOMAS McCULLOCH. Lawyer for Brian Dugan.

MARY ANN G. McMORROW. Illinois Supreme Court justice, 1992–present.

RONALD MEHLING. DuPage County circuit judge at 1995 trial.

RONALD MENAKER. Lawyer for Robert Kilander.

MICHAEL METNICK. Lawyer for Alejandro Hernandez.

JAMES MONTESANO. DuPage County sheriff's lieutenant.

KERRY MORRICK. Witness testifying about finding Jeanine Nicarico's body.

JEANINE NICARICO. Ten-year-old girl from Naperville, Illinois, murdered in 1983.

PATRICIA AND THOMAS NICARICO. Parents of Jeanine Nicarico.

NAN NOLAN. Lawyer for Rolando Cruz.

ROBERT A. NOLAN. DuPage County circuit judge for Stephen Buckley's 1986 evidentiary hearing.

REVEREND MICHAEL O'KEEFE. Pastor of St. Raphael's parish in Naperville.

BARBARA PREINER. DuPage prosecutor in Hernandez appeal.

JANE RALEY. Lawyer for Alejandro Hernandez.

DANIEL REIDY. Lawyer for Patrick King.

LOUISE ROBBINS. Shoeprint witness.

GEORGE RYAN. Governor of Illinois, 1999–2003.

JIM RYAN. DuPage County state's attorney, 1984–95.

JOHN RUIZ. Early suspect in the Jeanine Nicarico murder, never charged.

JOHN SAM. DuPage County sheriff's detective.

DONNA SCHNORR. Woman from Geneva, Illinois, murdered in 1984.

RICHARD STOCK. Helped prosecute 1990 trial. First assistant DuPage County state's attorney, 1991–95.

JED STONE. Lawyer for Rolando Cruz.

THOMAS SULLIVAN. Former U.S. attorney for the Northern District of Illinois, headed death penalty reform panel. (Not the same person as Thomas F. Sullivan Jr., assistant Kane County state's attorney.)

JAMES TEAL. Naperville police chief, 1973–89. Died May 6, 2000.

BRIAN TELANDER. Chief DuPage County criminal prosecutor 1984–88; later lawyer for Thomas Vosburgh.

PATRICK TUITE. Lawyer for Robert Kilander.

ROBERT TURNER. Witness who testified against Rolando Cruz.

SCOTT TUROW. Well-known author, lawyer for Alejandro Hernandez.

JEFFREY URDANGEN. Lawyer for Alejandro Hernandez.

THOMAS VOSBURGH. DuPage County sheriff's detective. Testified about "vision" statement.

ROB WARDEN. *Chicago Lawyer* editor and publisher. Later, executive director of the Northwestern University School of Law's Center on Wrongful Convictions.

FRANK WESOLOWSKI. Public defender for Alejandro Hernandez.

WARREN WILKOSZ. DuPage County sheriff's detective. Lead detective for the Nicarico case.

ROBERT WINKLER. DuPage County sheriff's lieutenant.

VICTIMS OF JUSTICE

REVISITED

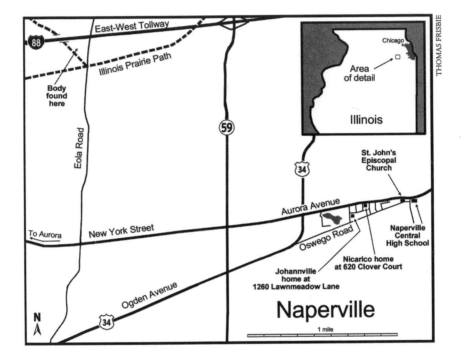

East-West Tollway

88

Illinois Prairie Path

Body
found
here

Eola Road

59

34

Chicago

Area
of detail

Illinois

St. John's
Episcopal
Church

Aurora Avenue

To Aurora

New York Street

Oswego Road

Naperville
Central
High School

Nicarico home
at 620 Clover Court

Johannville
home at
1260 Lawnmeadow Lane

Ogden Avenue

34

Naperville

1 mile

N

PART ONE

———————

VICTIMS

1

JEANINE NICARICO

Any criminal who acts alone and doesn't tell anybody has a very good possibility of escaping detection.

Thomas Atchison, former Kane County,
Illinois, sheriff's investigator

T HE SPUTTERING PLYMOUTH Volare irritated the scruffy young man like a stubborn lock that wouldn't give during a break-in. He'd already started the day in a sullen mood. That's why he'd skipped work that morning, why he was driving aimlessly and smoking marijuana. He wanted to forget that Denise had broken up with him, forget that he had no money, forget that nothing was going right. But the 1980 dark-green Volare wouldn't let him. Instead, it coughed at stoplights and hiccupped during low-speed turns, threatening to die. Something was wrong, he later said, probably the carburetor.

It was Friday, February 25, 1983, a bright winter afternoon, just a week after Denise had decided he wasn't the man she wanted. He was still living in the unfinished basement of her family's white frame house, where he had been staying for several months. Denise's father wanted the young man to move out, and on some nights he slept outside in his car in a dark sleeping bag he always carried in the trunk or on one of the seats in the car's tan interior.

Denise's house was in Aurora, Illinois, an old river town

being engulfed by metropolitan sprawl from Chicago, some thirty-five miles to the east. Around the young man, big money was coming to the area. Aurora and its next-door neighbor, Naperville, were rapidly adding spacious subdivisions and gleaming office buildings quite unlike the run-down rooming houses and apartments in the old Aurora neighborhood called East Aurora that he'd occupied before Denise's family had taken him in. The people moving to the area also were different—well educated, on their way up economically and eager to create a safe environment far from big-city violence. With about seventy-five thousand residents, Naperville had become the largest city in DuPage County, which was itself the fastest-growing county in the Midwest and the fifth wealthiest in the country. In 1997, Naperville would be selected in a national survey as the most "kid-friendly" city in the United States.

He was a medium-built man with medium-length dark brown hair and no beard or mustache. For nearly three months, he'd had a job as an ink mixer at the Art Tape & Label Corp. It wasn't a bad job for an unskilled laborer who'd just gotten off parole for burglary and arson, but he detested it. It didn't pay enough to solve his money problems, and he had always resented being told what to do. That was partly why he had decided to skip work for the fourth time in seven weeks. Today he was going to do what he felt like doing.

In a better-run criminal justice system, he would have been in prison or getting help in turning his angry life away from burglaries, violence, and drugs. Three times he'd been sent to a state penitentiary, but when he got out, his time behind bars seemed only to have made him worse. Aurora straddled the borders of two counties—DuPage and Kane—and the courts in each seemed uninter-

ested in him as long as his case records reflected successful prosecutions through plea bargaining. Several times, serious charges
against him were dropped for no clear reason. On other occasions,
authorities settled for a guilty plea with no jail time. No one relished risking an acquittal, which would erode the high conviction
rates that prosecutors liked to tout during elections.

In fact, he was a prime example of the problems caused by
the prosecution complex, a mind-set that spurs some prosecutors,
police officers, and judges across the country to pursue convictions at all costs in high-profile cases while settling for routine
treatment of lesser crimes that don't generate publicity. The
complex—in which public relations and concerns about political
ramifications can sway decision making, perhaps unconsciously—is most noticeable when an angry community is
demanding justice. In those cases, it can lead juries to demand less
evidence to convict unpopular defendants than they would normally require. It can make authorities believe it is their duty to
win a conviction. They begin to see the defendant and the criminal justice system's burdensome proprieties as foes that must be
outwitted.

The prosecution complex can lead police officers to tell a witness whom to pick out of a police lineup. It can encourage assistant state's attorneys to make deals with dubious snitches or
suppress information that would help a defendant. It can assure
expert witnesses that it's all right to fudge test results. It can push
judges to ignore the law if adhering to it would help a defendant
too much. Those suffering from the prosecution complex respond
to community pressure rather than focusing on the facts.

For the young man, the prosecution complex provided loopholes that often kept him out of jail. Time and again he'd been

arrested for crimes that were treated as routine, only to find himself right back on the street.

Six months previously, on August 23, 1982—just ten days after he'd gotten out of jail for burglary and arson—he'd attacked a twenty-two-year-old Clark service station clerk. He'd grabbed her late at night after she'd locked up her station on the east side of Aurora. He'd been in and out of the gas station much of the evening, saying he was trying to call his brother from the pay phone. After he'd grabbed her, he'd tried to drag her behind the building, covering her mouth with his forearm. She'd kicked and bitten him and had escaped when they'd tripped over a parking curb as they struggled. Police arrested him, but the case was dismissed. Had he been convicted of battery and found to be in violation of his parole for the earlier burglary, he still would have been in prison.

For him, that was a good break, but he didn't feel lucky. Looking back, he thought, it seemed he'd always been lonely and without enough money. When he was a child, his father's heavy drinking and unsteady employment meant the family never could stay in one place long. Later, people recalled that he was a sad child; some neighbors even took him with them on vacation to Minnesota to try to cheer him up. In the first high school he attended, he tried to hang out with the "greasers"—teenagers who fiddled with car engines, looked tough, and ignored schoolwork— but he'd been too quiet and too much of a follower. In his sophomore year, his family had moved twice, winding up in Aurora. He had registered at Aurora East High School but rarely attended and then dropped out.

Perhaps that background explained why he was attracted to the themes of alienation that ran through much of the music by the rock group Pink Floyd. He believed that Pink Floyd was the greatest rock band of all time, which annoyed Denise, who thought it was the Beatles. He listened to Pink Floyd's songs over and over, often with friends with whom he smoked marijuana.

He owed money to just about everyone. He'd bought the four-door Volare on February 14 for $5,600, and he would never make a single payment on his car loan, nor would he ever pay his car insurance bill. He hadn't replaced a hubcap that had been missing since a previous owner had changed a tire. He owed money to Denise's mother. He'd never even repaid his own mother for the scarce dollars she had contributed to his legal bills and fines.

He had hoped to marry Denise, but she had ended their relationship because he broke his promises. He had vowed to stop smoking. He had sworn he would stop using drugs. But he still smoked, and he used almost every paycheck to buy drugs. He didn't pay back most debts. Denise had decided he would never amount to anything.

Denise didn't know it, but he had long since become a habitual criminal. He had kicked in doors of businesses and grabbed what he could. He had been arrested in several home burglaries and told friends he'd committed dozens more. When he saw a chance, he took what he wanted. On occasions when he was feeling angry or depressed, he had attacked women and children, too.

"On or about February 25, 1983, [he] reached a point of anger that drove him to rage," an FBI psychological profiler later wrote, before the young man's identity was known. "A continuing problem with his life, possibly associated with a significant female . . . reached its peak."

At 620 Clover Court, not far from the streets where the scruffy young man was cruising, Patricia Nicarico, an outgoing school secretary, came home at noon to make lunch for her ten-year-old daughter, Jeanine. (It was her second trip; she had also come home at about 9:45 A.M. to check on Jeanine and make her a glass of chocolate milk.) On her way home, Patricia had stopped to buy Orange Crush and chocolate chip ice cream, special treats for Jeanine, who had stayed home from school after a bout with the flu.

Theirs was a pleasant house in which to spend a winter morning. In the paneled family room on the lower level, a metal TV stand held a color television set and videocassette recorder. Facing the TV set was a comfortable L-shaped sofa. Carpeting covered the family room floor and the stairs leading down to it. All seven rooms in the house, in which the family had lived for about eight years, were thoughtfully decorated and freshly painted. On the top level, one bedroom had been redone the previous spring after a debate over whether the new sheets should be rust- or ivory-colored. In the dining room was an elaborate sterling silver tea set.

Next door, Shirley Steck was making bridesmaid dresses in her sewing room. Shirley's daughter, Sonya, was Jeanine's good friend, and Shirley was fond of Jeanine, whom she described as all sweetness and bubbles. Shirley made breakfast for her on school mornings while Jeanine and Sonya waited for the bus. Jeanine hadn't shown up for breakfast that day, however, and Shirley knew that Patricia Nicarico had brought Jeanine home sick from school the previous morning. Shirley figured Jeanine was home by herself sick, and from time to time she peeked out a window to make sure everything looked okay.

Jeanine was cheerful, dimpled and pretty, the darling of the neighborhood and popular at Elmwood Elementary School, where she was an average student in the fifth grade. Her long, brown hair was shoulder length, her eyes were large and brown, and a small space between her front teeth added a wholesome charm to her bright smile. She loved horses, and her academic performance had improved after her fourth-grade teacher found a way to link horses to Jeanine's studies.

Jeanine's father, Thomas Nicarico, had left at about 6:45 A.M. for his engineering job with DeLeuw Cather & Co. in downtown Chicago. Her thirteen-year-old sister, Kathy, had caught a school bus at about 7:15 A.M. Her mother, Patricia, departed at about 7:20 A.M. to drive Jeanine's other sister, Christine, age sixteen, to high school. Then Patricia had headed to Ellsworth School in Naperville, where she was secretary to the school principal. She felt obligated to go to work because surgery had sidelined her for most of December.

The houses on tree-lined Clover Court had been dusted with a trace of snow early in the morning, but by now that snow had melted. Although the sun was shining, it was the chilliest day since early February, and the wind was gusty. Later that afternoon, the temperature would reach a high of thirty-one degrees Fahrenheit.

In a somewhat querulous mood after waking up that morning with nobody else home, Jeanine now greeted her mother by declaring that she wanted a grilled cheese sandwich.

"The only kind of cheese I have is Velveeta," her mother said, knowing her daughters disliked Velveeta cheese sandwiches.

Jeanine said she didn't care. Her mother fixed the sandwich, and Jeanine, cheered by the company of her mother, declared that it tasted good.

Patricia said, "See? If you'd try it once in a while, maybe you'd like it."

Jeanine munched quietly on the sandwich for a moment. Then she looked up at her mother and said something had happened that morning.

"Now, promise you won't get mad," she said.

"No. Tell me, Jeanine. What happened?"

"Well, somebody came to the door, Mommy."

"You didn't open it, did you?"

"Not really, but I guess I did."

"Jeanine, I told you—why did you open the door?"

"He was a nice man, Mommy. He came to the back door, and I didn't really open the door. I opened the inside door, but the storm door was locked, and I talked to the man through the storm door."

Jeanine, who was wearing a faded pink nightshirt with blue trim and a picture of the dwarf Sleepy, from Disney's *Snow White*, and the words, "I'm Sleepy," explained that the man was from the gas company, looking for a meter. Patricia was upset that Jeanine had opened the door, but she was pleased that her daughter obviously was feeling better.

"Here, Mommy," Jeanine said, handing Patricia her raincoat when lunch ended at about 12:30 P.M. "See? Don't worry. I'll be okay."

"I really don't want to go, Jeanine, but I have to," Patricia said. "Just be a good girl, and don't open the door for anybody. Remember, even if they ring the doorbell, nobody needs to come into the house when I'm not here. Just keep the door locked and call me, and I'll come home whenever you need me."

Patricia kissed Jeanine good-bye, locked the door, and drove off.

———

The young man was still driving through the area. He stopped at a church less than a mile from the Nicaricos' house and asked a church secretary about job openings. It was the second time a church employee had seen him there recently, and during the same period there had been several unsolved burglaries. His appearance made the secretary nervous. She told him there were no openings, but she wrote his name down on a piece of paper and stuck it into her desk. Later, after correcting her initial estimate, the secretary said she thought he'd left at 1:23 P.M.

According to the account the young man later provided to police, he was keeping his eye out for a place to steal tools. His usual method was to knock on a door. If someone answered, he asked if they needed yard work done or if he could use the phone. If no one answered, he broke in. At one point he had stopped at a house in Naperville, but the occupants were home, so he couldn't just kick in a door and take what he wanted. Instead, he borrowed a screwdriver.

The green Volare was acting up again as the young man reached Clover Court. A neighborhood woman later said she saw a car making a clumsy turn just after 1:00 P.M. Another woman said she thought the driver might be driving slowly so he could case her house for a burglary. She thought she saw him as she was watching a soap opera that ended at 1:30 P.M.

The young man decided to stop at another house, ring the bell, and see if anyone was home. He braked in front of a yellow split-level on a half-acre lot at 620 Clover Court.

The main entrance opened off the very wide, blacktop driveway, and the front of the house was lined with large evergreens. A gaslit black yard light flanked the driveway, which led to a two-car garage. A rural-style mailbox with the Nicaricos' name on it stood at the curb. A twenty-two-foot sailboat was parked on a trailer on the edge of the driveway, near the garage. A large tree partly screened the front door from the street.

He walked up the driveway. According to the account the young man later gave police, Jeanine answered the door when he rang the bell. She didn't open the door, but he could see her through a small window in it.

He asked if he could borrow a screwdriver or use the phone. She told him to go to the neighbors' house. She wouldn't open the door, and her answer made it clear she was home alone. He turned away but then changed his mind. He was frustrated and angry. He knew she was alone. He knew from experience he could kick open a locked door. He took what he wanted, and right now he wanted her.

Just a few minutes later, the green Volare was gone, and so was Jeanine. The front door of the house was hanging open, the splintered jamb recording the force that had smashed it. A Naperville man, Louis Jerman, saw a dark, medium-size car pull out of Clover Court onto Aurora Avenue that afternoon without stopping at the stop sign. Besides the driver, Jerman saw what he thought might have been a smaller person pushed up against the passenger door. Jerman had to brake his eastbound car to avoid a collision. Moments later, in his rearview mirror he saw the dark car head west down Aurora Avenue, pull around two cars stopped at a traffic light, run the light, and continue west.

Next door to the Nicaricos' house, Shirley Steck was still working on the bridesmaid dresses. She hadn't seen or heard a thing.

2

JOHN SAM

*A conviction cannot be supported by assumption, specula-
tion, or conjecture.*

People v. Schultz, Illinois Appellate Court, 1987

T HE VIOLENT-CRIMES UNIT at the old sheriff's office in
Wheaton, the DuPage County seat, was an uninviting
place to kill time on a Friday afternoon. The room was
cramped, the furniture battered, and the desks jammed together.
A new building was under construction on the west edge of the
city, but it would not open its doors for several months.

John Sam and the four other detectives in the DuPage
County sheriff's violent-crimes unit were relaxing at their desks at
3:30 P.M. They had little left to do in the half hour before their shift
ended, and they were making plans to go to the lounge at the
Viking Restaurant. Wheaton was the home of many evangelical
organizations, including Billy Graham's, and in 1983 liquor sales
were prohibited. The Viking, just outside the municipal limits, had
a liquor license and did a brisk business among the lawyers, judges,
and business executives who ran DuPage County.

When Patricia Nicarico's missing-child report came in from
Naperville with no details, it didn't particularly alarm Sam. He figured the kid was playing at a friend's house. On the other hand,
there was no particular reason to hang around the sheriff's small

offices. Sam and the other detectives got into a squad car and headed for Naperville, eight miles to the south. More than likely, Sam thought, the radio dispatcher would tell them the kid was back home before they got a third of the way there. Then, they could go straight to the Viking Restaurant.

Sam was, many people thought, DuPage County's best detective. During the previous year, he had led his unit in felony arrests, as he would that year and the next. There were no citizen complaints against him in his file. At age thirty-three, he already had silver hair, but he jogged regularly and kept himself in good shape. His clothes were informal on his own time and fashionable when he was on the job. He rarely carried a gun or badge, partly because it was hard to dress stylishly while carrying a gun and partly because he didn't want to seem like a heavy-handed cop. He bowled and socialized with the other detectives in violent crimes, but his blunt habit of speaking his mind kept him from being close to any of them.

Sam had learned to coax admissions out of people, to wrap up a case with a signed confession, while working child-molester cases. In those days, Sam wanted to avoid putting the youthful victims on a witness stand where they would be forced to relive their humiliating experiences. Even as a violent-crimes detective, he devoted most of his energy to interrogating people, winning their trust, and encouraging them to tell him their secrets. Physical evidence didn't much interest him, except as an aid in interrogation. Interrogations were his specialty.

Years later, other cops still talked about the way John Sam broke the Maurice Chevalier case. Chevalier, who had the same name as the French entertainer, was an executive at a suburban landscaping firm whose wife, Shirley, had been missing for three days. It hadn't been Sam's case, and Sam had been instructed not to waste time on it. Sam figured he'd take a crack at it anyway after his supervisors had gone home. He took Chevalier out for a couple of drinks while they were waiting for a polygraph operator, and by the end of the evening, Chevalier had told the whole story, including that his wife's body was buried near a highway in Michigan. Sam called the Michigan state police, who found the body. Chevalier pleaded guilty and was sentenced to forty years in prison.

The Chevalier case was an example of how Sam liked to work—on his own, without interference from the sergeant or lieutenant or the sheriff and following a personal code that said you didn't have to follow every rule in the book, but you did have to be sure that the right person went to jail.

"I hated having someone tell me what to do," Sam would say. "Don't tell me how I'm going to go about solving my case. Give me my case, give me the direction I need and the assistance I need. Help me solve my case. Don't tell me bullshit to do."

By the time Sam and the other detectives arrived, Jeanine had not returned to Clover Court. Moreover, it was immediately obvious that it was not a routine case: the front door had been kicked in. Nothing else seemed to have been taken, although Patricia Nicarico later noticed that a sheet and a small blanket from an upstairs bed were gone. The small family dog, Ruffles, had been found cowering in the laundry room.

A shoeprint on the door had been discovered by Naperville police officer John Bootz, the first police officer on the scene. Using his flashlight, Bootz had seen the mark in the dust that had been left by the bottom of a right shoe. Bootz had cordoned off the door with chairs to preserve it for the evidence technicians, who later photographed it with a special laser camera the sheriff's department had just purchased. The laser photo showed a curving pattern of rays in the heel area not visible to the naked eye. Bootz also had walked around the inside and outside of the house, checking doors and windows, but had seen no other indication that anyone had tried to get in.

Clover Court by now was crowded with sheriff's deputies, Naperville police officers, and FBI agents. Sam figured the FBI agents were there because the local newspapers and television stations had been making a fuss about missing children. There were not, in fact, many missing children in DuPage County. Still, the FBI was under a lot of heat, Sam knew, and its agents needed to look like they were doing something.

As Sam arrived, the Naperville police were leaving angrily, ordered away by the sheriff's officers. The Nicarico house was just outside Naperville's borders, so the missing-child case was technically in the county's jurisdiction. The Naperville police had been called first, but when the county officers had started arriving before Sam got there, they'd abruptly made it clear that the Naperville officers were not welcome. Now, DuPage County sheriff's detective Warren Wilkosz was in charge. Together with Sam, Wilkosz and another detective, Dennis Kurzawa, were considered the county's top detectives.

Sam wondered if Jeanine had disappeared during a burglary that had fizzled. Aurora, a short distance to the west, still had old, seedy neighborhoods along the Fox River, areas where street gangs could develop and flourish. Sam's experiences had taught him that burglars emerged from Aurora to raid the spacious houses in Naperville. He had described the pattern to others: "They grab the shit and run back where they can sell it. You don't go out to the boondocks to sell a VCR. In Aurora, there is a pawnshop on every corner."

At 5:00 P.M., Lewis Stonehouse, an evidence technician in the sheriff's department, arrived. Stonehouse took photographs of the outside of the house. As he did so, he noticed small footprints in the dirt outside the dining room window. Judging from the soil around the footprints, Stonehouse decided they must be fairly fresh. He photographed the footprints, which ran parallel to the house. Then he dusted the area around the door with a fine powder to look for fingerprints and took photographs of the shoeprint on the door.

At about 6:00 P.M., police brought two bloodhounds to the scene. Both dogs were given Jeanine's pillow to scent. Starting at the front door, they tracked a scent partway down the driveway and across the lawn to a point about eight feet from a tire track on the lawn near the curb. Another shoeprint was in the depression made by the tire track. There the trail ended. After scenting the shoeprint on the door, the dogs followed the same trail from the door to the street. One dog followed a slightly different trail from the street back to the front door.

Some of the sheriff's detectives started canvassing the neighborhood to find out if anyone had seen anything. No one had. With Naperville police already gone, the remaining officers could cover only a limited area. Some police officers made it as far as the church where the young man had stopped, given his name, and asked for a job, but they didn't go into the church or rectory to ask questions.

Louis Jerman, who had seen the car speed out of Clover Court, was not available for questioning. After spending a short time with his wife to celebrate their anniversary, he had left town for a business trip without ever hearing of Jeanine's disappearance.

After talking to Patricia Nicarico and getting a photo of Jeanine, Sam didn't wait to learn what the evidence technicians or bloodhounds might find. His first assignment was to find the meter reader about whom Patricia Nicarico had told him, the one for whom Jeanine had opened the door early that morning. Sam and Detective Thomas Vosburgh drove to the local office of Northern Illinois Gas Co. to obtain the meter reader's name. That evening, they found Henry Dunlap, age twenty, in his apartment in Aurora.

Dunlap said that he had been at the Nicaricos' house between 8:30 and 9:00 A.M. and that he had asked a girl at the house for the location of a meter. He gave Sam and Vosburgh permission to search his apartment and car. The detectives looked through drawers, behind furniture, in cabinets. There were no girl's clothes, stolen merchandise, blood, or weapons. There was nothing to indicate Dunlap had been involved in a crime.

The boots Dunlap had worn that day were in a NI-Gas van parked at the utility's offices. After some wrangling on the telephone with a nervous supervisor, Sam and Vosburgh confiscated the boots and took them to the sheriff's crime laboratory, where FBI technicians were on hand. The technicians said the boots didn't match the print on the door.

It was after midnight. Jeanine was still missing. Sam was worried, but there were no other leads. The detectives went home.

Next morning, there still was no sign of Jeanine. A plea for information put out by police set the telephones ringing. Sam started the day fielding calls. Some were bogus and others, though well intentioned, were of little help.

VICTIMS OF JUSTICE REVISITED :: **21**

Sam thought Jeanine might still be alive. Maybe some gang members from Aurora had driven off with her and then just dumped her somewhere. Maybe she was still wandering around, wondering how to get home. He couldn't imagine a burglar keeping her captive for long.

Another detective did get an intriguing call. Joann Johannville, the wife of a man who had an upholstery business in a garage behind the Nicaricos' house—the garage that had the extra gas meter that NI-Gas employee Henry Dunlap had been looking for—said she recalled seeing a rusty, light-colored automobile on Clover Court at about the time Jeanine disappeared. The front of the car appeared to sag downward somewhat on one side, she said. It had turned onto Clover Court, she said, and then had driven down the middle of the street.

Sam drove to Naperville to interview her. The Johannvilles lived in a one-story white ranch-style house on Lawnmeadow Drive, around the corner from the Nicaricos' house. Mrs. Johannville, a woman in her sixties, told Sam she had driven her husband, James, to his garage behind the Nicarico house. As she was returning home, Mrs. Johannville said, she saw a smooth-complexioned man in his twenties or thirties driving the intriguing car. He had been wearing a wool cap and granny glasses and had no facial hair. She had passed him at the corner of Clover Court and Lawnmeadow Drive. The driver's vacant, half-crazed expression had given her nightmares. She said he had looked "drugged out."

"I looked right at him when my car passed him at the corner," Mrs. Johannville said. "There was something like a blanket bunched up on the front seat next to him. He looked creepy."

For Sam, it was an unsatisfying interview. Mrs. Johannville

could provide few useful details. She could not describe the car very well and had not seen its license plate. Sam asked her to help an FBI artist create a composite image of the suspect. Mrs. Johannville didn't think she had seen him well enough, but she agreed to try.

Another neighbor of the Nicaricos, Carol Gheen, also said she had seen a four-door car driving down the middle of Clover Court at about the same time, but she thought the car was a dark color. She couldn't describe the driver and thought he might have been wearing a ski mask. Gheen said that the driver appeared to be looking right at her house.

Eola, a small hamlet northwest of Naperville and north of Aurora, was outside the booming real estate market of those cities. Its small cluster of old frame houses was surrounded by fields of corn and soybeans.

On the north edge of Eola, a nature trail called the Illinois Prairie Path ran along the abandoned right-of-way of a defunct interurban railroad. The rails and equipment had been pulled up years before, and trees and brush had overgrown the gravel bed. Part of the trail near Eola was lonely and little used because it was a dead end, cut off by a new tollway built to connect the fast-growing DuPage suburbs to Chicago. Most of the bicyclists and hikers who frequented the nature trails went farther east, where there were long stretches of unbroken trail, or west across the Fox River.

On February 27, Sunday afternoon, Charles Bryant, Kerry L. Morrick, and Gary Anderson called the sheriff's police from a farmhouse and said they'd seen a body near the Prairie Path. Sam and several other detectives drove out immediately.

The three men told the detectives that Bryant and Morrick had been hiking on the Eola trail with Morrick's two-and-a-half-year-old son. The men, both in their twenties, knew the trail generally was secluded. They said they hadn't minded because they'd been planning to smoke marijuana.

In a story that lawyers and investigators later came to believe omitted significant details, the three men said Bryant and Morrick had parked Bryant's blue van on the shoulder of Eola Road and had started walking west along the old gravel railroad bed. Tall towers carrying high-voltage power lines ran along the south edge of the trail. It was a bright winter day, and the ground, although frozen on the surface, was free of snow.

After the men had walked for a while, they'd arrived at a fork in the trail. They had chosen the path to the right and walked for about a mile to the end of the trail.

After they turned around and headed back toward the van, Bryant and Morrick said, they spotted a man and a woman in jogging clothes, standing at the edge of the path, looking down the embankment toward something on the east side. Bryant and Morrick said they did not stop walking, but as they approached, the couple turned and jogged away.

Bryant said he looked to see what had absorbed the joggers' attention. At first, he said, he thought he saw a long white box in a gully. Beyond it he saw something that looked like a dummy or mannequin. It was pale white, but it had a human shape to it. He took a few steps off the path and peered through the brush.

According to his story, Bryant climbed part of the way down the gully. He was pretty sure he saw a small corpse lying chest down in the brush. The head was resting on its right cheek and the face was visible. Bryant thought he saw a grotesque split in the forehead and scratches on the calves. There appeared to be a bandanna used as a blindfold, but it was pushed up over the left eye. The corpse was naked but seemed to have something pink, like a nightgown, underneath, with just a small section showing.

It was no mannequin. It was something that sent Bryant and Morrick off to Gary Anderson's house so someone else could see it, too. It was the brutally beaten body of a little girl.

Sunday had been a long day at St. Raphael's Catholic Church in Naperville for the young pastor, the Reverend Michael O'Keefe. Friends and relatives of ten-year-old Jeanine Nicarico were gathered for the second day of a prayer vigil, which had lasted through the previous afternoon and into the early evening. Neighbors, friends, and Jeanine's classmates were there to pray for her safe return.

Jeanine was a popular girl, and many of the pews in the church were full. Most of the children in her class at Elmwood School were there. So was her friend Sonya, who was seated next to her mother. Jeanine's parents were not present. They had stayed at home, waiting hopefully for news of their daughter, even if it came as a ransom demand. To prepare for any call from kidnappers, police had put monitoring equipment on the Nicaricos' phone line.

Father Mike, as he was known to the congregation, was close to the Nicarico family. He knew a few details of what had happened. At about 1:00 P.M. two days before, Jeanine had telephoned her mother and said she was watching TV. She'd heard her grandparents' hometown mentioned on a program, and Patricia suggested that Jeanine write and tell them about it.

But when one of Jeanine's friends had called at 2:40 P.M. to see if Jeanine was feeling better, no one had answered. When Kathy, one of Jeanine's two older sisters, arrived home at about 3:05 P.M., she had found the front door ajar, the striker plate knocked to the ground, and the molding inside the door frame almost totally torn off. An unfinished letter to Jeanine's grandparents was on the coffee table downstairs, and the TV was on. A dish of melted chocolate chip ice cream was on the table in front of the TV.

A short time later, Chris, Jeanine's other sister, was driven home in a car with some friends. Chris and her friends had searched inside and outside the house for Jeanine. There was no sign of her, however, and Jeanine had not been seen since.

As the congregation prayed, an FBI agent came to get Father Mike. The FBI wanted the priest present while they told the Nicaricos that they believed they had found their daughter's body. They also had to tell the family that Jeanine's body would be left in place overnight so technicians could inspect the area in daylight.

After recovering from hearing the shocking news, Patricia Nicarico asked if someone would please stay overnight so Jeanine wouldn't be alone, and the police assured her that someone would remain on the scene. Another officer went back to the church to bring Jeanine's sisters home to tell them.

Back at St. Raphael's, the pews still were full. Those attending the vigil saw someone walk up to the front of the church and talk to the Reverend Richard Bennett, an assistant parish priest. Suddenly, all eyes were focused on the front of the church. Was it good news? Had Jeanine returned home?

Sadly, the Reverend Bennett addressed the congregation. "I'm afraid our prayers are not going to be answered," he said. "The police have found a body. They are ninety-nine percent sure it is Jeanine's."

A moment later young girls were wailing and even men were crying. Their hopes were not going to be realized. Jeanine would not come home again.

At about 3:00 P.M. on Monday afternoon, John Sam stepped quietly into the morgue at Central DuPage Hospital, where an autopsy of Jeanine Nicarico was already under way, led by pathologist Frank Cleveland, who had come from Hamilton County in Ohio, where he was the coroner. Some of the other detectives were a little squeamish about autopsies, but Sam made it a point always to attend. He could get information at an autopsy that wouldn't be available in reports for days or weeks. Evidence of sexual assault, for example, could help point an investigation in the right direction.

The autopsy room was rank with strong chemicals. Two pathologists were methodically making incisions and taking notes. On the steel table, ringed by the coroner, deputy coroners, an assistant state's attorney, deputy sheriffs, an FBI agent, and hospital personnel, lay Jeanine's body. It had already been removed from the body bag in which it had been transported from the nature trail. The bag was discarded next to the table, littered with bits of twig and bracken.

Sam did not notice the bag. His whole attention was riveted on the stiff, pale body lying on the table. Its shape and size so closely resembled Nicole, the older of Sam's two daughters, that for a moment Sam imagined it was his own child before him. He felt instantly overwhelmed.

Sam pulled out a photo of Jeanine from his wallet, a color yearbook photo taken the previous fall. It was hard to see a resemblance between the dimpled girl with the radiant smile in the photo and the lifeless figure in front of him.

The injuries to Jeanine's head were fully visible. They were unimaginably brutal. Her face had been struck so hard that the underlying skull had been shattered. Later, Cleveland would say he had previously seen such wounds only in airplane crashes. Fragments of bone and cerebral tissue extruded from the gaping wounds. Her nose was broken and flattened and her hair was matted with dried blood. Blood had trickled from her pubic area, a likely sign, Sam knew, that she had been raped. (Swabs the pathologists took from her mouth, pubic area, and rectum would later confirm that.) Outlines of the twigs and leaves her body had lain on were imprinted on her skin. Her hands were a pure white. Still visible despite the blood and bluish-purple skin was the haunting face of a little girl, a little girl who looked as though she had been badly frightened.

Now that he knew Jeanine was raped and murdered, Sam figured he was looking for a sex criminal. A burglar wouldn't have abducted a young girl and left valuables in the house. A scared burglar, surprised by Jeanine, might have killed her to keep her from identifying him, but then Jeanine wouldn't have been sexually attacked.

A wave of bitter resentment and anger swept over Sam. He had investigated many vicious crimes, but nothing as savage as this. How could anyone do such a thing? As long as he carried a police badge, Sam knew, nothing would stop him until he found the inhuman monster who had murdered Jeanine Nicarico.

3

JOHN RUIZ

In almost every examination of a crime that goes
unsolved, there often is a tip or lead that particularly per-
plexes detectives, stubbornly defying their best efforts to
authoritatively confirm it or completely shoot it down.

Maurice Possley, *The Brown's Chicken Massacre*

OR AN INVESTIGATION to succeed, police need good
leads. Three days after Jeanine's abduction, though, they
didn't have any. Over the next few days they did everything they could think of to get the investigation on track.

Before the autopsy on Monday, authorities had converged on
the scene at the Prairie Path to process it as carefully as possible.
They cleared a path so they could approach Jeanine's body from
the east side, where a farmer's field separated the Prairie Path from
Eola Road. They noted that Jeanine's head rested next to an indentation as if she had been hit so hard that her head was driven into
the ground. She was facedown, and only her hair and a blindfold
wrapped around her head were visible. Her feet pointed toward
the Prairie Path. They took photographs and then moved the body
from the wooded area lining the path to the edge of the field. They
went through the area inch by inch on their hands and knees from
the edge of the field all the way to the Prairie Path, looking for
anything that might be evidence, but they found nothing but spat-

ters of blood. At about 12:25 P.M., they carried Jeanine's body in a body bag across the field to a waiting vehicle.

Authorities also sent a plane overhead to take aerial photographs of the scene, and a television news helicopter filmed it as well. Fresh tire tracks from an automobile ran down the path, and technicians made plaster casts of them in five places. They also made casts of two footprints found near the body. Bloodhounds brought to the area indicated that the killer had gone back up to the Prairie Path after dragging Jeanine's body to the place where it was found. Then the dogs stopped and raised their noses, indicating that they had lost the scent. The police surmised that the perpetrator had left the scene in a car or other vehicle.

Meanwhile, back in Wheaton, authorities announced they were forming a task force led by deputy chief Robert Soucek of the DuPage County Sheriff's Department and FBI special agent Joseph Burke. The new team, whose sole responsibility was to investigate Jeanine Nicarico's murder, was assigned an office in the new DuPage County government building on the west side of Wheaton. At least thirty officers from the Naperville Police Department, the Aurora Police Department, the DuPage County sheriff's office, the FBI, and the Kane County sheriff's office were assigned to the task force.

Also on Monday afternoon, police received a call from two tollway workers named Frank Kochanny and Roger Seppi, who said they had seen a car near the Prairie Path sometime between 2:45 P.M. and 3:00 P.M. on the day Jeanine had been abducted. They said the car, dark green with a tan or green interior, was visible from where they were working on the shoulder of the tollway. They saw the car turn around in a grassy area just off the path and head back down the path, away from the tollway. Kochanny thought it was a Ford Granada, but Seppi thought it might have been a Ford Fairlane or a Mercury Monarch, although he later agreed it might have been a Granada. One person was in the car, they said, a white male with medium-length, dark brown or black hair and no facial hair. He was in his late twenties or thirties. The car had Illinois license plates, and a hubcap was missing.

After the autopsy was completed at 5:35 P.M., Jeanine's body was released from Central DuPage Hospital to the Friedrich-Jones Funeral Home of Naperville. Deputy Coroner Edward Ley had used John Sam's photo of Jeanine to identify the body so that her parents would not have to view it. Thomas and Patricia Nicarico, however, insisted they wanted to see their daughter. They arrived at the funeral home at about 6:30 P.M., and at first Patricia did not recognize the body and thought there might have been a mistake. Then she saw a familiar scar on Jeanine's chin and a small gap in her front teeth, and she knew she was looking at her daughter.

On Monday night, an incident occurred that seemed significant only in later years. A dark green car with a missing hubcap pulled up at the Eola Road entrance to the Prairie Path. Inside were a young man and several friends, including a young woman. A police officer approached the car and asked its occupants what they were doing. The young woman, who did all the talking, said they had heard about Jeanine's murder and wanted to see where it had taken place. The officer told them that there was nothing to look at and that they couldn't stay, and the car drove off. Police made no note of the incident.

The next day, Tuesday, a volunteer group called Crime Stoppers of Naperville offered a $5,000 reward—its largest ever— for the arrest and conviction of Jeanine's killer. Also that day, an

FBI agent interviewed Kochanny and Seppi, who helped an FBI artist draw a second composite sketch of the suspect.

On Wednesday, the task force went back to the Prairie Path and swept through the area again, keeping an eye out for a murder weapon. This time, they found a piece of denim on a branch at the side of the path. It appeared to have been torn in passing from someone's jeans or coat. Some distance down the path, they also found a pair of sunglasses, an empty pack of Kool Light cigarettes, and a rusty license plate. They cataloged the items, but none of them appeared to be of any significance.

On Wednesday evening, visitation for Jeanine was held at the Friedrich-Jones Funeral Home from 4:00 to 9:00 P.M. Detectives photographed everyone on their way in and out. A sheriff's officer and an FBI agent saw one man briefly stay in his car after a second man got out and entered the funeral home. The first man remained in the car for a bit, then got out and wandered off. The plainclothes officers followed him, and when he noticed them, he began running. They ran after him and tackled him. It turned out that the man who had gone into the funeral home, James Raymond, was Jeanine's bus driver. The other man, an Aurora resident named Bradley Ross, had given Raymond a ride. When police asked him why he started running, he said it was because he saw men he didn't recognize following him. He said he didn't know they were law officers.

On Thursday, Jeanine's funeral was held at 10:00 A.M. at Friedrich-Jones, followed by a mass at St. Raphael's Catholic Church in Naperville. Once again, police photographed everybody.

Later, at an afternoon press conference, Deputy Chief Soucek read a statement saying, "We feel [the slayer] placed himself in a situation in which he went further than he planned." That wasn't what the evidence showed necessarily. The statement was designed to give the perpetrator an out if he felt inclined to make a confession. He could say that he didn't mean to kill Jeanine and at first had planned only a burglary.

Soucek said police were looking for a Ford Granada or Mercury Monarch, possibly missing a left front hubcap. Soucek also said authorities had determined that a shoeprint "significant in the investigation" was made by a type of hiking shoe called a Cloud Climber, which he said was sold by Morse and Fayva shoe stores.

On Saturday, Detective Warren Wilkosz interviewed James Johannville, who operated the upholstery shop behind the Nicaricos' house. Johannville said he was at the shop on the afternoon of the crime, but he kept the door to his shop closed because of the cold weather and had heard nothing.

Information was streaming in, and the crime lab was turning out test results, but so far nothing added up. The authorities needed a real suspect.

On March 8, nine days after Jeanine's body was found, detectives John Sam and Dennis Kurzawa went to visit John Ruiz. Ruiz was the son of Janie Ruiz, a cleaning woman the Nicaricos had hired a couple of weeks before Jeanine had disappeared, and police, Sam said, had discovered that Ruiz had a burglary record. Perhaps, police conjectured, Ruiz had heard something about the Nicarico house from his mother and had gone to burglarize it, not realizing Jeanine would be home. Then, panicked, he might have abducted the girl. Moreover, his Mercury Capri was green, the color of the car the tollway workers had reported seeing on the Prairie Path.

Ruiz lived in an apartment building in Aurora with his wife,

Elaine, and a baby daughter. When Sam and Kurzawa showed up, Ruiz told them that he'd been at work on the afternoon of the crime and had had nothing to do with it. But then he added something more intriguing. He said he'd had a dream in which he saw the victim lying dead in the woods near a creek.

"I thought we had something with Ruiz at first," Sam said later. "And then he came up with his vision—the dream. The dream was good enough for me at the time. You've got to fall off the chair—how did he know this stuff? Plus his mother was the ex–cleaning lady."

Ruiz said he'd had the dream the night the girl had disappeared but that he didn't tell anyone but his wife.

"Wasn't that the way it was?" he asked his wife, who was in the next room.

"Yes, that's right," she said.

But there was a flaw in Ruiz's dream story. He'd claimed he'd had the dream *after* reading about the crime in a newspaper, but he said he'd had his dream the day *before* the stories had appeared. Ruiz's story didn't add up. Ruiz couldn't have had the dream after reading a newspaper because no edition with the story had been published yet. Sam figured the dream story was bogus.

Other information continued to come in. Deputy Sheriff Paul Sahs determined that one of the shoeprints found near the body was made by Gary Anderson, one of the men who had called the police. The finding fit Anderson's story that he had walked close to the body.

On Wednesday, March 9, an Aurora man named Dean Schmunk called police to say that on the previous day he had seen a car similar to the one police were looking for. The car was driving on the east side of Aurora, Schmunk said, but he couldn't identify the driver. As it turned out, when Schmunk saw the car it was in the vicinity of the address where the young man with the dark green Volare had moved after Denise's family kicked him out. Police did not interview Schmunk for more than a year, however, and the car he saw never was identified.

Also on Wednesday, John Ruiz came to the task force offices, where he was read his rights, formally making him a suspect. He was taken to Central DuPage Hospital, where a crime lab worker took hair, saliva, and blood samples.

The DuPage County detectives were going to make sure they checked thoroughly into the Ruiz angle. The detectives quizzed him repeatedly. Detectives Sam and Kurzawa also took Ruiz to see a polygraph examiner from the Chicago firm of Reid and Associates. The examiner told Sam that Ruiz was too upset to produce a reliable test. That was no surprise; Sam and Kurzawa had done their best to upset Ruiz to see if he'd let anything spill. In fact, while they were in the car on the way to the polygraph office, Sam felt sure that the detectives had persuaded Ruiz that he was unlikely to survive the rest of the day. If Ruiz knew anything, Sam was certain, he would have let it slip right then, but nothing had.

Meanwhile, Frank Cleveland turned in the autopsy report, in which he concluded that Jeanine had died as a result of massive, crushing blows to the head. Cleveland said that three blows to the back of her head resulted in V-shaped lacerations and that the murder weapon was a blunt, cylindrical object one and one-half to two inches in diameter. There also were two larger blows to her forehead, he said. He also said that she had been raped vaginally.

Detectives continued to investigate John Ruiz. The next day, Detective Warren Wilkosz went to talk with Thomas and Patricia Nicarico and asked for more information about Janie Ruiz, the cleaning lady. But a few days later, when Wilkosz and Detective Albert Bettilyon took John Ruiz back to Reid and Associates for another polygraph exam, the investigation received a big setback.

Denying once again any involvement in the crime, John Ruiz passed the lie detector test. Sam figured Ruiz was just after the reward money. The authorities were going to need a better lead.

4

ALEJANDRO HERNANDEZ AND STEPHEN BUCKLEY

Most of the confession later proved to be inconsistent with the various facts of the murder. All of it having to do directly with the crime itself was worthless. Yet both police and the prosecution believed, perhaps in part because they so badly wanted to.

Willard Lassers, in *Scapegoat Justice,* on the 1956 conviction in Canton, Illinois, of Lloyd Elton Miller Jr., who was freed in 1967 and whose indictment was dismissed in 1971

EIGHBORS OF ALEJANDRO "Alex" Hernandez knew better than to believe all the stories he told. Alex, who lived in a working-class area on the east side of Aurora, had been diagnosed by experts as someone who, among other things, sought lots of attention and invented facts. Four years before, he'd told staff members at a school where he was enrolled in classes for students with emotional disabilities that he'd been chased by a guy in the neighborhood with a trunk full of guns. He'd also said someone had chased him and pointed a gun at him but hadn't had the guts to pull the trigger. Alex said he had kicked the gun out of his assailant's hand and considered killing him but hadn't. Two people tried to break into Alex's house the next day, he'd said, but when Alex had told them he was going to shoot them, they'd run away. The stories, staff members knew, were not true.

Alex "fantasizes himself as more powerful and capable than he really is," one psychological examiner had written when Alex was fifteen. "[He is] frequently observed telling tall tales, which seem to serve the purpose of building him up."

Another report, written by a social worker when Alex was nine, had said of Alex: "[He had a] tendency to tell tall tales in order to make you feel that he was someone special."

On one occasion, Alex had boasted that he was an undercover aide to police during a drug arrest at his school. School officials, who knew the story was bogus, were worried by his behavior. They arranged for a counselor to talk to Alex, but that didn't stop him from fabricating stories. He'd enjoyed the fleeting respect his yarns had brought him.

Now nineteen, Alex had an agreeable manner and a fondness for smoking marijuana and sniffing glue. He had a naive ambition to be a police officer, although he had dropped out of Aurora East High School almost as soon as he entered it and had a rap sheet with minor arrests and a theft conviction. One of his uncles, Robert Estremera, was a police officer, and Alex couldn't help noticing how much respect that commanded within the family.

Alex's IQ had been measured at various times in the mid- and low 70s, and he had a hard time grasping simple facts. At one point, for example, he argued that the city of Rock Island in northwestern Illinois couldn't be on the Mississippi River because the Mississippi bordered southern Illinois. It couldn't be in both places, he said. He'd never managed to get a driver's license or register to vote. When he had been involved with other people in minor crimes, he'd done stupid things. Once, police arrived just as a break-in was beginning. Alex tried to run away but tripped and was caught. On another occasion, in February 1981, he cut his foot while stealing an air conditioner from a house that was being rehabbed. Police followed the trail of blood through the snow and caught Alex and his partner, Arthur Burrell. Alex, who at that point had no criminal history, turned state's evidence and got off with probation, which he completed successfully. Burrell, who had a long record, wound up in prison. Later, he would get a chance to even the score with Alex.

Alex lived with his parents, a younger brother, Ephraim, and sister, Iviliz, in a four-flat belonging to his aunt on Sumner Street in Aurora. He had been born in Adjuntas, Puerto Rico, on October 10, 1963, and his parents had taken him to the United States two months later. He'd lived in New York and New Jersey before moving to Aurora when he was five. One of his former neighbors described Alex as a nonaggressive pest. He never held a job for long and never had any money. He frequently asked others for drugs, especially joints, and was often trying to sell little odds and ends, some of which had been stolen. People didn't dislike Alex; they just didn't want him around. His nickname was "Crazy Alex."

"I always approached Alex as if I were talking to a three- or four-year-old," said Jane Raley, a lawyer who later would help represent Alex. "He was very childlike. He was very innocent. He always had something wrong with him physically. If it wasn't his eyesight, it was health, it was his arms. He was sort of a hypochondriac."

Early in March 1983, two weeks after Jeanine's murder, Alex told his mother, Haydee, he had inside information about a sensational crime. Haydee was a stocky, warmhearted woman who spoke English with a thick accent. Like her husband, a lift truck driver, she had never gone past the eighth grade. Alex, she thought, resented the favored treatment his father, Tomas, seemed to give his younger son, Ephraim, and she blamed that for the occasional bitter fights between Alex and his father over the past four years. On several occasions, Tomas had kicked Alex out of the family home for short periods. At times Alex sneaked home and slept on the open-air rear porch, where Haydee would bring him food. Once, in winter, Alex had slept in a car briefly before he was permitted to return.

Haydee wasn't sure what to make of Alex's claim. She asked if the crime in question was the murder of the little girl from Naperville, which had recently been described on the radio. Jeanine's killer had disappeared without a trace, and almost everyone wanted to know what had happened. News of the murder had been updated frequently on radio news shows and on TV. The newspapers carried stories every day. The offer of a reward for information leading to an arrest had been widely publicized as well.

Alex told his mother that a young man named Ricky was Jeanine's murderer. Alex said that while they were sitting in a car, drinking beer, Ricky had motioned Alex over and said, "I didn't mean to kill the girl, but she wouldn't stop screaming."

Alex hadn't notified the police. Haydee, perhaps too familiar with Alex's record of tall tales, didn't call, either. But Richard Kepner, a coworker of Alex's uncle, thought differently when he learned from the uncle what Alex had said. On March 14, Kepner called the Naperville police, the FBI, the DuPage County sheriff's office, and the sheriff's office in adjoining Kane County. Without leaving his name, Kepner gave Alex's address and said: "Alex Hernandez has information about the murder of Jeanine Nicarico."

To the frustrated police, Kepner's anonymous message sounded as though it might be the break they needed. Calls had poured in and the task force had been following leads, none of which had panned out. Publicly, authorities said that Jeanine had not been sexually molested. Although that wasn't true, they hoped it would mislead anyone pretending to know details of the crime.

The investigators, knowing that most crimes are solved quickly or not at all, were worried. John Ruiz, perhaps the most significant suspect uncovered so far, had just that day passed his second polygraph test.

Sam figured he was on the trail of a sex killer, probably someone who had acted alone. The FBI profiler had said the crime probably was committed by a lone killer, as well as predicting that the killer might return to the crime scene. Two neighbors of the Nicaricos—Joann Johannville and Carol Gheen—each said they had seen someone suspicious in a car on Clover Court about the time that Jeanine had disappeared. Their vague descriptions differed, but that wasn't surprising; they'd had no particular reason to be paying close attention, and eyewitness accounts were notorious for being off the mark.

The medical examiner said Jeanine had died two to four hours after she'd eaten lunch, which meant the killer probably took her straight to the Prairie Path. There, two state tollway workers had seen the Caucasian man driving the car. But no one had found the man driving the car on the Prairie Path. And none of the other leads had gone anywhere. Now, even John Ruiz didn't seem to have anything to do with the crime.

Then came Kepner's tip about another Hispanic from Aurora—Alex Hernandez. Maybe there was an Aurora connection to Jeanine's murder after all. John Sam and another sheriff's detective, Dennis Kurzawa, promptly went to talk to Alex.

Sam and Kurzawa were familiar with East Aurora and had little trouble finding Alex Hernandez's address. It was an old four-flat occupied by Alex's family and other relatives.

At first, Alex wouldn't cooperate, but when Sam and Kurzawa drove him in their squad car to a shopping center parking lot for a chat, he soon opened up. By the time they had brought him to the task force headquarters, he was telling them a story about "Ricky," quoting Ricky as saying that he didn't want to kill the girl, but she wouldn't stop screaming. He said Ricky was about seventeen, wore cowboy boots, and had black hair. At first, he'd said he didn't know Ricky's last name; now he said it was Benevides. At first, he hadn't mentioned that anyone else was in the car, now he said two other young East Aurora men were there—Stephen Buckley and Mike Castro. He said the car was a green Oldsmobile Cutlass, the same model that happened to be driving by the detectives at the moment. Ricky, Alex said, kept a police club in the trunk of his vehicle.

Alex, Sam noticed, repeatedly quoted Ricky in the first person so that it almost sounded as if Alex were making the statements himself. Sam and Kurzawa listened for significant details that weren't public knowledge, details that would show Alex wasn't just spinning a yarn. There were none.

Sam had been around police work too long to put excessive faith in stories from people of Alex's stripe. Whenever there was a big case, especially one in which reward money was offered, there was always someone willing to string police along with a fabricated story, just as there was always someone in jail eager to get a lighter sentence by testifying against a fellow inmate. But right now, Alex was the best lead police had.

Over the next seven days, Deputy Sheriff Dennis Kurzawa brought Alex again and again to the task force headquarters in the new county building. The detectives spent hours with him, talking about the case and frequently buying him lunch. Alex was excited; he felt as though he was helping to solve a crime, just like a real police officer. Even on days when he wasn't invited, he showed up. The detectives encouraged him and hinted he might be offered a job in the county highway department. "Come on, Alex," they would say when they arrived at his home to pick him up and he was still in bed. "Real police officers don't sleep late."

"I'm going to be a detective," Alex told his mother. "I'm going to solve this case."

On March 16, Alex told FBI agent Jeff Bogan the Ricky story. He said that Ricky carried a nightstick in the trunk of his car and that Ricky had said he hadn't meant to "kill that bitch."

Detective Warren Wilkosz showed Alex a picture of Jeanine's body as it was laid out in the autopsy room, hoping he'd provide some details or blurt out a confession. Alex, though, could add nothing more.

Sam spent plenty of time trying to get Alex to tell more about the crime. He figured there was no street kid in Aurora he couldn't crack if he put his mind to it, but Alex was beginning to frustrate him. Finally, he was fierce with Alex. He asked him how he would like to see his sister's head crushed as Jeanine's had been. Alex was so upset he was crying. Sam knew he had Alex at the breaking point. "Say the words, Alex," he thought to himself as he grilled Hernandez. "Say: 'I did it.' " But Sam could not get Alex to confess.

Alex had been happy to talk to the detectives at first, saying that he had heard details about the crime from "Ricky." His stories, though, were implausible and inconsistent. Sam started to doubt that Alex knew anything about the crime.

At another point, Alex said that he was supposed to meet the mysterious Ricky the following Saturday. He signed an affidavit authorizing a hidden recording device that he would wear to the meeting. But no Ricky ever appeared.

On March 17, DuPage authorities decided it was time to try a little subterfuge. Police brought Armindo Marquez to the task force headquarters. Marquez, known to his East Aurora friends as "Penguino," had known Hernandez since childhood. He'd been jailed when police had smashed a burglary ring that was suspected of more than a hundred break-ins throughout northeastern Illinois. After his arrest, he called Kane County detective Thomas Atchison and said he'd heard about Alex's involvement in the Nicarico homicide from a friend who visited the jail. Penguino made it clear he was ready to help.

The sheriff's deputies planned to put Penguino and Alex into the same partitioned area to see if Alex would give away incriminating details about Jeanine's murder, details that he might have been holding back. Getting a suspect to talk to someone he trusts is a tool investigators often use. It wasn't a ploy likely to furnish a statement that would hold up in court, they figured, but it just might produce some leads.

They instructed Penguino to say that he knew who had killed a boy in a nearby suburb—Bolingbrook—on the same weekend Jeanine had died. Penguino supposedly was going to collect the reward, which had been raised to $10,000, and get out of jail by telling police all he knew. A box full of cash, purportedly the reward, was left in a cubicle with Alex and Penguino, who was wearing a prison uniform. The police exited, although Detective Albert Bettilyon (who didn't understand Spanish) tried to listen from a spot ten to twelve feet down the hall and around the corner. Bettilyon managed to hear bits and pieces of the conversation.

The Kane County officers who had transported Penguino to DuPage thought the setup might violate Hernandez's Miranda rights because Penguino was acting as an agent of the police. They left promptly, wanting no role in the questioning.

Alex later said he promptly told Penguino that the partitioned area might be bugged and that they should speak in Spanish. The two young men wound up alternating between Spanish and English. Later, Alex said the statements he made during the forty-five-minute conversation were made at the behest of authorities. Sam confirmed that, saying that Penguino was told to get information about the Nicarico homicide from Alex, and Alex was told to get details of the Bolingbrook crime from Penguino.

Bettilyon heard Alex say that Saturday was a good day to do burglaries. Alex said, "I'd drive for burglaries." Alex also said he had hired an attorney because he had bopped someone on the head. He said he was going to San Diego at 1:00 A.M. the next day.

"On Saturdays, we do houses," Bettilyon later said he heard Alex say. "We have a good day and do houses because everybody leaves home for the weekend. . . . I am a big thief. I only got caught once because I tripped while I was running. . . . I steal from cars and houses."

The young men also discussed the crimes in Bolingbrook and Naperville. Penguino said he could lead police to the knife that was used in the Bolingbrook murder. Alex said he knew how Jeanine was killed. Penguino said he was present when the

Bolingbrook boy was killed. Alex, as far as Bettilyon could tell, said he was present at Jeanine's murder.

"All I did was hold her down," the detective heard Alex say.

When Bettilyon repeated the admission to the others, Sam's reaction was furious and primal. "Let's kill that little son of a bitch," he said to himself. "Let's take him and throw him out the fucking window."

Here was a young man who'd had a hand in those wounds Sam had seen during the autopsy. How could he go on smiling after committing such a horrible crime? Alex had told Penguino that Jeanine had been taken to an abandoned farmhouse or stable where the girl was beaten to death with a bat or club. Sam felt Alex deserved the same treatment.

"You got forty guys standing out in the hallways wanting to throw that little Puerto Rican out the window," Sam said later. "Now we're all motivated. We want that little bastard. He just said the key words: 'I held her down.'"

Anger and a thirst for retribution weren't enough. The next step was to build an airtight case. For starters, the detectives asked Alex and Penguino to lead them to the farmhouse or stable where Jeanine had been taken. The detectives got out a squad car and took Alex and Penguino for a ride. As they drove, one of the detectives, Thomas Atchison, heard Alex and Penguino discuss splitting the $10,000 reward.

Although Penguino said he had been to the building before to sell stolen merchandise, neither he nor Alex could find it. They led detectives from place to place. Atchison didn't think Alex knew north from south, east, or west. Alex certainly didn't know street names. Eventually, the detectives gave up looking and went home.

Later, police studied aerial maps to try to identify a building resembling the one Alex and Penguino had described, but they never were able to find one.

On March 18, Alex signed an affidavit for the police detailing his story about "Ricky." When shown photographs of people named Ricky, he picked out the picture of another East Aurora man, Ricky LeRoy Byrnes, as the person most like the Ricky he had seen in the car. But he was still unable to say who exactly Ricky was, and no Ricky who fit Alex's story was ever found. Police questioned Ricky Byrnes, but he knew nothing about the crime.

Sam decided to talk to the other people in Alex's story, Stephen Buckley and Mike Castro, the young men who supposedly were in the car with "Ricky." On March 21, Sam went to Stephen Buckley's home in Aurora. It was an old house in a well-kept working-class neighborhood. The furnishings were comfortable but not lavish. Stephen's father, John, had retired from a job as a lineman at the local power utility, and the family didn't have much money. Even so, the house had a warm, relaxed feeling.

Although Steve's sister, Norma, had been caught selling drugs with her boyfriend and had later spent time in prison, the Buckleys were a solid working-class family. Stephen's older brother, Michael, worked for the city as a firefighter. His older sister, Carol, was married and lived in a newer house on the west side of the city.

Stephen was a mild-mannered twenty-year-old who, like Alex, had dropped out of Aurora East High School. He'd once been arrested for breaking down a door in the basement of a neighboring house with a friend and stealing a shotgun, but he had no other criminal record. He smoked marijuana regularly. Like Alex, he didn't have a job.

Sam asked Stephen Buckley to come down to the sheriff's headquarters with his friend Mike Castro. Buckley agreed, and the two young men duly arrived. Questioned separately, both denied knowing anything about Alex's story. They said they had never been in any car with anyone named Ricky discussing a murder.

Sam showed Buckley a hiking shoe with a heel pattern similar to the print on the Nicaricos' front door.

"Got any shoes like that?" Sam asked.

"Sure," Buckley said, "I have a pair like that."

"May I see them?" Sam asked.

"Okay," Buckley said.

After Buckley had gone home, Sam drove to the Buckley house. Steve's mother had put the shoes in a paper bag so Sam wouldn't get dirty. He took them back to the sheriff's headquarters, but he didn't hold out much hope that anything would turn up.

"It was too easy," he said later.

At the sheriff's headquarters, DuPage's shoeprint expert, John Gorajczyk, was out for the afternoon. However, Don Schmitt, the quartermaster at the jail and a fingerprint expert, saw some similarities between the bottom of Buckley's shoes and the print on the door. So the next day, March 22, Sam and Detective Thomas Vosburgh went back to the Buckley home, where Sam gave Buckley a receipt for his shoes. He asked Buckley where he was on the day of the crime. Buckley said he thought he was babysitting for his sister, Carol. The two detectives talked to Carol, who told them she was not sure if Steve babysat that day, but that she would check with her husband and let Sam know.

Next, the two detectives went to the Continental Can Company in the DuPage County suburb of West Chicago. There they learned that Mike Castro was at work on the day of the murder and did not leave until after 5:00 P.M. He could not have been present at Jeanine's abduction and murder.

Meanwhile, John Gorajczyk, the shoeprint expert, was back in the lab. He studied the shoes and noticed significant differences between them and the print on the Nicaricos' door. They weren't the right shoes.

"They don't match," Gorajczyk told the lab chief, Philip Gilman, who had tested the shoes for signs of blood. The extremely sensitive test could detect even minute quantities, but it was negative.

Gilman told Gorajczyk to tell the sheriff about his conclusion.

The sheriff was Richard Doria, a short, stocky ex-Marine with a big ego and a dictatorial management style that made him unpopular among his employees, although they also knew that in a pinch they could count on him to back them up. Some DuPage authorities were surprised by how jealously Doria guarded what he perceived to be his territory. He was known as something of a loose cannon, which angered other DuPage politicians at times but also earned him some respect for speaking his mind. "He's no-nonsense; he doesn't give a damn about what anyone thinks about him," one of his top aides said.

Doria had made a name for himself as an effective drug investigator and had become undersheriff to the previous sheriff, Wayne Shimp, the grandson of a DuPage County sheriff who had run on the 1864 Union party ticket topped by Abraham Lincoln. Doria also owned a trucking company. When Shimp left office, Doria was ready to spend whatever it took to win the Republican primary, which in conservative DuPage County was tantamount to winning office. Opposing candidates backed off, and Doria was elected to run Illinois's second-largest sheriff's department.

Underlying Doria's tough veneer, some people thought, was an attitude that police could do no wrong. In a way, that was a welcome change. For one thing, Doria put a stop to escapes from the county jail, something that had plagued previous sheriffs. When one former sheriff was asked on television how he could explain why so many escapes had occurred under his administration, he could only theorize that the jail was getting a lousier class of prisoners. Wayne Shimp also had a flawed record; at one point, in apparent violation of state law, he had an ex-con running the county's police force on the night shift.

Gorajczyk's conclusion posed a problem. It was standard policy for a report to be written on any test or comparison that was made in the crime lab. On the other hand, if Gorajczyk wrote a report, it would make it difficult to send the shoes to an outside lab because most crime laboratories would not handle material already examined by another lab unless the first lab couldn't reach a clear conclusion. That helps to prevent "lab shopping"—the practice of sending material to different labs until the desired result is secured. Gorajczyk said he decided not to write a report, even though Gilman wanted him to. He hadn't had an opportunity to fully examine the shoes, and they were not returned to him for further testing. Later, he said he regretted not writing a report.

Sam heard of Gorajczyk's opinion and wasn't surprised. It had been too easy to get the shoes. If Buckley had been guilty, he probably would have tried to keep his shoes from getting to the police. Instead, he'd just handed them over.

"I ain't that good a cop," Sam said.

Other detectives were continuing to investigate Alex Hernandez. An evidence technician obtained a hair sample, mouth swabs, and fingerprints from Alex, who also took—and failed—a lie detector test. An FBI agent named Barbara Babcock posed as Mrs. Nicarico and talked with Alex. She cried, and asked if Jeanine was raped. Alex told her that he did not know if the girl was raped because he was not there but that he would help find the killers.

Detectives Dennis Kurzawa and Thomas Vosburgh went to talk to Ricky LeRoy Byrnes again, the young man whose photo Alex had picked out. But Byrnes again denied knowing anything about the murder except what he'd heard on the news.

Police went to Alex's house and confiscated his clothes and his brother's clothes. They took the clothes to the crime lab, but tests were negative for blood.

At one point, Sam ran across Lewis Stonehouse's slides of the two shoeprints in the dirt outside the Nicaricos' dining room window. Sam thought the shoeprints might be significant, but he was assured they'd been made by friends of Jeanine's sisters as they ran around the house looking for Jeanine.

The investigation was not going well. DuPage sheriff Richard Doria told the task force members that if they did not solve the case by the end of the month, they could not keep their space in the new county building. The shorthanded Kane County sheriff pulled his officers out of the task force and reassigned them to regular duties. No other strong leads had been uncovered.

On March 28, the sheriff's office asked Edward German of the Illinois State Police Crime Laboratory to examine Buckley's shoes and crime scene photos.

On March 30, DuPage and Naperville detectives met with Pete Kochanny, one of the tollway workers who had seen the green car near where Jeanine's body had been found. Kochanny had said he thought the car was a Granada. The police officers showed him photos of Granadas, and he picked out the model year 1975.

Sheriff's Sergeant John Zaruba got a printout listing all

green Ford Granadas registered in the area and checked them out one by one. Another detective was assigned to look for a farm-house that matched Alex's description. He spent weeks looking, without success.

As far as Sam was concerned, the case was going nowhere, but the detectives kept trying. Throughout early April, they combed Aurora, looking for leads, trying to find someone who would talk. By mid-April, the investigation seemed stalled. The task force had broken up and the FBI had dropped out. It was time for John Sam to grill Stephen Buckley to see what he really knew.

On April 20, Sam called Buckley and asked to meet him for breakfast at a Denny's near Buckley's home. Sam figured Buckley would be more likely to agree to meet at a neutral site, rather than at a police station—not that it made much difference. Sam planned to take Buckley to the sheriff's headquarters anyway.

Sam and Detective Warren Wilkosz already were at the restaurant when Buckley showed up. The detectives ate a relaxed meal, but Buckley was too nervous to take a bite. He knew he was a suspect and knew Hernandez had named him. He'd been given a receipt for his shoes, and he knew they were considered evidence. He didn't know enough about the legal system to know that it was long past the time to get a lawyer. Instead, he was following his mother's advice: you didn't do anything wrong, so just be honest with the police.

After breakfast, the detectives took Buckley to a small inter-view room in the old jail building, leaving the van that Buckley had borrowed from his father at the Denny's. John Sam had one goal in mind: he was going to "bust Stephen Buckley's balls."

Sam and Wilkosz were used to working together. They had known each other since they'd attended the same Catholic grammar school in Cicero, a tough suburb bordering Chicago's West Side whose most famous former citizen was Al Capone. Sam's father had been a Cicero policeman; Wilkosz's father had been a firefighter. The two detectives now worked in adjacent cubicles.

The detectives knew the interview was going to be a rough one. Everyone had been cleared from the area except Sam's direct boss, Lieutenant Kenneth Lepic, and the chief of the detectives, Robert Soucek. Later, Soucek and Lepic told Sam he had been yelling so loud, they could hear him down the hall.

The room had a table covered with files and photos of Buckley's shoes. Sam and Wilkosz sat down and told Buckley they knew he was guilty. Wilkosz especially came on strong. Unlike Sam, who alternated between intimidation and charm, Wilkosz always came across as a hard guy—"a drill instructor," Sam would say, "or a Chicago cop." Wilkosz was tall, lean, and muscular, a detective, Buckley felt, who did not like him. He was a sheriff's detective, and Buckley didn't doubt that Wilkosz could kill him if he wanted to.

The detectives wanted Buckley to make a mistake, to change his story, to let something slip. They told Buckley that tests had *proved* his shoes left the mark on the Nicaricos' door. They showed him diagrams and the inked bottoms of his shoes. Buckley was at a loss. He couldn't explain why his shoeprint was on the Nicaricos' door.

The shoes were his, all right. Buckley could remember the day he'd bought them at Payless Shoes; when he'd gotten home, he'd seen his friend Marty Brusatori with a similar pair. Marty's shoes had those same high tops of imitation suede, the same tan rubber soles and heels with swirling patterns, but they were a size smaller. Buckley's matched the size of the print left by Jeanine's abductor.

The hiking shoes were called New Silver Cloud shoes. The detectives said they had scientific proof that Buckley's New Silver Cloud shoes had made a print on the front door where the little girl lived. They knew he had kicked in her front door, abducted her, and killed her. They did not care where he'd bought the shoes.

The interrogation room was uncomfortably warm. Vaguely, Buckley wondered if the detectives could control the temperature. His shirt collar was wet with sweat under his long, stringy hair, and his hands felt hot and damp. At times the detectives ordered him to stand, and Buckley was embarrassed at the way his legs trembled.

Sam had seemed friendlier at first. He was as tall as Wilkosz, but his blue eyes and blond hair with streaks of silver seemed less threatening. Sam liked to laugh, but he was not laughing now. He wanted Buckley to talk about killing the little girl.

"Your friends, these mutts, what do you think they're going to do?" Sam demanded. "Did you think they're going to sit in jail and take all the heat? No fucking way. They'll say: Get your ass right down here with us, buddy. You come down here with us."

"I didn't do it," Buckley said. "I know you don't believe me, but I didn't do it."

Wilkosz shook his head slightly and glared at Buckley. "Your shoeprint is on the door. You know that. *We* know that. Tell us how it got there."

"I don't know," Buckley said. "Maybe somebody took my shoes, I don't know. All I know is that I wasn't there. I didn't hurt anybody."

The detectives didn't believe him. They wanted to know where he was on Friday, February, 25, 1983, the day Jeanine was abducted. Buckley was not sure. He didn't have a job, and he had dropped out of Aurora East High School. Usually, on Fridays, he went to his sister Carol's house to babysit for her children. But Carol had checked, and Stephen had not been there that Friday.

"You weren't there," Sam said. "Don't you understand? This is a death case. The state's attorney will deal with the first person who talks. The others are going to die. They're going to kill you."

"I didn't do it," Buckley said. "I didn't kill her."

Wilkosz pounded the table and threw things off it. Sam pounded the wall. They asked Buckley whether he knew John Ruiz. They asked about Alex Hernandez and his story about "Ricky." Over and over, they asked where he was on the day of the crime. Buckley stuck to his story. He didn't know anything about Alex and Ricky and drinking in a car. He didn't know where he was on the afternoon of the crime.

"Take your shoes off," Sam said. "Take off your shoes and socks."

"Why?"

"Don't ask me why," Sam said. "I didn't ask for any whys. Take them off."

Sam wanted to show Buckley that the detectives had total control over him. They made him sit on a table. They took away the chair and made him sit on the floor. They told him he wasn't good enough to have a chair. In anger, Sam threw a chair. They threatened to take him out to a field and beat him. They brought out the photographs of Jeanine's body and spread them on the table.

"Look at your handiwork," they said. "This is the result of what you did."

Then they left the room.

The pictures were horrible. Buckley glanced at them, but he

didn't want to see more than that. Finally the detectives came back. Buckley didn't change his story. He said he'd had nothing to do with the crime.

They told Buckley they'd put his name on television so the family of the victim could find him and kill him. There was no doubt in Sam's mind that Buckley thought his life was close to ending.

Several times the detectives told Buckley he was free to leave, but he was too frightened to move. He was sure they would never really let him go. Finally, in late afternoon, the exhausted detectives insisted he leave. They drove him back to the Denny's and released him.

"He never got off the story," Sam said later. "He just said: 'I didn't do it, I know I didn't do it, someday you guys will know I didn't do it. If you're going to kill me, kill me. If you're going to put me in jail, put me in jail. I didn't do it.' He's crying and everything. The guy's very emotional, but nothing changes. Nothing changes. All those hours, he never changed his story, he never changed his attitude. Nothing.

"He had me totally convinced that he didn't do it."

5

ROLANDO CRUZ

---

*The police became convinced that [William Marvin]
Lindley was the murderer. They diligently searched for
any evidence that would enable the prosecutor to build a
good case against Lindley in court, and they brushed
aside any evidence that might have pointed to developments that would have been in Lindley's favor.*

> Author-lawyer Erle Stanley Gardner, writing about
> his California client, whose death sentence
> for a 1943 murder was overturned

TOM KNIGHT DID NOT share John Sam's belief that
Stephen Buckley was innocent.

Knight was DuPage County's hard-driving, charis-
matic chief of criminal prosecutions. Some defense lawyers didn't
like Knight. They thought he was the kind of lawyer who could
fall victim to the prosecution complex, who could get so focused
on winning a case that no amount of evidence could convince him
he had the wrong suspects. They felt he saw everything in black
and white and considered himself to be on the side of the good
guys. Once, he said that he couldn't go home and kiss his wife at
night if he were a defense lawyer who had put a criminal back on
the streets. His pugnacious manner had become well known in his
thirteen years as a prosecutor. In his earlier days as a prosecutor in
central Illinois, he had been nicknamed "The Black Knight."

Others, though, were impressed by his abilities in the court-room.

"He was a good prosecutor, and everybody had a lot of respect for him," said James Teal, the Naperville police chief. "Once he took a position, he would argue it very well in favor of whoever he was arguing it for. He was an exceptional trial lawyer."

J. Michael Fitzsimmons, a wealthy political maverick who had beaten the regular Republican organization to become state's attorney, had brought Knight from Champaign-Urbana to be his chief criminal prosecutor. Knight needed a job; his boss and mentor was leaving office, and Knight didn't want to work for his replacement.

People in DuPage County soon learned that Knight got results. On one occasion, the family of a slain boy had complained to John Sam that the prosecutor assigned to the case was planning to charge the killer with aggravated battery instead of murder. Sam had told the victim's mother to go to Fitzsimmons's office and insist on having Knight prosecute the case. He's the best one, Sam had told her. Knight did take on the case. An alleged accomplice was acquitted, but the killer was convicted of murder.

This time, Knight wanted to make sure the investigation into Jeanine's murder was handled properly right from the start. Sometime before, Sheriff Doria had said on television that he was treating the disappearance of an eleven-year-old boy as a routine runaway. Shortly afterward, the boy had been found stabbed to death in a suburban forest preserve, a huge embarrassment for Doria and the county. Burglars who had broken into the apartment where the boy was home alone later admitted they had found him hiding under a bed and killed him so that he wouldn't identify them. Another case had been thrown out because a judge ruled that Detective Dennis Kurzawa had questioned a suspect while in custody but hadn't given him his rights. Knight was having no such mishaps on this case.

For one thing, it wouldn't be good politically for his boss, J. Michael Fitzsimmons, the state's attorney. In less than a year, Fitzsimmons would face a tough regular Republican candidate, Jim Ryan, in a primary election. When Fitzsimmons was first elected, he had beaten Ryan by just three hundred votes, and the election coming up on March 20, 1984, wasn't likely to be any easier. If Fitzsimmons were defeated, Ryan would be sure to replace Knight, who'd already lost a job once when his boss at the time was replaced.

A week before John Sam and Warren Wilkosz's marathon grilling of Stephen Buckley, Tom Knight had started working with a special grand jury. It was a controversial step. Some people in the county thought he should leave the investigating to the police and go to a grand jury only when police had found solid suspects. On the other hand, more than a month had gone by since the crime had been committed. That was much too long; the case was in danger of going unsolved. Something had to be done to get things moving forward.

Using the grand jury, Knight could run his own probe, getting information that the sheriff's investigators couldn't seem to come up with. The special grand jury had subpoena power, which gave Knight power, too. He could threaten uncooperative witnesses with indictments. He could order that they be picked up by police and brought before the grand jury. That gave him the leverage he needed to pry loose testimony that could solve the case.

Eventually, Knight focused his probe on Alex Hernandez,

Stephen Buckley, and another young Aurora man, Rolando Cruz.

Cruz was a good-looking, arrogant gang member who told police he sometimes was called Chinaman because he liked to use martial arts moves while scrapping with other young East Aurora men. He'd grown up with two older sisters and a younger sister in a middle-class family; his father, Robert, was an auto body shop foreman and his mother, Dora, was a factory worker. Their home, Cruz said, was in a "Beaver Cleaver" Aurora neighborhood. According to Dora, no one in the family had ever been in serious trouble with the law. Rolando was a member of the Latin Kings street gang, although he had no record of criminal gang activity. His entire criminal history consisted of one conviction for criminal trespass to property, for which he'd served twenty-six days in jail, and several burglary arrests. He had spent six months in the army reserves before coming back to Aurora and telling people he had been in the Marines.

Cruz's name came up when police interviewed Arthur Burrell, Alex's partner in the air conditioner theft and Cruz's partner in the case of criminal trespass to property. Later, Cruz admitted also burglarizing drug dealers with Burrell three times in 1982. Burrell had reason not to like either Alex Hernandez or Rolando Cruz; Hernandez had turned state's evidence against him in the case of the stolen air conditioner, and Burrell believed Cruz had turned him in for stealing traveler's checks.

Burrell had served time for the burglary he'd committed with Hernandez, and he was finishing his sentence in a halfway house for another burglary. He was happy to implicate both Hernandez and Cruz. While he was incarcerated, he claimed, Cruz had written him letters that said Alex was burglarizing places in Naperville near a high school and an A & P store. He said that he used to ride bikes on the Prairie Path with Alex and others and that they had partied and built a clubhouse there. Burrell could not produce the letters, but police figured they should talk to Cruz anyway.

When DuPage County sheriff's detectives Dennis Kurzawa and Thomas Vosburgh had gone to visit him on April 19 after leaving an earlier message saying they wanted to talk to him, Cruz had told them he knew nothing about the crime, but after hearing about the reward money, he had said he would check around. Cruz and the detectives met several times in the following days. On April 22, Cruz started telling the detectives about burglaries other young East Aurora men had committed. On April 29, nine days after Sam and Wilkosz had tried to "bust Stephen Buckley's balls," as Sam had put it, Cruz contacted the detectives and told them that another East Aurora man, Ray Ortega, knew that Alex Hernandez had committed the crime. That call brought Cruz directly into the case, a development that he would have plenty of time to regret afterward.

Three days later, on May 2, Cruz sat down with detectives and—in a tape-recorded statement—again said that, according to Ray Ortega, Hernandez was the murderer. Sam talked to Cruz, and when Cruz said he'd served in the Marines, Sam and Wilkosz asked him about Chesty Puller. Marine lieutenant general Lewis "Chesty" Puller was the most decorated Marine in the corps's history, but Cruz had never heard of him. He'd never heard the term "semper fi," a shortened form of the Latin phrase *semper fidelis,* the Marine Corps motto. With that, Sam knew Cruz had never been a Marine.

Cruz had an insolent air about him that made Knight and some of the detectives think he knew more than he was telling. (Later, it would turn out he knew Hernandez—he'd said he had a schoolyard fight with him in fifth grade; he knew who Buckley was because Buckley had dated a friend of Cruz's sister in junior high school; and he'd lived down the street from John Ruiz.) Detectives Vosburgh and Kurzawa told Sam they thought Cruz was holding back significant information. Sam had a high regard for the other detectives, particularly Kurzawa, but he thought they were wrong about Cruz, whom he considered an impudent liar. Cruz had lied about his age. He had claimed his ancestors were Native American, when in reality they were Mexican.

On May 6, a Friday, authorities went to a DuPage County judge and secured grand jury subpoenas. Subpoenas were served on Monday for Cruz and other young East Aurora men.

Three days later, Cruz called the sheriff's office and said that he had been shot at. It was Monday, May 9, 1983, a date that would later become important. Vosburgh went out to pick up Cruz. Back at sheriff's headquarters, Cruz said that Hernandez had threatened him that evening. Hernandez, Cruz said, claimed Cruz knew "way too much" and said Jeanine had been hit with a bat. Cruz also quoted Hernandez as saying he "didn't do it . . . [but] I just finished it 'cause I was getting blamed for it anyhow." Cruz hinted that he knew more. The detectives showed him two pictures of Jeanine, one of her when she was alive and one after the murder. They left the room, and Cruz looked at the pictures. Then Detective Kurzawa called Knight, and Knight told him to let Cruz sleep at the jail. The next day, May 10, Kurzawa took a tape-recorded statement from Cruz. Later, DuPage County authorities also put Cruz into a witness protection program, giving him money and paying for him to stay first at a motel and later at apartments in Glen Ellyn and Wheaton.

In his May 10 tape-recorded statement, Cruz said he got his information from another young East Aurora man, Emilio

Donatlan. According to the story, Hernandez brought Jeanine to Donatlan's apartment in Aurora. (Later, he added that Donatlan was having a birthday party for Ray Ortega.) Donatlan raped the girl and hit her with some kind of bat or club because she would not shut up. She was knocked unconscious, and he continued to rape her, but then she regained consciousness and began screaming again. So Donatlan hit her again, and Ortega kicked her down a long stairway. The fall broke her nose. Then she got up. Alex Hernandez walked her to a car and drove her to the Prairie Path and finished her off so he wouldn't get blamed. Cruz thought the murder had taken place in the dark.

Sam didn't think much of Cruz's account. First, Jeanine's head wounds had been too brutal to allow her to reawaken and start screaming again, much less walk to a car. Any one of the blows would have been fatal, the medical examiner had said. Second, the medical examiner had said Jeanine had died two to four hours after eating, which meant she had died during daylight, not after dark. Third, there were too many people involved. They couldn't all be the kind of person who goes along with the murder of a little girl. Somebody there would be testifying against the others. Instead, Sam was certain, there was a lone killer out there who had to be found before he committed more crimes.

Sam was even more sure Cruz was lying when police later that day visited Donatlan's small second-floor apartment. There was no sign of any disturbance. There was no blood. The couple living on the first floor had heard nothing. The flight of stairs Jeanine supposedly had been kicked down was an exterior staircase, visible for a long distance in a busy area. If Cruz's story was accurate, somebody would have seen or heard what was happening.

"I thought Cruz was just a bullshitting asshole the first time I met him," Sam said later. "That's all I ever thought he was—that, and someone looking for a free ride."

On May 12, Knight started calling witnesses before the special grand jury. The three main witnesses to appear that day were Ray Ortega, Wilfredo Estremera (Alex Hernandez's uncle), and Rolando Cruz.

Ray Ortega had become part of the case when Cruz mentioned his name. (Later, Cruz said he hated Ortega because Ortega had dated Cruz's ex-girlfriend, Cindy, while Cruz was in basic training for the army reserves.) Ortega was eighteen and had dropped out of Aurora East High School two weeks into his freshman year. He'd spent eleven months in prison after escaping from a youth facility, and, since then, he'd never worked. Instead, he said, he just got high with his friends.

In front of the grand jury, Ortega denied having anything to do with the murder, and he called Alex Hernandez goofy and a liar. He said he hadn't talked to Cruz in four years. One day, he said, while he was walking with a friend, he saw Cruz, but the friend said, "Don't call to Rolando. He's a big liar. He says he's got cars and a mansion and a good job, and he doesn't have anything."

After Alex's uncle testified about Alex's original story, Rolando Cruz took the stand, the first of five appearances he would make before the grand jury. Cruz was happy to cooperate. His family had moved to Texas, and he had no income. Now that he was helping the investigation, however, the county was paying his rent for an apartment in Wheaton and was even footing the bill for classes in cable TV installation at the College of DuPage.

Without that help, he wouldn't have a place to live. Plus, there was the chance of getting that $10,000 reward.

Cruz repeated the story he had told detectives. Knight took him over the story again and again, probing for any new facts that might help the case. But Cruz didn't have any.

The grand jury met again the following week and each Thursday throughout the summer and fall. Knight called Hernandez and Buckley to the stand. He called John Ruiz, Armindo "Penguino" Marquez, and Emilio Donatlan. The two women who'd seen the strange car on Clover Court and the two state tollway workers who'd seen the green car at the Prairie Path testified.

Alex Hernandez testified on July 7, 1983, and again on January 12, 1984. A good part of Hernandez's testimony was disoriented or incomprehensible. He said that Sunday was a weekday, and he said during his second appearance that he had been before the grand jury several times, when in fact he had been there only once. He described "Ricky" in several ways—as Hispanic and white, with long hair and short hair, and driving a car of three different colors. He referred to him as "Ricky from Oswego," "Ricky Byrnes" and "Ricky Benevides." Authorities never found anyone named Ricky Benevides.

At his second appearance, he said that all he had done was lie to investigators, hoping to get the reward. By then, it had finally occurred to Hernandez that he was a target of the investigation.

"I wanted the money, see?" Hernandez testified. "I am trying to do—I made the whole damn thing up. I wanted some damn money. That is, you know, I lied, and look where the lies got me to, possibly murder, which I never even did or had anything to do with. . . . I am just trying to tell you I lied. You know, it is hard when you don't have a place to stay, especially in the winter, when you have to stay in the car outside."

To buttress the grand jury probe, Knight passed along assignments to the detectives. Most of them hated the idea of being errand boys for Knight's grand jury, and Sam, now convinced that Buckley, Cruz, and Hernandez had nothing to do with the crime, refused point-blank.

"Nobody wanted to do this shit," he said later. "It was: find this asshole, find that asshole. Go find this guy over here, see what this guy's got to say. Who wants to go to Aurora and find a bunch of assholes every day and try to get them to talk to you? They used to come up with these lists of stuff to do, and I would say, 'I'm not doing it because these guys didn't do it.' I got other things to do."

The assignments generally fell to Detective Wilkosz. Eventually he was released from other duties and worked full-time with Knight.

Gradually, Knight's theory of the case began to emerge. Hernandez and Cruz were involved; that's why they had made so many statements. Buckley was, too; it was his shoeprint on the door. Because the two people who had seen a strange car on Clover Court and the two who had seen the green car at the Prairie Path had all seen a lone white man, that must have been Buckley. Ruiz couldn't have been directly involved because he'd been working. But perhaps he had taken a hand indirectly, maybe as the mastermind who'd told the others which houses to break into.

Evidence was piling up, but some of it was contradictory and some seemed irrelevant. In fact, the case was reaching a point at which the prosecution complex can be a dangerous force because the facts were few—and a thin case is always a hazard for a prosecutor.

"You really become kind of a prisoner of the thin case," said

Scott Turow, an author and former federal prosecutor who would enter the case several years later. "You want to believe in it so much because it is the only way you can go forward. You just make yourself believe it."

Knight was determined to move forward. He knew that John Sam thought he was on the wrong track. Sam repeatedly argued with him, saying Knight was chasing the wrong guys. But Knight was just as passionate in arguing his case, passionate to a degree that surprised Sam. Knight had always taken Sam's opinions seriously before, but now he just seemed to be ignoring them.

"The police worked countless hours—uncompensated hours," Knight later told the CBS program *60 Minutes.* "The prosecutors—everybody who was involved in this case—did their level best to find the people who committed this crime."

At another time, Knight added, "I know the record better than anyone. I got input from all quarters. I would not want to do anything to the wrong person."

Knight, however, had to recognize that there were holes in the case. Buckley didn't fit the descriptions of the lone white driver. None of the witnesses reported seeing any Hispanics. DuPage County's expert, John Gorajczyk, had said it wasn't Buckley's shoeprint on the door. None of the many tests done in the crime lab had connected any of the three suspects to the crime. And though Alex Hernandez and Rolando Cruz had made statements implicating other people, nobody else had implicated them.

Faced with those flaws, someone trained as an investigator might have reacted by casting a wider net, looking for other suspects. But as a prosecutor, Knight tended to focus on improving the case at hand. Over the summer and fall, Knight went to work. Buckley's right shoe had been sent to the Illinois State Police

Crime Laboratory, where Edward German examined it. German had said it was impossible to be sure whether the shoe was the correct one. The shoe also went to the Kansas Bureau of Identification, where it was examined by forensic scientist Robert Olsen. He, too, said he couldn't be certain that the shoe had made the print. In between, however, the shoe went to yet another expert, Louise Robbins. Her conclusion was much more direct.

Robbins was a physical anthropologist at the University of North Carolina at Greensboro. She'd had an undistinguished career and until recently had had no particular knowledge of shoeprints. That had changed in the 1970s, when she'd been called on to study numerous 4,700-year-old footprints in two Tennessee caves. By measuring the prints, Robbins had concluded that all of them had been made by just a few individuals.

That led to a call from Mary Leakey, a renowned anthropologist unearthing traces in Tanzania of ancient human ancestors. Leakey's field scientists had found old footprints and Leakey wanted another expert's opinion of them. Robbins flew to Africa and concluded that a newly discovered, clearer print had been made by a ruminant, an even-toed hoofed mammal in a suborder that includes cattle and deer. It proved to be an embarrassing misidentification. A maintenance man working with Leakey soon discovered more of the prints, and eventually they were determined to be an important find—the footprint trail of ancient hominids, or human ancestors.

Robbins had, in a sense, put her footprints in her mouth, but she soon learned that it didn't matter in the legal world of forensic testimony. At any given time, there are a number of high-stakes trials going on around the country, and the lawyers involved in those cases need experts willing to testify. Many of those "experts" are not really experts at all, but the courts are so lenient that such people are allowed to testify anyway. Suddenly Robbins was getting calls from lawyers asking her to appear in criminal trials.

Robbins had noticed that people wear down the bottoms of their shoes in various ways because they walk differently. Some people wear down the outside of the heel first, for example, while others rub away the inside. She also knew that the bone structures of people's feet vary. Robbins decided this meant each individual has a unique "wear pattern" that could be used to match a person to any of his or her shoeprints, even if they changed shoes. That meant she could look at a leather shoe and determine whether the wearer had left a particular set of gym shoeprints. Carried away with her new notions, she claimed she could determine the sex, race, and socioeconomic status of a person just by looking at a shoeprint.

Some prosecutors were ecstatic. They wouldn't necessarily use her in a solid case, of course, where doubts about her claims would be an unnecessary risk. But in a case where there was nothing much else to go on, why not? And so Louise Robbins found herself in courtroom after courtroom, testifying for both prosecutors and the defense. In every case, her conclusions favored the side that had paid her to do the testing, usually the prosecution. She helped put people in prison for life, even though she had never actually proved that she could match up a single unidentified shoeprint with the person who had made it.

Buckley's shoeprint was a big challenge, though. The pattern of curved rays on the bottom of the heel was similar to the pattern on the Nicaricos' door, but most of the rays on Buckley's shoe curved in the opposite direction. Buckley had bought his New Silver Cloud shoes at Payless Shoes, which was supplied by a

Spanish factory that had done a cheap knockoff of a hiking shoe popular at the time. Another Spanish factory had done a similar knockoff to the same specifications called the Cloud Climber shoe, which was supplied to Fayva shoe stores. The rays on the door were more like the Fayva pattern, but none of the suspects had a Fayva shoe.

Robbins's technique was neither high-tech nor especially scientific. All she needed was a ruler and a protractor. She measured the shoes, looked at the bottoms, made some test impressions, and came to her conclusion: only a shoe worn by Stephen Buckley could have made the print on Jeanine Nicarico's front door.

Knight's case was starting to come together. Using Robbins's shoeprint testimony, he could argue that Buckley had kicked in the door. Because Buckley had kicked in the door, Knight could argue that Buckley also was the Caucasian man who was driving the car on Clover Court and the Prairie Path.

Of course, no one had seen Buckley abduct Jeanine, and no one could say he was the one who had murdered her. That was where Alex Hernandez and Rolando Cruz came in. Knight suspected they had been involved in the murder; it was just a matter of getting the evidence. The special grand jury gave Knight the ability to get that information. He could use it to compel testimony from associates of Cruz and Hernandez, working-class Hispanics off the street who, Knight was sure, knew or had heard something of the murder. They weren't people who would show up with lawyers or file motions to quash subpoenas. If Knight subpoenaed them, they would have to come. And if they came, Knight knew, they would have to talk.

For six months, Knight and the grand jury trudged their way through hours of testimony from police officers, eyewitnesses, and various young East Aurora men with criminal records who knew Stephen Buckley, Rolando Cruz, or Alex Hernandez. Finally, a young East Aurora man who knew Rolando Cruz tied Cruz to the crime.

Ramon "Chuck" Mares, the nephew of Cruz's aunt's ex-husband, testified that early on a June 1983 evening, he and Cruz had gone for a two-hour ride northward from Aurora and back again, during which they had smoked a joint and drunk a twelve-pack of Budweiser. During the drive, Mares said, Cruz admitted that he had been present when Jeanine was murdered but said that he hadn't done it himself.

Now Knight had a piece of the puzzle, someone who could link Cruz directly to the crime. His next piece came from Dan Fowler, who had met Cruz in the Kane County Jail. At first, Fowler said only that Cruz claimed to have known who'd committed the crime. But after the grand jury took a lunch break, Fowler said he had held back some details. He said that Cruz was at the scene of the murder and knew the location of a bat that was used to kill Jeanine. Later, a defense investigator said Fowler had claimed that Knight had pressured him for more information during the lunch break and had threatened to indict him for perjury. Knight later denied pressuring Fowler.

The case was coming together. Louise Robbins, the shoeprint witness, was ready to say that Buckley had kicked in the Nicaricos' door. Ramon Mares and Dan Fowler had testified that Cruz had admitted he was present at the murder. All Knight needed was something to tie Alex Hernandez directly to the crime. Finally, Knight found that link.

It came from Jackie Estremera, Alex Hernandez's young cousin. Estremera had testified before the grand jury at an earlier time, but he had said little of significance. Now, fearful because Knight had threatened to jail him over the weekend for missing a grand jury appointment, he was ready to say more. He testified that he'd heard Alex Hernandez admit to being present when he and Cruz had broken into the Nicaricos' house to commit a burglary. They had gone to Naperville because the people there had nicer things to steal, he said. Both of them had been high after sniffing paint fumes. They had found the girl and Cruz had killed her so that she couldn't identify them.

Now, Knight had the basis of a case, but it was uncomfortably shaky. The testimony from Mares, Fowler, and Estremera was critical but also vague. On January 26, almost a year after the crime, Knight's boss, J. Michael Fitzsimmons, issued an appeal to the public for more information.

No significant new information surfaced. The primary election was rapidly approaching, and Jim Ryan was running a strong campaign against Fitzsimmons. On March 8, just twelve days before the election, Knight asked the grand jury to indict Buckley, Cruz, and Hernandez.

That evening, John Sam got a call from Detective Warren Wilkosz telling him he was to come back to the sheriff's headquarters later that night. "One of Tom Knight's bullshit adventures," Sam thought to himself, but he agreed to go. When he showed up at headquarters, he saw it wasn't another pointless East Aurora hiking expedition. The grand jury had indicted Knight's three suspects, and Sam was to help round them up.

Cruz was no problem; he was already in jail. He'd gone in on a felony theft charge Knight had pressed, claiming Cruz had stolen a stereo from an apartment unit in the building where the county had put him up. Police had brought Cruz back from Ohio, where he'd gone after completing training as a cable TV installer. He had been visiting a young woman, the daughter of the local mayor, and had been lounging on a recliner in a pool at the moment he was picked up. After Cruz's sentence for felony theft had run out in January, Knight had kept him in jail by charging him with perjury for lying about his birth date (he'd put 1960 on his driver's license so he could buy liquor even though his real birthday was May 26, 1963) and saying he'd served in the Marines. He also was charged with obstruction of justice for going to Ohio.

Sam and the other detectives headed to Aurora to get Buckley and Hernandez.

Hernandez recently had been discharged from the Elgin Mental Health Center after admitting himself voluntarily. His father had thrown him out of the family home again, so he was staying at a Catholic mission in Aurora. When the detectives got there, Hernandez wasn't in. It was an odd feeling for Sam as the detectives waited in the parking lot. Here he was with his boss, Sergeant James Montesano, and a third detective, all waiting to arrest someone Sam thought was innocent. Montesano, Sam was sure, thought Hernandez was innocent, too, although he wouldn't come out and say it. Instead, he would caution Sam to keep his opinions to himself. Rather than talk about Hernandez, the men chatted idly about neutral topics. Finally, they saw Hernandez cross the mission yard, and they called him over to their squad car. You're coming with us, they told him.

Back at the jail, the detectives presented Hernandez with his stack of indictments. "You win them all, these are all yours," Sam said. "You're going to get a lethal injection, but if you want to make a deal to save your life, Tom Knight is right here. If you want a lawyer, whatever you want, we have everything right here. We'll make it real easy. All you got to do is tell us who was with you and everything about it, and that way we guarantee you don't get the lethal injection."

Hernandez realized he was in big trouble, but he still insisted he was innocent. Five people, including Detectives Sam and Wilkosz and Assistant State's Attorneys Tom Knight and Patrick King, grilled Hernandez for about three and a half hours, pushing him to make a deal, but all he said was that he didn't do it. Finally, at about 3:15 A.M., they gave up and sent him to the jail's booking chute, a room separated from the booking office by a glass partition. Hernandez was crying and shaking, saying, "Not me, not me." It was time to go pick up Stephen Buckley.

This time, the sheriff's deputies notified the Aurora police, who sent six officers to help arrest Buckley at his home. To Sam, it seemed as though half of the Aurora Police Department was there, along with the four DuPage County detectives, all prepared for a middle-of-the-night shootout with John Dillinger rather than picking up a young man so mild mannered he'd walk up to an electric chair and sit down if he was told to.

The procedure with Buckley was the same as it had been with Hernandez. They brought him back to the sheriff's headquarters, showed him the stack of indictments, and told him he would die if he didn't make a deal with Knight. As did Hernandez, Buckley continued to protest that he was innocent. Finally, Knight and the detectives gave up trying to get an admission and sent him to be booked.

The indictments were announced on March 9, the day after they were returned by the grand jury. To the public, it sounded as though the case had been solved. But Knight had many weaknesses in his theory that three Aurora burglars killed Jeanine after they found her home alone. The four eyewitnesses who saw a car reported seeing just one white man. Their descriptions of that man did not match any of the suspects. Joann Johannville, the only witness to be shown a photo lineup, could not identify anyone. Except for the shoeprint that John Gorajczyk had said wasn't Buckley's, there was no physical evidence, and the theory that Louise Robbins used to match the print to Buckley was controversial. The blanket and sheet taken from the Nicarico home and Jeanine's missing underpants never were found. The unidentified fingerprints found in the Nicarico home did not belong to Buckley, Cruz, or Hernandez. The three men had no known access to any car matching the descriptions given by witnesses. The three suspects also had no history of violent or sexual crimes and had never been accused of committing any kind of crime together. Cruz and Hernandez had spun stories for authorities, but none included inside information, none matched the facts of the case, and they were all different. The witnesses ready to testify that Cruz and Hernandez had admitted taking part in the crime similarly were unable to provide any inside information.

"I can't believe they indicted them on the evidence they have," a top DuPage official familiar with the investigation told a reporter.

Even though Sam believed the men he'd arrested were innocent, the indictments didn't bother him that much. "Hell, I ain't infallible," he said. "Maybe these guys do know something, and the indictments will jar it loose."

As long as he thought he might be on the trail of the real killer, Sam didn't mind if Buckley, Cruz, and Hernandez were miserable. Still, when Buckley and Hernandez had been sent down to the jail, Sam knew a line had been crossed. The criminal justice system had, he believed, imprisoned three innocent people. Now Sam had two jobs: tracking down a killer who no one would admit was still at large, and helping to free innocent men charged with what was sure to be a capital offense.

The next morning, Sam made an unusual trip. He went to the cell where Stephen Buckley, now incarcerated, was wearing a prison-issue orange jumpsuit.

"Steve," Sam said, "I know you didn't do it. And if you can think of anything I can do to prove you're innocent, let me know what it is."

Buckley didn't have any suggestions. That didn't surprise Sam. Probably, he thought to himself as he left, this guy thinks this is just another bullshit plot to get him to talk.

Sam was at a dead end. Three young men he believed were innocent were in jail. A killer was on the loose. And nobody seemed to care.

6

DONNA SCHNORR

Serial killers . . . spread their depredations from jurisdiction to jurisdiction, knowing that separate police departments have difficulty coordinating their investigations of such crimes.

Stephen G. Michaud and Hugh Aynesworth,
Murderers among Us

O N JULY 15, 1984, FOUR months after Stephen Buckley, Rolando Cruz, and Alex Hernandez were jailed, Donna Schnorr was driving home in the wee hours of the morning. Schnorr had been at a volleyball party with more than sixty people, including coworkers, in a small town south of Aurora called Oswego. A coworker and friend, James Hames, was driving behind to keep an eye on her.

Donna, age twenty-seven, was popular with staff members at Mercy Hospital in Aurora, where she was a floor nurse in the cardiovascular unit. She had grown up in Waterman, a small Illinois farm town, and gone to work at the hospital after graduating from Rockford Memorial School of Nursing in Rockford, Illinois.

"The first thing that comes to mind about Donna is that she was so well-liked by so many people," her younger brother, Roger, recalled later. "She made everyone feel comfortable around her. She had a lot of friends at work and on her softball team, and of course she was very close to her family. She was the type of person you would love to be around."

Hames didn't follow Donna all the way home. Instead, nearing his own home, he turned off in Aurora, and Donna continued north on Randall Road alone. Behind her now was a scruffy young man, a lone killer, driving an old brown Impala.

The man should have been in jail. Two months before, he'd been released from the DuPage County Jail on a $20,000 recognizance bond for burglary, even though he had a long history of offenses.

That very evening, in fact, police in the Kane County city of Geneva had released him after stopping him again. He had been pulled over for a traffic offense and charged with "depositing injurious material on the highway," although the nature of that material was not specified in the police report. He was released on his own recognizance and had hitchhiked back to his car, which he'd left near the shoulder of the road.

The young man had first seen Donna, alone, at a stoplight in Aurora. He'd decided to follow her north on Randall Road.

Moments later, at around 4:00 A.M., the calm of the rustic night was shattered. A farmer, out having an early morning glass of lemonade at his picnic table, heard a car horn honking wildly and saw two cars on Randall Road that he thought were drag racing. The young man's Impala then crashed into Donna's car and knocked it off the highway.

Donna's light green 1979 Monte Carlo came to rest on a grassy area just off the shoulder. The young man pulled up directly behind her, trapping her car between his car and a fence. Quickly she locked her driver's side door, but the window was rolled down because her air-conditioning was not working. As

Donna slid toward the passenger-side door, desperately trying to get out, the man reached inside her car and turned off the ignition.

He crawled through the open window, and just as Donna got the passenger-side door open, he grabbed her. The two fell struggling onto the grass, but the man was too strong and forced Donna into his own car. Then he made her lie down on the front seat and tied her hands behind her back. He returned to her car with a rag and wiped the area around the driver's door to remove fingerprints. Then he took her purse, removing the money and wallet and leaving the rest lying in the middle of the road. The last thing the farmer heard was a loud scream.

Moments later, a patrol car happened on Donna's car. The patrol officer saw an abandoned car with the door open, the interior lights on, and the key in the ignition. The engine was not running. The patrolman assumed the car had been abandoned by a drunken driver who had wandered off, and he radioed for a truck to tow the car away.

About one hundred yards to the south was a cornfield-lined gravel lane called Mooseheart Road. The next day, Dan Davis, the husband of one of Donna's cousins, a man trained in tracking while performing reconnaissance duties in Vietnam, found the fresh tracks of a barefoot woman next to a man's shoeprints leading from a spot along Mooseheart Road where a car clearly had pulled over. Possibly, Davis theorized, the perpetrator had led Donna from the car at that point, or perhaps she tried to escape before he forced her back into the car. Some distance away, he found a wooden bat, which he later turned in to police.

The young man who had abducted Donna, in describing the incident to police later, said nothing about Mooseheart Road. Instead, he said he first had decided to drive Donna to Lake

Geneva, a resort city in Wisconsin, but changed his mind. By the time he could get there, it would already be getting light outside. So instead he took her eleven miles to the Seavey quarry, a water-filled abandoned gravel pit on land owned by the Nagel Excavating Company where he had often taken his former girlfriend, Denise, and other friends swimming that summer.

At the quarry, the young man later told police, he led Donna through the area, forcing her to perform oral sex and raping her at least twice. Although he'd removed her clothes, he let her put her blouse back on because the mosquitoes were so bad. Finally, he dragged her into the water. At some point, he also struck her head with his fist or a blunt instrument. She resisted, but she was not strong enough. She did get a big breath of air before he forced her head underwater, but he struck her on her back to force the air out of her lungs as she struggled furiously. After a few minutes, she stopped struggling, and he knew she was dead. It was about 4:40 A.M. He dragged Donna's body out of the water but did not leave right away.

Finally, he decided it was time to go. As he drove out of the Seavey quarry at about 5:00 A.M., three other young men were just arriving to swim and fish. They were surprised to see another car. The car leaving the quarry flashed its brights at them, which made it hard for them to read the license plate, but they did manage to see some of the numbers. They also noticed that the car was a Chevrolet that they thought was maroon. They saw Donna's body as soon as they reached the water.

The next morning, Clara and Bernard "Bud" Schnorr, Donna's parents, were surprised when Donna did not show up at church. Donna traveled every Sunday to her parents' home in Waterman, and the family would go to Trinity Lutheran Church in nearby DeKalb. This Sunday the Schnorrs planned to have their photo taken for the church directory after the service. Then they planned to have lunch at the local Ponderosa Steakhouse.

Donna did not show up for the photo shoot, either. At the Ponderosa, the Schnorrs nervously watched cars pull in and out of the parking lot. Their uneasiness increased as they drove back home to Waterman.

When they arrived, a uniformed DeKalb County sheriff's deputy was standing in the driveway. He told Bud and Clara that Donna's car, with the gearshift still in drive, had been found on the shoulder of Randall Road and that the contents of her purse had been scattered on the pavement. Then he told them that Donna's body had been found in the Seavey quarry.

Donna's brother, Roger, was sitting in his living room in a small Illinois town near the Iowa border, watching a Chicago Cubs baseball game, when the phone rang. His wife, Karen, was lying outside in the sun when she heard Roger start to scream. When Karen took the phone from her shocked husband, she learned from her brother-in-law, Kurt, that Donna was dead. Roger threw a suit into his car, and he and his wife headed for Waterman.

Howard Jacobsen, the pastor of Trinity Lutheran Church, and his wife, Lois, were already at the Schnorr home when Roger and Karen arrived. Bud and Clara were just sitting, hunched over and crying. Roger had never seen his father cry before, except in happiness at Roger and Karen's wedding.

"That was a terrible scene," Roger recalled later. "To witness the uncontrollable crying by your dad and mom and sisters—I just could not believe that this had happened. And to actually absorb the fact that Donna was dead, to just try to imagine that someone would kill her, was just unbelievable. It was just too much to take at one time."

On Monday, Bud Schnorr, who'd had no history of heart trouble, had a sudden heart attack. He never recovered fully and was able to attend his daughter's funeral for only a short time while confined to a wheelchair. He died of a second heart attack two days after Christmas of that year at age sixty-two, another victim, his family was sure, of his daughter's murderer.

"[Bud] died when Donna died," Clara later told a reporter. "He never got over it. That killed him. She was his pride and joy, and they found her like that."

At Donna's visitation and funeral, police tailed her former boyfriend, who operated an auto body shop near the small village of Big Rock, west of Aurora. Police theorized that his skill as an auto body repairman might have allowed him to disassemble or repair his car, hiding any evidence of a collision with Donna's car. Police repeatedly searched the farm where he lived and also searched nearby ponds where they thought he might have dumped damaged parts of his car. When investigators learned that the former boyfriend had put a note in Donna's casket, they exhumed her body and read it. It said simply that he loved her and missed her.

Meanwhile, Donna's family was growing increasingly frustrated at the slow pace of the official investigation and its focus on Donna's former boyfriend, whom they believed to be innocent. Roger and Bud Schnorr drove around the area, looking for a car matching the description of the one seen at the quarry. They were frustrated that police didn't seem to take seriously the wooden bat that Dan Davis had found some distance from the footprints along Mooseheart Road. The bat appeared to have blood on it, and they thought it might have been used in the crime. (Authorities did test the bat for blood, but the test was negative.)

Police asked Donna's parents to invite the former boyfriend over and to intentionally irritate him so that he might make some kind of statement admitting his involvement in Donna's murder. The plan called for putting a microphone under the kitchen table. The police were to wait outside, in a van near the house, while one officer was to be stationed in the basement. But the family refused, fearing that a sneeze from the policeman in the basement could give away the ruse and make it appear the family had no confidence in the man who had loved their daughter. Finally, the Kane County authorities hired a polygraph expert from New York who had been featured on national news programs. The expert tested the former boyfriend and said the results conclusively showed he was guilty.

The Schnorr family was shocked. Roger thought, "God, this is unbelievable. How could he have done that to Donna?"

John Sam did not know much about the Donna Schnorr murder, which had happened in another county. Under Sheriff Doria's administration, DuPage did not coordinate murder investigations with the state police, as some other counties did. Sam couldn't start assuming that every murder had been committed by the killer he was pursuing. But he was sure Jeanine's killer was on the loose, and he was determined to find him.

Sam wasn't alone anymore. He'd been joined in his off-hours investigation by James Teal, the Naperville police chief.

The Naperville Police Department's role in the investigation had been limited ever since the day of Jeanine's abduction, when the county sheriff's deputies curtly ordered the local police off the scene. Naperville officers had put in plenty of hours anyway, combing the area for Jeanine until her body was found. Teal had seen how the horror of the murder had impacted Naperville.

"This crime affected little children for life," he said. "You could see the mood change in people."

When the task force was formed, Naperville contributed a dozen officers. Now, the more Teal learned about the special grand jury's work, the more he feared that the suspects were innocent.

Teal had spent the early years of his career on the street in Pontiac, Michigan, where police dealt daily with much more crime than occurred in affluent and relatively quiet DuPage County. After coming to Naperville, Teal had tried unsuccessfully to create a countywide DuPage murder task force so there would be at least one police agency experienced in investigating murders. Teal was familiar with people he referred to as "street bums" who lie to police, and he felt the special grand jury had focused on three suspects more quickly than the evidence indicated it should have. He had contributed Naperville police officers to the task force, but he felt they'd been used almost as decoys while authorities focused on Buckley, Cruz, and Hernandez. Teal didn't think the investigation was going in the right direction, and he wanted to get it back on track.

Teal had met first with Sheriff Richard Doria. Doria had been autocratic and scornful, acting as though Teal were a meddler who didn't know what he was talking about. Teal left feeling foolish. Perhaps, he thought, he just didn't know as much about the case as Doria did. Later, however, he heard that after he'd left, Doria had summoned Robert Soucek, his second-in-command, and demanded to know why Teal seemed to know *more* about the case than the sheriff's police did.

After Buckley, Cruz, and Hernandez had been indicted, Teal took Tom Knight to lunch at the Viking Restaurant, the same place Sam had been headed to on the day of Jeanine's murder.

"Look at the shoeprint evidence," he'd told Knight, "you can tell just by looking that Buckley's shoeprint is different from the print on the door." Teal held up shoeprint photos that he'd brought with him to demonstrate that the rays in the pattern on the heels curved in opposite directions. Knight, though, just put the photos aside and didn't look at them.

Knight had not been scornful, as Doria had been. Instead, he'd been earnest. He'd talked with such certainty about reverse negatives—about the inverting effect of a shoe hitting a door as the door fell away, wear patterns and other technicalities—that Teal became confused and almost believed he was wrong. When he got back to his office, he reviewed the data and assured himself that he wasn't crazy, that there really was very little evidence against the suspects. But Knight, he saw, was a man really convinced that he had the right defendants.

Now Teal was ready to help Sam find the real killer. Both of them were sure that if they could get a good lead, Teal could bring the resources of the Naperville Police Department to bear on the case until the killer was tracked down.

The two men decided to start by taking another look at a lawyer's son Knight had discarded as a suspect early in the case. Although there was nothing directly linking the lawyer's son to the crime, they wanted to make sure he'd been checked out thoroughly.

The lawyer's son lived in a prominent Naperville neighborhood. He'd sneaked out of Naperville Central High School on the day of Jeanine's abduction and was known to have been walking by the Nicarico house that afternoon. Data that turned up in the first few days after Jeanine's murder showed that he'd known Jeanine's sisters, that he had been to the Nicarico home in the past, and, more intriguing, that his girlfriend had torn her entry for the day of the murder out of her diary. The diary was significant because the girlfriend was his alibi—she'd confirmed his story that he spent the afternoon with her.

In addition, Sam had been told that the lawyer's son had at one time had a green Granada, the kind of car the tollway workers thought they'd seen on the Prairie Path on the day of the murder. Sam and Teal figured that he was the right place to start their investigation.

Sam started by talking to some of the suspect's friends one evening to see what he might learn. The next day, he came to work at three o'clock, and his captain, Kenneth Lepic, and lieutenant, Robert Soucek, said they wanted to talk to him.

Lepic had had an idea that Sam was doing his own investigating and had been studiously looking the other way, so he didn't talk much. But Soucek had plenty to say.

"What the fuck are you doing?"

Sam was forthright. "I'm looking into this guy."

Soucek wasn't pleased. "The sheriff's on my ass. What the fuck are you doing? His lawyer called here and wanted to know why are we harassing his client and all this shit. The case is solved."

Soucek told Sam that Sheriff Doria wanted to talk to him, so Sam went to the sheriff's office. Doria was on the phone, talking with the suspect's lawyer.

"I got him in here now, and I'll find out the story," Doria was saying to the lawyer.

Sam was disgusted. "What's the problem?" he asked, when Doria hung up the phone.

Doria gave Sam an angry look. "This lawyer said you were at the school yesterday, telling everybody that his client killed Jeanine Nicarico."

Now Sam was angry, too. "So what school was I at?"

"I don't know, some school in Naperville."

"What school do you know that has students in it at six or seven o'clock at night?" Sam asked. "Who did I tell, the janitor? Because I was here in this office until five-thirty, six o'clock. I took another guy with me, and we didn't even talk to this guy till about nine o'clock at night."

Doria really didn't care whether Sam was at the school. He just didn't want any more calls from lawyers.

"Why are you doing this?" he asked Sam.

"Because these guys in jail didn't do it," Sam replied. "I'm looking for the killer. I don't know if this guy did it, but I'll tell you what. What's this guy calling a lawyer for, already? Shit, I go out one night, and the lawyer's on the phone the next day? If I were you, I'd kinda wonder about *him,* not me."

Doria didn't care about that, either. "Tom Knight's mad at you, everybody's pissed off," he said. "This case is solved. We've got the guys."

"Bullshit," Sam said. "Tom Knight, my ass."

Now Doria was firm. "I'm telling you, we got this case solved. This is a case—we did everything we possibly could. We beat every tree in the forest, and it's a big goddamned forest. What do you think we should do?"

"I don't know," Sam said. "Maybe just sit back and wait. I don't know. But we can't sit back and throw three guys in jail who didn't do it."

Doria was tired of arguing. "Well, from now on, anything you do, you check with Tom Knight," he said.

"Who do I work for, Tom Knight? Or do I work for you?"

"On this case," Doria said, "I want you to go through Tom Knight."

Sam was furious.

"The guy that did this is still out there, and I'm being told not to look for him," he would say to anyone who cared to listen. "Well, if we ain't looking for him, who is?"

Buckley, Cruz, and Hernandez had been in jail for months. Their trial would start in less than two months. Time was running out, and he was nowhere close to finding the killer.

"I'm sitting back thinking, what the fuck am I going to do?" Sam said later. "I never thought this was going to trial."

Going to trial was a big problem, because Sam would be expected to testify for the prosecution, helping to convict three men he thought were innocent. As the trial neared, Sam worried more and more about what he should do.

Then came the big blow. Sam was taken off felony investigations and reassigned to patrol convenience stores to make sure minors weren't buying liquor.

Sam had had enough. His investigation had been shut down. If he remained a detective, he would be expected to testify. Sam said he was going to quit. He'd made the same threat in the past when he was upset, and Doria had always talked him out of it. This time, Doria didn't argue. Sam gave his notice, and on December 1, 1984, he ended his career as a police officer.

"I wasn't going to hold his hand anymore," Doria later told a *Washington Post* reporter. "He was aggressive. He did his job. He was a good dick. But he's got a very big ego. Mine's big, too. Only I admit it, and I'm the boss."

It was a decision Sam regretted in some ways in later years, because he never made it back into police work and never found another job he liked as much. At the time, however, he felt he had little choice, even though he had to admit he'd failed to find the killer.

"You know, maybe deep down they all hoped I would have found something," Sam said later. "I don't know."

7

GARY JOHNSON

---

*A trial is not a sporting event where [participants] should
concern themselves with notches in their belt but instead a
fundamental method used by our society to determine the
truth.*

Supreme Court of Kansas, in re *Sue Carpenter*, 1991

G ARY JOHNSON KNEW HE couldn't win a trial by calling
everybody a liar. Yet it was hard to see another way to
free his client, Stephen Buckley.

It was January 1985, and the trial John Sam had dreaded was
about to begin. *The People of Illinois v. Stephen Buckley, Rolando
Cruz, and Alejandro Hernandez* was set to start in DuPage County's
crowded old courthouse in downtown Wheaton. Each defendant
was charged with twelve counts of murder, rape, kidnapping,
deviate sexual assault, aggravated indecent liberties with a child,
home invasion, and residential burglary.

Johnson, a tall, slim young lawyer handling his first big criminal defense trial, had happened on the case almost by accident. In
fact, after graduating from Drake University Law School in Des
Moines, Iowa, he'd interviewed for a job as a DuPage County prosecutor, a job that might have brought him into the Nicarico case
on the prosecutors' side. Johnson had made it through three
rounds of interviews and was waiting one afternoon to see Tom

Knight for his final meeting when Knight came bounding down the stairs of the state's attorney's office with a racquetball racket in his hand.

Embarrassed, Knight realized he'd forgotten about the interview and asked Johnson if they could reschedule. Johnson had agreed, but before the new interview could take place, he had received a call from the state's attorney in adjoining Kane County. The state's attorney there, Gene Armentrout, earlier had given Johnson an interview because Johnson's parents lived next door to the mayor of one of Kane County's larger communities. It was Armentrout who had persuaded DuPage County officials to interview Johnson. Now, Armentrout had an opening and offered it to Johnson, who took it.

Johnson proved to be an excellent trial lawyer. Like Knight, he was aggressive and passionate and had a good instinct for how juries looked at evidence. He worked for four years as a prosecutor and then joined a small law firm, where he handled personal-injury lawsuits and other civil cases.

One day, Johnson ran into another lawyer, Cliff Lund, at the Kane County Courthouse.

"We were waiting in line to get our cases heard in a civil courtroom," Johnson recalled later. "I was a couple of years out of the state's attorney's office. I knew him just as a lawyer roughly my age. He said, 'Do you like being at the firm you are at?' I said, 'Yeah, they are good people, but it's all civil.' I said that I would like to get back involved in some criminal work, that I miss some of that. And his exact words were, 'Well, boy, do I have a case for you.'"

Lund had represented Stephen Buckley's sister, Norma, in an earlier case. When it finally became clear to the family that Stephen was likely to be indicted, Norma had called Lund. He'd immediately recognized the seriousness of the case and how much of an edge he'd lost by coming into it so late. Almost all of the witnesses had already testified before the grand jury, and, as he put it later, "What was down in ink was down in ink."

Lund, whose courtroom presence was more subdued than Johnson's, thought Johnson's fiery personality would help him represent Stephen Buckley.

"I'd had cases against Johnson, and I felt that his was the kind of physical dynamic and intellect that we needed for the case," Lund said. "I felt that this was a case that required two lawyers. And I felt two blond, blue-eyed lawyers in DuPage County would be very effective."

Tom Knight was the lead prosecutor, which was a surprise to just about everyone. Knight's boss, State's Attorney J. Michael Fitzsimmons, had, despite Knight's efforts before the grand jury, lost the election to Jim Ryan, and people had assumed Ryan would fire Knight because during the campaign Ryan had drawn support from local attorneys who disliked Knight. Fitzsimmons had tried to turn that against Ryan by proclaiming that "the defense lawyers want to move back into the state's attorney's office." He'd promised that wouldn't happen if he was reelected. Fitzsimmons also had stressed his independence from the county party chairman, James J. "Pate" Philip, who would later become the Illinois Senate president. But those tactics didn't win over enough votes. It appeared that once again, a change in administration would cost Knight his job.

In addition, as a criminal defense lawyer, Ryan had gone up against Knight in the courtroom, and the friction had sparked enough voltage to split atoms at the nearby Fermi National Accelerator Laboratory. In one case versus Ryan, Knight had asked that the record reflect that Ryan's face was just inches from Knight's and that Ryan was glowering at Knight. It wasn't surprising, then, that once installed in office, Ryan had announced that he would turn the Jeanine Nicarico murder case over to his capable new chief of criminal prosecutions, Brian Telander.

The prosecution complex, however, had worked itself too deeply into the case. The Nicaricos, together with their friends and neighbors, had become a political force in Naperville, and they thought taking Knight off the case was a bad idea. They collected thousands of names on petitions asking that Knight be retained. The Nicaricos had grown to trust Knight, and their friends and neighbors feared that a new prosecutor might take the case in a different direction, lose it, or even drop the charges. Ryan, a cautious politician who instinctively chose the path of least resistance, capitulated and kept Knight on temporarily as a special prosecutor.

As the opening day of the trial approached, Knight had most of the advantages. He and the second-chair lawyer, Patrick King, had been preparing for two years. Through his work with the special grand jury, Knight had familiarized himself with the intricate details of the case and, through his questioning, had weakened some potential defense witnesses' testimony. Affected by the prosecution complex, juries anywhere are likely to lower the conviction threshold for a crime as horrible as a child's murder, and in conservative DuPage County, the jury would be even more inclined to find a defendant guilty. Moreover, as is often the case in a crime that angers the public, Knight could count on favorable rulings from the judge on procedural issues.

"In this kind of a case, the prosecutors look like white knights going after a baby killer," Gary Johnson said later. "Even if they get caught doing something unethical, the judge is not going to punish them, because of the kind of case that it is. The judge is going to cut them a whole bunch of slack."

Because the three defendants were to be tried together, Lund and Johnson had to coordinate their efforts with the public defenders representing Cruz and Hernandez. Cruz's public defender was Tom Laz, a nine-year veteran of the office. Hernandez had Frank Wesolowski, the chief of the public defender's office. Wesolowski usually didn't handle cases anymore, but his staff was so burdened by its regular caseload that no one else was available.

Both Laz and Wesolowski faced serious constraints. Wesolowski still had to deal with the administrative matters of the office. And Laz was expected to handle a full load of about eighty other cases while he was preparing for the biggest trial in the county. It wasn't easy. At one point Laz found himself in court waiting for a case to be called when he noticed something familiar about a defendant who was talking to the judge.

"It seems I should know this guy," Laz whispered to Eugene Wojcik, another public defender.

The discussion at the bench continued. "Who's your lawyer?" the judge wanted to know. The defendant turned and pointed at Laz, who'd had so many things going on that he'd totally forgotten about the defendant's case. He hadn't even brought a case file with him.

It was no surprise that the public defenders had fewer resources than the prosecutors. That's how the county wanted it. In fact, some county officials thought the imbalance wasn't great enough. Wesolowski found himself stopped in hallways and criticized by members of the DuPage County Board who thought he shouldn't have assigned a separate lawyer to each of the two defendants who needed a public defender. One lawyer for both defendants would have been enough, they said.

Lund and Johnson were private lawyers, but they soon realized that they faced limitations, too. They wouldn't have the resources to put on the kind of case they wanted unless they spent all of their fees on defense experts and worked virtually for free. Early on, that's what they decided to do.

The prosecution did have one major weakness—a lack of evidence. The only physical evidence in the case was the shoeprint on the Nicaricos' door. The cases against Cruz and Hernandez consisted largely of the testimony by various young witnesses of dubious credibility who would say they heard Cruz or Hernandez admit they were involved. There also were statements to authorities by Cruz and Hernandez that didn't jibe with the facts. Several of the witnesses had changed their stories at least once, which would make it harder for the jury to believe them.

Not one of the defendants had admitted to police that he had taken a direct part in the crime. An admission to a police officer would carry far more weight with a DuPage County jury than vague statements from young men off the street who couldn't keep their stories straight or jailers repeating statements that didn't directly show guilt. But it seemed there was no such admission.

And then the prosecution got a boost that was going to be a nasty surprise for the defense lawyers.

On January 3, 1985—four days before jury selection was set to begin—the defense lawyers got a pretrial filing called Supplemental Disclosure X that said Rolando Cruz had made an oral statement to Detective Thomas Vosburgh that no one had heard about before. Later, Vosburgh would say that in that statement, which practically amounted to a confession, Cruz had described a vision in which he saw the victim sodomized—a fact that hadn't been made public—and her head struck so violently that it left an indentation in the ground. Cruz also had said the girl was dragged from her house by her ankles and left near a field. However, there was no mention of a vision or dream in the supplemental disclosure.

Cruz told his lawyer, Tom Laz, that he never had made such a statement. But the "vision" story still was a nightmare for the defense. Because it included four pieces of inside information about the murder, it tied Cruz directly to the crime and, by implication, made the case against Hernandez and Buckley stronger, too. For the defense lawyers to win, they would have to persuade a DuPage County jury that police officers were mistaken or lying. That would not be easy to do.

"In DuPage County, the juries seem to think that the prosecutors are always right," said Janet Petsche, a political candidate-turned-reporter who covered the DuPage County courts before becoming a lawyer herself. "They think that where there's smoke, there's fire. The juries are not as particular as they should be. They don't look at it as if the prosecutors have to prove their case. They want the defendants to prove their innocence, particularly in a place like DuPage County, which is law-and-order Republican."

The "vision" statement wasn't the only problem shaping up for the defense lawyers. They also started to see that they were likely to lose the key procedural battles in the trial. That became apparent when the defense found out about John Gorajczyk.

Under a rule called the Brady Rule (based on the U.S. Supreme Court ruling in *Brady v. Maryland*), prosecutors are supposed to give defense lawyers any information indicating that defendants might be innocent or that could raise questions about the prosecution's evidence or witnesses. The fact that John Gorajczyk—the county's own shoeprint expert—had looked at the shoeprint on the Nicaricos' door and concluded that it wasn't Buckley's was important information for the defense, but the prosecutors had never said anything about it. The defense lawyers learned about Gorajczyk's conclusion only a month before trial through a tip from another county employee.

Normally, a judge might penalize prosecutors for withholding such evidence, but the judge, Edward Kowal, did nothing.

Kowal was a respected jurist whose leniency toward parole violators had given his courtroom the nickname the Last Chance Garage. But Kowal had also been a longtime assistant state's attorney, and criminal defense lawyers who practiced in his courtroom felt that was where his sympathies lay. Moreover, Kowal knew he would have to run for reelection within a year.

"Kowal was a nice fellow—probably under most circumstances a good judge—but I got the idea that there was a lot of public pressure on him not to rock the boat in this case," Gary Johnson said.

Johnson knew that meant he was also likely to lose the most important pretrial issue: severance, or splitting the single trial sought by prosecutors into three separate trials, one for each defendant.

Severance is a question that comes up whenever there is more than one defendant in a trial. Often, if defendants are indicted together, they are tried together unless they have made accusations against each other. If there have been accusations, the trials often are severed, because every defendant has the constitutional right to cross-examine his accusers. That's not possible if a codefendant who made the accusations exercises his right not to testify.

Gary Johnson and the other defense lawyers wanted the trial severed because they thought their clients would have a better chance to win. In a single trial involving all three defendants, the jury would tend to apply evidence against one defendant to all three. "Guilt by association," Gary Johnson called it, and he wanted to prevent it if he could. Separate trials would help the jury focus on how little evidence there really was against each of the defendants.

On the other hand, a joint trial would present a parade of witnesses before the jury. Each of their stories might be suspect, but together, they might be convincing. And if the defense lawyers called all of them liars, the jurors would start to suspect that the defense was simply attacking every witness, no matter what he or she said.

"Oftentimes, if jurors believe a guy made a statement, then they will sweep in everybody," Johnson said. "We didn't want Steve Buckley sitting in a trial where Alex Hernandez's and Rolando Cruz's statements were coming in."

Tom Knight wanted a single trial, however, so he suggested an alternative. Whenever a statement by Hernandez or Cruz that implicated the others was mentioned during the trial, the names of the other defendants would be edited out. This process, called redaction, would protect the defendants' constitutional rights while allowing a single trial, Knight argued.

Kowal accepted Knight's plan and ruled that there would be a single trial. That touched off more debate over how the statements would be edited. The defense lawyers feared it would be done in a way that would make it clear to the jury whose names had been left out.

"We kept asking the judge every time we went to court: if you are not going to allow us to have the trials severed, we would like to see these redacted statements," Cliff Lund recalled later. "And every time Kowal would turn to Knight, and Knight would say, 'I'm not done with it yet.' And we objected, and Kowal just said, 'Well, Tom's a busy man.' "

The next step was jury selection. The defense lawyers tried to pick jurors who seemed educated and thoughtful, on the theory that they would be less swayed by emotion and more likely to see how scant the evidence was.

"Our theory of the case from the very get-go was that Stephen Buckley didn't do it and that no evidence showed that he did do it," Lund said. Public defenders Laz and Wesolowski, meanwhile, hoped to bring out the contradictions and unreliable nature of the evidence against their clients, Cruz and Hernandez.

And then the opening day of the trial arrived.

The trial started on January 14, 1985, on the second floor of the old courthouse. A jury of eight men and four women had been selected. Thomas and Patricia Nicarico attended, accompanied by their pastor, Father Mike, and several friends and relatives. The Nicaricos sat expressionless in the benches behind the prosecutors' table.

The morning session was devoted to a final battle over the editing of statements by one defendant that implicated another. Gary Johnson wanted Judge Kowal to forbid Knight from linking Buckley to Hernandez by saying they had had a social relationship or mentioning that Hernandez had said Buckley was in the car with the mysterious "Ricky." After much argument back and forth,

Judge Kowal said he would ensure that the statements did not cause a problem. And then, after lunch, it was time for the trial to begin.

Criminal trials start with an opening statement by the prosecutor, followed by a statement from the defense. The opening statements give lawyers a chance to outline their cases so that jurors will understand the significance of what they later see and hear during the presentation of evidence, or what lawyers call the "case in chief."

The prosecutors entered the courtroom and walked to their table on the left side of the courtroom, near the jury box. Steve Buckley, Rolando Cruz, and Alex Hernandez, wearing street clothes instead of their prison-issue jumpsuits, were brought to a table on the right side of the courtroom, where they sat with their defense lawyers. The twelve jurors and two alternates filed in. Judge Kowal, in his black robe, sat at a raised bench in the center.

"The main thing I remember about the trial was the atmosphere," Gary Johnson recalled later. "You could really feel the hatred. You could cut it with a knife. The anti–Hernandez, Cruz, and Buckley sentiment was very steep."

Knight used his opening statement to weave together the stories of Buckley, Cruz, and Hernandez. He argued that they planned to burglarize Jeanine Nicarico's house but wound up abducting, raping, and murdering the girl instead. Referring to a large map that showed Naperville and the Prairie Path, he drew a picture of a day that had started out as an average morning in a quiet residential neighborhood.

"The only thing the least little bit out of the ordinary that morning was the fact that ten-year-old Jeanine Nicarico was staying home with what may have been a touch of the twenty-four-hour flu," Knight said.

He mentioned how Patricia Nicarico had come home to fix lunch and had later talked to Jeanine on the telephone at about 1:00 P.M. He described how Jeanine was missing by 3:05 P.M., when her sister Kathy came home and how Jeanine's body was found at the Prairie Path two days later.

"There would be no safe return of Jeanine Nicarico," Knight said. "They determined she had been brutally assaulted and murdered."

Next, Knight told how police had traced an anonymous caller with the tip about Alex Hernandez. Then he quoted Hernandez as saying that when the mysterious "Ricky" claimed to be the killer, "My two friends, Mike Castro and Steve Buckley, [were] present."

Friends. That was just what Johnson had been trying to prevent. He objected immediately, and Judge Kowal reminded Knight to leave out other names, but it was too late. The connection between Hernandez and Buckley had been drawn.

Knight went on to talk about the shoeprint and the experts who had examined Buckley's shoe. He talked about statements that Hernandez had allegedly made about the actions of himself and his "partners." He also said that the shoeprints by the dining room window showed that more than one intruder had been present.

"I submit that the evidence will show that they went to the home, that one or two of them peeked in the dining room window at the southwest corner of the home where the curtain was open and [they] could see some silver service sitting on the buffet there in the living room, a prime item for the burglary that they were scouting out," Knight said. "I submit that they then went around to the front door, where, protected from view, at least partially, by a large evergreen tree in front of the front door at the Nicarico home, the defendant Buckley kicked the door."

He then described how Jeanine had been caught and dragged from her home, getting one hand free long enough to make a last desperate grab at the wall by the front door.

"Where they took her immediately from there, the evidence may not completely show, but the evidence will show that in [a] short time she was raped, sodomized, blindfolded, beaten, and murdered by probably three o'clock in the afternoon," he said.

As soon as Knight finished, Johnson asked that a mistrial be declared. Knight, he argued, had linked Buckley to Hernandez's statements by using the term "partners" and by revealing that Hernandez had said Buckley was in the car with the mysterious "Ricky."

"It was in direct violation of the court's earlier order not to refer to names," Johnson said. Judge Kowal, however, denied the motion for mistrial and ordered the case to proceed.

Giving the response were Tom Laz for Cruz and Gary Johnson for Buckley. Frank Wesolowski decided to reserve his opening statement on behalf of Hernandez until later in the trial.

Laz and Johnson told the jury that there was no real evidence in the case, that the jurors would be left with a puzzling litany of doubts. But even as they gave their arguments, they knew they were fighting the prosecution complex. They knew the jurors would hesitate to put the defendants back on the street if there was any chance, however remote, that they were guilty. The bar for a guilty verdict would be set very low indeed.

The first week of the trial was devoted mostly to setting the scene and providing details of the crime that had occurred. Alternating between smiles and sobs, Patricia Nicarico talked about her last lunch with her daughter and identifying her badly disfigured body at the morgue by a scar on her chin and a little space between her teeth. Jeanine's sister Kathy described how she ran to get a neighbor when she got home from school and realized Jeanine was missing. The neighbor had telephoned Patricia at work and told her to come home. Detectives and evidence technicians testified about their methods for obtaining and preserving evidence. The men who found her body told how they saw it blindfolded and almost nude at the Prairie Path. Mohammad A. Tahir, a forensic scientist for the Illinois Department of Law Enforcement, said too little semen was found to determine the attacker's blood type.

On Friday, the fifth day of the trial, Dr. Frank Cleveland of Cincinnati, the coroner of Hamilton County, Ohio, testified. Cleveland, who was considered an expert on determining time of death, said the victim died two to four hours after eating lunch on the day she was abducted. He said the five blows to her head were so strong that they would have killed her almost immediately. He said she was killed at or near the place where her body was found.

In the second week of the trial, Knight started calling witnesses to the stand who could repeat incriminating statements they said had been made by Cruz or Hernandez. The crux of the cases against Cruz and Hernandez had begun.

Jackie Estremera, Hernandez's sixteen-year-old cousin, said Hernandez had told him of a longstanding plan to burglarize the Nicaricos' home. "[He said] they were all messed up on paint [fumes]," Estremera said. "He said that they went up to the house, but he never got out of the car. . . . They knocked the door down, they kicked it in."

On cross-examination, Frank Wesolowski asked, "Did you

make up the contents of the conversation because you were being cited before the grand jury?"

"Yes," Estremera said, before the judge could sustain the prosecutor's objection.

Under subsequent questioning from Knight, however, Estremera reverted to his original story.

Next, Dan Fowler, age twenty, who had met Cruz in the Kane County Jail, said that while he was driving with Cruz and drinking beer in the spring of 1983, Cruz had broken down in tears and admitted to having been at the scene of the crime.

"He said he was there, but he wasn't involved in what happened," Fowler said.

Fowler also explained why he had changed his testimony from what he had said at his first appearance before the grand jury, when he'd testified that Cruz had never said anything about being involved, but had only said he knew the people who did it and was testifying against them.

"I was holding back," he said. "I didn't want to get so involved, like, so I'd end up here today."

Unlike some of the other witnesses, Fowler came across as reluctant but believable.

Knight also used Fowler's testimony to help link the three suspects when Fowler testified that the people who committed the crime were "friends" of Cruz's.

"Did he say where they were from?" Knight asked.

"Aurora," Fowler said.

Fowler was followed by Ramon "Chuck" Mares, age twenty-four, who told a story similar to the one he had given the grand jury, although now he said his conversation with Cruz occurred on a March night instead of a June evening, as he had told the grand jury.

"We were sitting there, joking, laughing, talking regular," Mares said. "He just said my name, and I said, 'What?' And he said, 'Do you remember the killing of the little girl from Naperville? . . . Chuck, don't tell nobody, but I was there . . . but I didn't kill her.' "

Armindo "Penguino" Marquez, age twenty, testified that during his conversation in the room with the box of money, Hernandez had admitted taking part in the crime. Hernandez had said his partner pulled the victim out of her house by her ankles and that the girl was killed because she was making too much noise.

"He held her and the other guy hit her," Penguino said. "She was dumped and stomped on the back of her head."

Penguino also testified that he had seen Buckley and Hernandez together almost every day. He said he saw Hernandez and Cruz together two or three times a week.

Gary Johnson demanded a mistrial for the second time.

"Armindo Marquez says that Alex and his partner go out and do this crime and then in the same breath, on questioning from the prosecutor, he said that Buckley and Hernandez are seen together every single day," Johnson complained to Judge Kowal outside of the jury's hearing. "If you can't get an inference that the partners are . . . Rolando Cruz and Stephen Buckley, there is something thick upstairs that needs work on. The inference is crystal clear that we are talking about Cruz and Buckley."

Judge Kowal, however, denied the motion.

To prove that Penguino was not testifying just to get a light sentence for all his burglaries, prosecutors put first assistant Kane County state's attorney Thomas F. Sullivan Jr. on the stand. Sullivan testified that Marquez had received no special treatment.

He also said he never had spoken to Knight about any such deal.

Then Frank Wesolowski showed Sullivan a transcript of the Kane County proceedings in which Sullivan had clearly spelled out why Marquez was getting a light sentence.

"I might comment at this time," Sullivan had said, "that this recommendation of four years, which is the minimum for residential burglary, Mr. Marquez, is based primarily upon your cooperation with the police . . . and also Assistant State's Attorney Tom Knight of DuPage County, who also recommended that your case be viewed with leniency. Otherwise, you would not be offered this four-year sentence."

Sullivan deferred to the transcripts, admitted he was wrong, and angrily stalked off the witness stand. Later, Sullivan said he had forgotten the statements made during Marquez's sentencing.

"I felt that someone should have refreshed my memory about the information prior to my testimony," he said.

The incident had little effect on the proceedings, however.

"Normally, that would have devastated a case," Gary Johnson said later. "In this case, where the bar was lowered, the state was not going to be held to the same standards. I don't think the jury cared."

Arthur Lee Burrell, age twenty-two, Alex Hernandez's partner in the air conditioner burglary, testified that while in Graham Correctional Center, he had received a letter from Cruz saying the Naperville area was a good place for burglaries. He also said he had frequented the area where the body was found many times with each of the defendants. He said he was "best friends" with Cruz, "like brothers" with Hernandez, and an acquaintance of Buckley's. He said he had seen Cruz at the Prairie Path three or four times a month, that it was a popular place to have parties, and that he and Hernandez had built a clubhouse there. (Police, however, had been unable to find any sign of a clubhouse. Later, when public defender investigator Manuel Alvarado asked Burrell to show him the place, Burrell led him to a spot behind an industrial building, one and one-half miles from the Prairie Path.)

Again, a Kane County assistant state's attorney testified that the witness had received no deal and got the sentence the judge wanted. This time, the defense produced transcripts of the judge saying that he wasn't happy with the sentence but that he would accept it because it was what the prosecutors wanted.

(Under the Brady Rule, prosecutors should have turned over to the defense any transcripts they knew documented deals with witnesses. Later, assistant Kane County state's attorney John Barsanti submitted an affidavit saying that while he was in the DuPage County prosecutors' office preparing to testify in the Nicarico case on February 1, 1985, he heard assistant prosecutor Patrick King ask if some documents should be disclosed to the defense. Barsanti said Tom Knight then replied, "The only Brady I know has got a hole in his head," an apparent reference to former White House press secretary James Brady, who was shot during the March 1981 attack on President Ronald Reagan, Brady, and two others. Barsanti said that remark was followed by laughter. Later, Knight and King said they had no recollection of such an incident and said no Brady material was withheld.)

Next, Stephen Ford, age eighteen, who had been in jail with Cruz, said that Cruz had said that "next time something like that happens, I'll just kill 'em and make sure there's no witnesses."

Then the transcript of Cruz's tape-recorded statement from May 10, 1983, was read in court. It was a chilling document.

In the statement, Cruz said he had spoken with Hernandez that evening after someone had shot at him while yelling, "What good is a dead Chinaman?"

"[Hernandez] started talking, and he started telling me how I knew too much, and then he touched me on my head . . . and he told me, he goes, 'Right here, right here is where, bust her head, she got hit with that bat,' and he goes, 'But I didn't do it,' he goes, 'I just finished it 'cause I was getting blamed for it anyhow.' And he goes, 'But you know too much. You know way too much.' And then he looked at me, he just like smiled, he goes, in a real funny voice he goes, 'What good is a dead Chinaman?' and I looked at him. I said, 'So, you're the one, huh?' He just looked and he just took off his way, and I went my way."

Then citing Donatlan as the source for his information, Cruz said that Hernandez and Ray Ortega were sniffing spray paint in a house in Aurora while keeping the ten-year-old victim captive. The girl, Cruz said, was raped and beaten by Donatlan, who knocked her out "in order to make love to her." Cruz said that Donatlan hit the girl with a bat, which broke, and that Ortega kicked her down a flight of stairs, breaking her nose.

"I don't know if they felt good because of that, like they got away with it [and] can do it again," Cruz was recorded as saying.

Jurors were told that Donatlan's house was searched shortly after Cruz made the statement, but no blood was found on floors or rugs.

The Cruz transcript ended the part of the trial dealing with testimony from young East Aurora men. To the jury, the effect was substantial. It almost appeared that every young man in East Aurora had testified against Cruz or Hernandez.

8

THE VERDICT

---

*[T]he Texas political climate . . .seemed to believe that the
public cried out for harsh judgment, demanding that
someone should die in retaliation for Officer Woods'
death.*

Randall Adams, with William Hoffer and
Marilyn Mona Hoffer, *Adams v. Texas*
(Adams was freed from death row in a case made
famous by the film *The Thin Blue Line*)

NEXT, IT WAS TIME FOR Stephen Buckley's defense attorney Gary Johnson to worry about the shoeprint testimony.

At the same time that witnesses were repeating what they claimed Rolando Cruz or Alex Hernandez had said, Knight started putting on the shoeprint witnesses. For the defense lawyers, the first major surprise in the trial came when Deputy Sheriff Donald Schmitt testified about Buckley's shoe. Schmitt was the quartermaster at the jail, and he had inked the bottom of the shoe when Sheriff's Detective John Sam brought it in. Schmitt had compared it with the print on the door. Now he testified that there were nine points of similarity. Buckley's shoe, he said, made the print on the Nicaricos' door.

"My opinion [is] that the impression on the door was made by the shoe impression that was submitted," Schmitt said.

Johnson thought that Schmitt's testimony was a violation of trial rules because he should have been notified of Schmitt's findings beforehand. But Judge Kowal let Schmitt testify.

On cross-examination, however, Schmitt did not do very well. The pattern of rays on the heel of Buckley's shoes curved in the opposite direction from those in the dusty print on the door. Schmitt explained that was because the dust moved as the door opened. But he couldn't explain why that wouldn't also affect the nine points of similarity he had seen. He also couldn't explain other variations. "That is why I recommended to the chief that we take it to a shoe expert," he said. At the end of the day, Johnson felt that on the whole it had been a good day for Buckley's defense.

He didn't feel that way, however, after Edward German testified.

German, who until recently had been a forensic scientist for the Illinois State Police Crime Laboratory, had examined the shoeprint and Buckley's right shoe after Schmitt and Gorajczyk. Before the trial, Johnson had talked to German, and he had seemed helpful and friendly. But when German got on the stand, he gave Johnson another one of the surprises that had characterized the trial. Without looking at the shoes again, German had changed his assessment. Now he testified that Buckley's shoe had "probably" made the print on the Nicaricos' door.

Schmitt had said the difference in the pattern of rays on the heel was caused by movement of the dust. German now claimed it was caused by the heel slipping as the door was kicked and fell open.

"I found the correlation of all the ray formations that are present here do match very well with the bottom of the shoe," German testified at one point.

For any other shoe to have made the impression, he said, it would have to have the same unique and general characteristics as Buckley's hiking shoe.

"I found that the right shoe, People's Exhibit Number 8A, probably made the impression that is present on the door," he concluded while being questioned by Knight.

During four hours of cross-examination, Johnson tried to pin German down, to show how he couldn't be sure of his findings, but German glibly slipped through every net. In all, German spent six hours on the witness stand, but for the defense it felt like six hundred.

That night, Gary Johnson and fellow Buckley defense attorney Cliff Lund went to a bar. Johnson felt that his cross-examination of German had been so bad that he'd lost the trial. Lund still had hope; he thought German might have seemed slippery to the jury.

German was followed by Louise Robbins, whom Knight touted as his central witness. Robbins testified about her theory that just as everyone leaves unique fingerprints, everyone leaves unique shoeprints, no matter what shoe they are wearing. Using her theory, she said, she was able to tell that the print on the Nicaricos' door was left by a shoe worn by Stephen Buckley.

Johnson had asked Judge Kowal to keep Robbins off the stand because her methods were not accepted in the scientific community. He'd lost that battle, but on cross-examination, he was able to establish that Robbins's theory was not accepted by other shoeprint experts. On the whole, Johnson thought, he'd done a pretty good job of discrediting her.

Then came the "vision" statement that the defense hadn't known about until just before the trial. Detective Thomas

Vosburgh testified that Cruz had talked of having a dream or vision in which Jeanine was dragged from her home, sodomized, and struck so hard that her head left an impression in the ground—details that never had been made public. Cruz, Vosburgh testified, also said her body had been left near a farmer's field. Vosburgh said that he had brought up the "vision" statement in a conversation with assistant DuPage County state's attorney Patrick King at a December 20, 1984, Christmas party at the Wilton Manor restaurant and banquet hall in Wheaton shortly before the trial.

The defense lawyers had been surprised to learn of the "vision" statement from Vosburgh. Now they got another surprise. Detective Dennis Kurzawa testified that he, too, had been present when Cruz made the "vision" statement. Tom Laz objected because the defense hadn't been notified of Kurzawa's role, but Judge Kowal let Kurzawa testify.

Both Vosburgh and Kurzawa said that Tom Knight told them not to write a report because the matter would come up before the grand jury in a few days. They both testified that Cruz had made the "vision" statement on May 9, 1983, an evening when Cruz was known to have met with the detectives but for which there was no record of what he said.

After Kurzawa testified, Deputy Sheriff James Roberson and Sheriff's Lieutenant Robert Winkler, a jail supervisor, each testified about conversations they said they'd had with Hernandez.

Winkler testified that Hernandez, while in jail, asked to talk with him. Hernandez then said that he "and two others" had planned a burglary in Naperville in February 1983 but that Hernandez had lost his nerve and that the others had dropped him off several blocks from the house.

Winkler took no notes of the June 6, 1984, conversation, nor was it recorded. He did not write a report until three days later. In his report, he wrote that Alex Hernandez had said a Mr. Coffee machine and other items had been taken from the house, that a Lincoln Continental had been the car used during the crime, and that Rolando Cruz had been driving the car.

Winkler continued that Hernandez said his companions had picked him up later and that he'd noticed a little girl in the backseat who was obviously frightened.

"Her lip was bleeding and she wanted to go home," Winkler quoted Hernandez as saying. Hernandez claimed he was dropped off at home and never saw the girl again, Winkler said.

Winkler's report had made no mention of the injury to the girl's lip. Winkler added another detail that was not in the report. He quoted Hernandez as saying the victim's house was near Route 65, the designation for Aurora Avenue. The bleeding lip and the location of the house, both missing in the report, were the only details in the story Winkler related that were corroborated by facts. Part of what did appear in the report—Hernandez's alleged assertion that a Mr. Coffee and other items were stolen—was known by the time of the trial not to be true.

Winkler also testified that about a week or ten days prior to his conversation with Hernandez, he had talked with Cruz, who also was then in jail. Cruz, he said, told him he was approached that February by some friends to help in a burglary. Cruz said he refused but offered to show them how to hot-wire a car, Winkler claimed. He said Cruz maintained he had not seen the others again for two days.

When they returned, "They asked him if he wanted to have sex with a little girl," Winkler said. "He said no, he wasn't into that."

Winkler had written no report of the interview, but Sheriff's Sergeant James Montesano testified that Cruz, in a subsequent conversation with Montesano, had referred to the interview with Winkler, confirming it had taken place.

Roberson testified that Hernandez had admitted going to the Nicarico home to commit a burglary. They took the girl from the house, but, Hernandez said, when he left the scene, she was still alive. Roberson said he put Alex's statement in writing two days later in a letter to a sheriff's sergeant. However, the letter did not mention any statement by Hernandez about the Nicaricos' house, nor did it include the word "burglary."

Knight's final shoeprint expert was Robert Olsen of the Kansas Bureau of Identification, who dealt the defense another blow from the blind side. In his initial report, Olsen had said Buckley's shoe was "similar" to the print on the door; now he said it was "highly probable" that the two were the same.

Then Lund had a brainstorm.

"Ask him for his notes," he whispered to Johnson.

"We took a break to look at his notes," Johnson recalled later, "and in those notes were some of the greatest sheets of paper I've seen in my career as a lawyer. He really didn't have many of his own writings at all, but he had Ed German's notes, which I hadn't known existed. Ed German's notes were just tremendous because it was just what I thought: there was substantial reason to doubt the validity of Ed German's testimony."

German had written that Buckley's shoe "could have at best" made the print on the door and that another shoe could very well have done so. While testifying, German had said that, as a state police expert, he could give only one of three conclusions: that the shoe in question didn't make the print, that it did, or that it could have. In his report, German had selected "could have." Having left the agency before the trial started, however, German had testified, he now was free to give a more precise description—that Buckley's shoe probably made the print. Yet here was his own report saying "could have at best." That made it sound as though even a "could have" conclusion was doubtful.

Johnson felt like doing cartwheels. Now he wanted to get Ed German back on the witness stand and confront him with what those notes said. German, however, had gone to Japan. It was late in the trial, and there wasn't time to bring him back.

"For the very first time, I saw Judge Kowal angry, because he knew how clever this was," Johnson said. "He knew that Ed German beat the crap out of me that day, he knew now that Ed German really, truly doesn't believe what he says, and he knows Ed German's in Japan and I can't get him back."

In the end, Judge Kowal ordered the lawyers to work out for the jury a summary of what the notes said. It wouldn't have the same impact as bringing back the witness, but from Johnson's point of view it was much better than letting German's testimony go unchallenged.

But still more surprises waited in the wings.

Joann Johannville was one of the two women who had reported seeing a car driving down the middle of Clover Court on the day of the crime. She had been unable to give a clear description of the driver and had not been able to positively identify Buckley in a photo lineup. When she took the stand, however, she pointed at Buckley and said he was the driver.

Johnson was stunned; he'd had no indication she would say that. Fortunately, he earlier had learned that Johannville had written some notes about what she saw, and he had obtained them. As he cross-examined her, Johannville faltered. In her notes, she had said the driver had smooth skin; Buckley's was rough and pitted. She had described a clean-shaven man closer to age thirty-five than twenty-five; Buckley, who had bushy muttonchops, had been twenty. In her grand jury testimony, she had said the main thing she had remembered was that the driver wore granny glasses; Buckley didn't wear glasses. As Johnson grilled her, she seemed unsure of her story. At the end of the day, Johnson felt she hadn't hurt his case.

Three more minor witnesses testified, and with that the prosecution rested.

Johnson opened his defense by putting on the stand Buckley's parents and a friend of theirs who had visited on the afternoon of the crime and remembered that Stephen was home.

Then, Joseph E. Nichol, who helped set up the Illinois State Police Crime Laboratory, testified that it was "highly improbable" that Buckley's shoe had left the dusty print on the Nicaricos' door. Biological anthropologist Owen Lovejoy, a professor at Kent State University, the Case Western Medical School of Ohio, and the Northwest Ohio College of Medicine, testified that there were "dramatic differences" between Buckley's shoe and the print.

Alex Hernandez's relatives asserted that he had been helping spread gravel in the driveway at the family home on the afternoon of the crime. Rolando Cruz's sister testified that he was babysitting her children.

Various other witnesses were called to support the defense's case. Then the defense rested. In all, more than a hundred witnesses had taken the stand.

Although each of the lawyers had been considering having their clients testify, they all decided against it.

Hernandez was too much of a risk; because of his limited mental abilities, no one knew what he was likely to say. Tom Laz, Cruz's lawyer, thought he had done a good enough job of debunking the witnesses against Cruz. He didn't think he needed to risk putting Cruz on the stand.

The decision on Buckley, though, was tougher.

"There was a little bit of a heated debate," Johnson said. "We thought we were way ahead, and that we should win. This is exactly where we want to be, we don't want to change it. Let's finish here."

Having presented their evidence, the lawyers now gave their closing arguments to try to persuade the jury to interpret the evidence in their favor.

Knight, as prosecutor, went first. Occasionally interrupted by noisy Chicago & North Western trains passing just outside the window, he spent much of his closing argument going over the testimony of Ed German and Louise Robbins. For Knight, that's where the case turned. He belittled the defense expert witnesses, saying Owen Lovejoy didn't have much experience and Joseph E. Nichol was an expert in ballistics, not shoeprints.

He told the jurors not to worry if they didn't see what the state's expert witnesses saw in the shoeprint. A World War II reconnaissance pilot would understand much more about the terrain he was seeing from an airplane window than an average person would, he said. Similarly, Louise Robbins would understand more about what she was looking at in a shoeprint.

"She can, indeed, see some things that we have difficulty seeing," he said. "There are so many things that match up so well that it's just got to be reasonable to conclude that no other shoe other than the Buckley shoe made that print."

Then Knight summarized the evidence against Hernandez and Cruz, saying that the only sensible explanation of their behavior was that they were guilty.

For Cruz, the proof was in the "vision" statement, he said. "There's no way [for Cruz] to know that information. He knows it because he was there. . . ."

"The evidence in this case, ladies and gentlemen, is complex," Knight said. "It's not a case where one piece jumps right out and says there's your answer. But it's the kind of case that with the analyses you can give it, along with your collective intelligence and experience, you should say beyond any reasonable doubt that these three men are responsible for the shockingly repugnant series of crimes that occurred.

"After you've heard all the arguments in this case and deliberate on this case, I submit the evidence dictates a verdict of guilty on all these charges."

Wilfredo Rios, an investigator for the public defender's office, headed to the courthouse restroom after Knight ended his emotional argument. Moments later, Knight entered the restroom, too, and Rios realized that Knight was crying.

"He was so distraught," Rios recalled later. "I think the idea of what had happened really got to him. When I heard him crying in the bathroom, I realized he really felt what he was saying."

Next, it was time for the defense lawyers to give their arguments.

Frank Wesolowski told the jurors they should ignore the

testimony of Arthur Burrell and Armindo "Penguino" Marquez because it just wasn't believable. Jackie Estremera, he said, had concocted testimony because he feared he would be jailed if he didn't.

Moreover, he argued, the prosecutors were asking the jurors to make guesses. They were being asked to guess that if Joann Johannville saw only one person in the car on Clover Court, that meant two more suspects were hiding in the car. They were being asked to guess that the reason Johannville's description of the light-colored car on Clover Court differed from the green one the tollway workers saw on the Prairie Path was because the defendants changed cars.

None of the defendants had access to a green Granada such as was seen on the Prairie Path, and there was no report of one being stolen, Wesolowski argued.

"I ask you to return a not-guilty verdict," he said. "Don't compound the injustice of this case."

With that, Judge Kowal sent the jury home for the evening. The next day, it was Johnson's turn for a closing argument.

In an emotional two-hour statement, Johnson pointed out that Buckley was fully cooperative with police during the investigation.

"The prosecutor would have you believe that the person or persons involved in this offense switched cars to dump the body in an effort to avoid being caught by the police. Is this the same person, when asked about a set of shoes, and they're questioning him about a homicide, he says, 'Yeah, I've got shoes like that. Test them. You can have them.' Is that the same person? Is it a reasonable inference? It is not. . . .

"Stephen Buckley had nothing to do with the case. He had nothing to hide."

Johnson also ripped the state's shoeprint testimony. Why didn't they trust their own expert, John Gorajczyk, when he said they had the wrong shoes?

"Then what happens? What happens to those shoes after John Gorajczyk has the gall to debunk their clue, their first clue? They're packaged up, and somebody else takes a look at them. . . . What does that tell you about the character of this case? What does that tell you about the length that these people will go to to make sure somebody pays for this crime?"

Finally, Tom Laz gave his closing argument on behalf of Rolando Cruz. Laz talked about how Dan Fowler had changed his grand jury testimony after a lunch break to say that Cruz admitted being at the scene of the murder.

"He tells you one thing in the morning, and one thing in the afternoon," Laz said. "It doesn't matter which one he sticks with. He's a liar."

Ramon "Chuck" Mares's testimony showed he also was lying, Laz said. According to Mares, Cruz had admitted he was present at the slaying. At one point, Mares said the conversation took place in the afternoon. At another point, Mares said it happened in the dark at 7:00 P.M. in June. In June, however, it's still light out at 7:00 P.M., Laz pointed out.

Laz criticized Sheriff's Lieutenant Robert Winkler for not writing a report about the statement he said Cruz made.

"I think the sheriff's office had paper in March of '84," Laz said. "I think they had pencils, typewriters, pens. Given a case of this magnitude and given the import of a statement like that, does it give you pause to question whether or not that statement was ever made if a trained police official can't sit down and even write a handwritten report?"

He also cast doubt on the "vision" statement. After Cruz allegedly made the statement, he tape-recorded an interview with police the next morning. He appeared before the special grand jury three days later and again the following month.

"No one asked him about a vision," Laz said. "Maybe it's because they didn't know about the vision because maybe the vision didn't exist."

In an Illinois criminal trial, the prosecution gets the last word in the rebuttal argument. In his rebuttal, Knight pointed out that the defense lawyers seemed to be calling everyone a liar.

"They put the police on trial for what they're doing and why, put the prosecution on trial for what they're doing," Knight said.

The evidence, however, called for a guilty verdict, he said. "I submit to you that when you consider it all, it shows beyond a reasonable doubt that these three men have committed an extremely repugnant series of crimes on Jeanine Nicarico."

Then the case went to the jury.

To the jurors, the cases against Hernandez and Cruz seemed pretty straightforward. The parade of witnesses recounting various ways in which they said Cruz or Hernandez had implicated themselves had strongly persuaded the jury.

Moreover, Cruz had a cocky air that made him seem like a hardened criminal, said juror Marianne Narro.

"Cruz looked so smug every day in the courtroom," Narro said. "It didn't make him look good."

Once a foreman was selected, the first juror to speak said, "This will just be a mere formality. We might as well get going and start signing these papers."

Juror Michael Callahan, an insurance broker, was appalled. He recalled that this was the same juror who, on the very first day of the trial, had said during the first recess that the three defendants must have done something or they wouldn't be there.

"I said, 'What do you mean, a mere formality?' " Callahan recalled later. " 'We just sat through a seven-week trial. Don't you think we ought to discuss the evidence?' Then he said, 'Is there anybody here who doesn't think these three did it?' And a few people said that, yes, we have to discuss this case."

Callahan knew it was going to be a tough decision. When the prosecution had rested, he had thought to himself, "This is it? This is all we're going to hear? We're supposed to send these three guys away for the rest of their lives based upon this?"

To Callahan, the trial had been a battle between two excellent lawyers, Gary Johnson and Tom Knight. The other lawyers had taken part, but it was Knight and Johnson who were passionate, persuasive, and quick to respond to surprises. Now it was time to decide which of them was in the right.

Some of the jurors argued that if they were really innocent, Buckley, Cruz, and Hernandez should have testified. Others reminded them that Judge Kowal had instructed them that should not be taken into consideration.

"Half the jurors made up their minds on the first day of the trial," Callahan said later. "There was a strong feeling that somebody had to pay for this."

For Callahan, the decision on Buckley was fairly easy because the evidence was so shaky. Louise Robbins, he argued, was just a charlatan who never should have been allowed near a courtroom. He would vote "not guilty" on Buckley. Reaching a decision on Cruz and Hernandez, however, was much more difficult.

Callahan wasn't 100 percent convinced that Cruz and Hernandez were involved, yet on the other hand, there were enough witnesses and police officers who testified against them that he decided he would find them guilty. He wouldn't vote for the death penalty.

Sooner or later, he figured, the truth would come out.

"If the truth was absolutely against Cruz and Hernandez, fine," Callahan recalled later. "If the truth was that they had nothing to do with it, that was fine, too. I wasn't totally satisfied, but I didn't see any other way out of it."

Moreover, he admitted to himself, he wasn't looking for the notoriety of being the only person on the jury to block a conviction.

With Callahan aboard, the jury reached a decision fairly quickly on Cruz and Hernandez: guilty.

Buckley was harder to settle. Eight jurors wanted to convict him; four wouldn't go along. Finally, after fifteen hours of deliberations, the jury decided it couldn't reach a verdict.

On February 22, the jury returned verdicts of guilty against Cruz and Hernandez for the offenses of murder, aggravated indecent liberties with a child, residential burglary, deviate sexual assault, rape, and aggravated kidnapping. The jurors said they couldn't reach a verdict on Buckley. The seven-week trial was over.

The Nicarico family and friends were present as the verdicts were read. The victim's mother and one of her sisters wiped away tears as they heard the verdicts. Hernandez whimpered as his hands were cuffed and he was led away. A bailiff patted Cruz's shoulder.

All that remained was to determine the sentence. Judge Kowal scheduled separate death penalty hearings for Cruz and Hernandez, who both waived their right to a jury decision.

Hernandez's hearing was set to be first, and Cruz's was to follow immediately.

During the hearings, the Nicarico parents testified about their family's pain.

"It's very, very difficult for me to put into words the tremendous effect on our family—the tremendous loss and emptiness in our family," Patricia Nicarico testified. "We still live in terror every day. . . . We never feel safe, ever."

She talked of many nights in which she had cried herself to sleep or didn't sleep at all.

"Jeanine was our baby. The last one will always be your baby. She was just a very, very special little girl."

Patricia also talked about the hopes that were taken away and the pain that wouldn't go away.

"You want to get on with your lives—want to go back to the joyful, carefree life. It just doesn't seem to get easier. The loss is always there—the void.

"You try to go about your lives. Even [when we're] away from here, we're constantly haunted: 'What if Jeanine were here? She would have enjoyed this.'

"Maybe the pain will be eased a little bit, but the loss will always be there."

Thomas Nicarico said the murder "put a cloud over our lives. It's the bogey man come to life.

"Jeanine was taken away from us when she was just starting to blossom. She was a tremendous joy in our lives. . . . The physical, emotional, and psychological pain she must have gone through tears me apart."

During the sentencing hearings, Steven Pecoraro, who had been in jail with Cruz, said Cruz admitted that he [Cruz], "Alex and Steve Buckley broke into the house. He didn't describe how they got in. He said they broke into the house and found the little girl there, and they took her away from the house and drove her to an abandoned house in Aurora."

Cruz, Pecoraro testified, said he was going to write a book titled *How to Kill a Little Girl, or Five Ways to Crush a Skull.* Pecoraro also said he had heard Cruz singing "Little Jeannie."

Deputy Sheriff Richard Brogan testified at the sentencing hearings that during the trial, Cruz had said, "I like to make faces at Mr. Nicarico. I like to wink at him and blow kisses to him."

Cruz also said, Brogan testified, that Thomas Nicarico "keeps staring at me, so fuck him."

Deputy Sheriff Joseph Kupsche testified at the hearings that, on the day before jury selection had started, Cruz had "said he was sick and tired of all this fucking shit going on, and he wanted to kill Knight and Alex Hernandez."

Kupsche testified that Cruz had said "he was going to get a weapon into court somehow" and told Kupsche that "he was going to kill my motherfucking white punk ass while out on the street. He said that he was convinced at that time that he would be found not guilty and be out on the street."

The two convicted defendants also spoke at the sentencing hearings. Hernandez testified that he had made up stories in hopes of collecting the reward. He also said that threats he received in jail prompted him to tell jail guards he had information about the crime.

"I lied about everything," he said.

Cruz started to read a statement in which he said, "The Lord

Jesus Christ and all my loved ones . . . do know I am not guilty in any shape or form. I never had any knowledge of the case until DuPage detectives came to me." While reading his statement, Cruz broke down, and his lawyer, Thomas Laz, had to finish it for him.

On March 15, 1985, it was time for Judge Kowal to give Cruz and Hernandez their sentences.

To Cruz, he said: "The trial . . . has revealed a child aged ten was taken from her home, sexually and physically abused in such a vicious manner that words are inadequate to describe. . . . She was then discarded in an inhuman fashion, disposed of in a manner that lacked total compassion, let alone any sympathy or consideration. This was a tragedy that affected everyone.

"Concerning the charge of murder, the Court finds that there are no mitigation factors such as to preclude imposition of the death sentence.

"The Court, therefore, according to the law, sentences you, Rolando Cruz, to the penalty of death."

To Hernandez, he read a similar statement, concluding: "The Court, therefore, according to the law, sentences you to the death penalty."

Cruz and Hernandez stayed seated, sobbing. Bailiffs had to help Cruz and Hernandez from their seats after the judge read their sentences.

Juror Michael Callahan was appalled. He had voted to convict, but he'd already made up his mind that he never would have voted for the death penalty because the evidence was so skimpy. At the last minute, the lawyers had decided to have Judge Kowal set the sentence instead of the jury. Callahan couldn't understand why Judge Kowal chose the death penalty.

"For a death penalty, the case should be rock solid," he said.

"It should be absolutely conclusive. You've got witnesses, you've got physical evidence, you got a whole bunch of stuff. In this case, there was none of that."

Judge Kowal also scheduled a new trial for Buckley. Knight said he had accepted a position with the U.S. Justice Department's Criminal Strike Force and probably would not prosecute Buckley during the retrial.

Sam was discouraged and depressed. Through the pretrial period and even during the trial, he had argued with Knight. Knight kept telling him, "They did it, John." Sam would say, "Don't tell me that shit, Tom. They didn't do it. Nothing you can do or say is going to change my mind. Nothing."

Sam didn't think Cruz had made the "vision" statement. Every day, the detectives had discussed the case, brainstorming and talking about leads. No one had ever said anything about a vision. Warren Wilkosz, technically the chief detective on the case, also said later that he had never heard anyone mention a vision.

"I remember we'd sit and drink sometimes," Sam said later. "The other detectives would talk about Cruz. Vosburgh and Kurzawa would say, 'Oh, I really think he knows something.' They really did believe that either he had something to do with it or he knew about it. But never once did they talk about this goddamned vision."

Knight was not deterred. Even after Sam quit, Knight would talk to him before pretrial motions were heard, going over what the testimony would be, and once again trying to convince Sam that the defendants were guilty.

"Tom," Sam had said, "I don't work there no more. Don't try that shit. I don't believe they did it, and you're not going to change my mind, so why keep saying it?"

Finally, the day had come during the trial when Sam had expected to testify for the defense. Knight had seen him in the hallway of the courthouse.

"I thought he was going to have a heart attack," Sam said. "He's asking in the hallway, 'What are they going to ask you, what are you going to say?' I said, 'I don't know. Whatever they ask me, I'm going to tell them what I think. I'm going to tell them the truth.'"

Knight was taking no chances. The next thing Sam knew, Knight had gone into the courtroom and obtained an order from Judge Kowal that would keep Sam from telling the jury what he thought about the case. The defense lawyers weren't surprised. From a legal standpoint, getting John Sam on the stand to talk about his conclusions was a long shot.

"We got toasted on it," Gary Johnson said later. "We got squashed on it, as we should have."

Now, Sam's efforts seemed so futile. He'd been taken off the job of looking for the killer—the killer no one would admit existed. He'd quit his job partly so he could testify for the defense, and they wouldn't let him testify. Nothing had made a difference.

"I wasn't expecting to get thrown out of the trial," Sam said. "My testimony was what I really believed. I'm sure it would have made a big difference to a jury. I was on the force ten and a half years. I solved a bunch of cases. I led the county in arrests for three years. It wasn't like they picked some yutz who just worked there for two years and says these guys didn't do it. I was one of the key investigators in the whole case.

"If I could have gotten up and told my story, they'd all have walked."

9

JOHN HANLON

Prosecutors are among the more important officials in the U.S. political system. They have the awesome responsibility of deciding whether or not to prosecute. With the power of the state behind them, they have the ability to shatter the lives of individuals wrongfully accused.

Steve Neal, late author and columnist,
Chicago Sun-Times, December 17, 1996

BOUT TWO MONTHS after Rolando Cruz and Alejandro Hernandez were sentenced to death and Stephen Buckley was sent back to jail to await a new trial, a bitter young man was driving through the town of North Aurora.

The young man was bitter because he'd been told that day that his former girlfriend, Denise, would never have anything to do with him again.

He'd gone back to Denise's home, as he had many times since he'd moved out. He still hoped to get Denise back and would spend time talking to her mother about the situation. At times, he would tell Denise's mother that he had given up drugs, because he knew that was one of the problems that had come between them.

The young man also talked about wanting to rear a daughter, a little girl like the one he occasionally babysat for one of his friends. Denise's mother told him that he'd better get married, but he said that he thought he could rear a child by himself, although he repeated his dream that someday he might marry Denise.

Then Denise's mother ended the young man's hopes. Her daughter, she had said, was completely over him and would never resume their relationship.

Now he was on the street again. Three months earlier, he'd bonded out after being arrested and charged with stealing jewelry from a home on Austin Avenue in Aurora. The patio doors had been pried open, causing about $700 in damage, and quite a bit of jewelry, some of it valued at more than $1,000, was taken.

About a week later, the young man had taken stolen jewelry to the home of Bruce Bartimes, a friend, and asked him to hide it. The young man also had tried to sell Bartimes a pearl necklace for $300. After the young man left, Bartimes—at the urging of his sister, Mary—had called police and turned over the jewelry.

When the young man had come back for the jewelry and was told Bartimes had turned it over to the police, he was furious. He slapped Bartimes in the face with a glove and threatened to hurt Bartimes and his sister, Mary. He threatened to put sugar in Mary's gas tank or firebomb the house. He also told them not to leave their dog outside alone.

Now, angry and bitter, he went for a drive in a friend's car. It was May 6, 1985.

Within hours, the young man followed a twenty-one-year-old woman into her apartment building's parking lot in North Aurora. He pulled up next to her and got out of his car. He began talking to her and eventually asked her out. She declined, so he pulled out a hunting knife. Threatening her with the knife, he forced her into his car. He gagged and blindfolded her and drove her to a remote

area, where he attacked her in the backseat. He forced her to perform oral sex and then raped her vaginally.

Then he drove her back to her apartment complex in North
Aurora, acting as though they had been on a date. He told her that
his name was Brian and that he had gone to Aurora East High
School and that he had a young daughter named Tanya. He let her
go without further harm and drove off.

Later that month, on May 28, 1985, a nineteen-year-old woman
was walking down Route 31 in Geneva, a road that runs down the
west bank of the Fox River. The young man stopped his beat-up
blue Gremlin and attempted to force her into the car. She managed to escape. As the young man drove away, she saw his license
plate number. She reported the incident to the Geneva Police
Department immediately, but authorities didn't track the young
man down until a later, more serious incident occurred.

The next day, a sixteen-year-old woman was walking down the
street in Aurora at about 8:00 P.M. when she noticed that a beat-up
blue Gremlin had passed her a couple of times. Then she noticed
that the same car had come across the yellow centerline and pulled
up just behind her.

She turned in time to see a young man get out of the car and
come toward her. She began to run, but the man grabbed her
around her waist. When she tried to scream, he put a hand over her
mouth.

The attacker threw her into the car through the driver's-side door so hard that she hit her head on the passenger-side door. He threw an afghan over her and held her head down with a tire iron. He told her that he was going to get "some tight, white pussy."

The man drove his car to a remote area, where he forced her out of the car. He kept the afghan over her head and tightened a belt around her neck. Leading her by the belt, he took her farther into a wooded area, away from any roads. At one point, the belt broke as she started to struggle. She was able to hit the young man in the forehead with a rock and scratch his face, but he was too strong for her and managed to get her clothing off. When he tried to rape her, she grabbed his testicles. He reacted by punching her hard in the face and continued his assault. After completing the rape, he let her get dressed and then apologized for the way he had degraded her.

On the way back to Aurora, the young man returned a ring he had taken from her earlier. He asked her what her name was and told her his name. He also asked whether she knew any kids from Aurora East High School. She had him drop her off a block or so from her house so that he would not know where she lived. She ran home and knocked on the front door, only to see the man's car coming around the corner.

She did not report the attack to police right away, fearing that the young man would come after her if she did. She told her mother and her boyfriend about the attack, but she could remember only the man's first name, Brian. She remembered the last name began with a "D" and thought it might have been "Duncan." Her boyfriend took her back out to find the scene of the attack. There, they saw a part of the broken belt.

Meanwhile, some 180 miles away in Springfield, the state's capital, three young lawyers in the Illinois appellate defender's office were assigned to represent Rolando Cruz and Alejandro Hernandez.

Because Cruz and Hernandez were sentenced to death, their cases automatically were appealed to the Illinois Supreme Court. Two of the young lawyers, Tim Gabrielsen and John Hanlon, were assigned to the Cruz appeal. The other, Larry Essig, was assigned to Hernandez. Their job was to persuade the court that their clients deserved new trials.

It was a daunting job. The case record on Cruz alone was about ten thousand pages. Cruz, the more vocal of their clients, was insisting that he was innocent while at the same time making it clear he didn't trust his two new lawyers.

"We were pretty young guys," Hanlon recalled later. "We were both a couple years out of law school. We handed him these business cards that had the seal of the State of Illinois on them, and we said, 'We are with the appellate defender's office.' And he views us, first, as state employees, and it's the state that's trying to kill him. Second, we are kind of like public defenders, and his public defender in his view had just screwed up the case."

Actually, Hanlon thought the public defenders had done a pretty good job considering their limited resources, but he knew it was natural for defendants to blame their lawyers if they were convicted.

For the first two to three months, the lawyers read through the transcripts, summarizing them and making notes about important issues.

"You get to page 1,000, then you get to 2,000, then 5,000, and on and on," Hanlon said later. "At some point you think, certainly there has to be evidence by which this guy has been convicted by twelve people and then sent to Death Row. And at some point you realize, it's just not here."

To Hanlon, Cruz's "vision" statement was perhaps the most vivid indication that there was something wrong in the case. How could police officers hear a suspect tie himself to such a sensational case and not say anything for nineteen months? From a legal standpoint, however, the strongest issue clearly was the guilt by association caused by having a joint trial instead of splitting it into three. The prosecutors, Hanlon thought, had used that to make their case appear much stronger than it really was. In some instances, the redacted statements had sounded more incriminating than the original ones would have.

"One witness says, 'I know that Cruz hung out at the Prairie Path,' and another witness says, 'I know Hernandez hung out at the Prairie Path,' " Hanlon said. "That becomes 'Cruz and Hernandez hung out together at the Prairie Path.' It was kind of skillful, the way they did it."

To buttress a legal argument, an appellate lawyer must dig through hundreds of cases to find ones in which courts have ruled on similar issues. The next step is to select those cases in which the rulings support the appellate lawyer's argument. The lawyer also must anticipate the cases that are likely to be cited by opposing lawyers and prepare answers to those arguments.

Fortunately, Gary Johnson had done a good job of assembling evidence on the severance issue for a posttrial motion. If a lawyer doesn't object to an issue in a trial or neglects to raise that issue in a posttrial motion, that issue cannot be the basis of an appeal. Had the trial lawyers not raised the severance issue and preserved it, the appellate lawyers' only course would have been to claim that the trial lawyers were ineffective or, under a concept called the plain error doctrine, that the mistakes were so obvious, a new trial was warranted. Winning an appeal that way, however, is much more difficult.

Gradually, the appellate lawyers plodded through the trial transcripts and records of Supreme Court decisions. They found one case, *People v. Buckminster,* that as long ago as 1916 had made it clear that a defendant has the right to cross-examine a codefendant who makes accusations. Another helpful case, *Marsh v. Richardson,* was handed down while they were working on the appeal. As the work progressed, Hanlon became persuaded that the Illinois Supreme Court would order new trials. The law clearly was on the side of Cruz and Hernandez.

In Hanlon's opinion, Knight had crossed way over the line. In theory, the jury was not supposed to know that Cruz and Hernandez had made statements implicating each other and Buckley. But any jurors who didn't realize Cruz and Hernandez had made such statements would have been too dull to find their way into the jury box. Knight and the witnesses had repeatedly referred to the "friends," "partners," or "named individuals" who took part in the crime. All the jurors had to do was look at the defense table to guess who those friends and partners were.

At one point, for example, Sheriff's Lieutenant Robert Winkler had helped link Hernandez to Cruz while relating a statement he said Cruz made while in jail:

> He [Cruz] stated that on the day—he was approached one day in February of '83, and that some friends of his asked him if he wanted to be involved in a burglary, be involved in it. And he said no, he didn't want to.
>
> And they told him that they had a problem. They didn't have a vehicle, and they would like to know if they could borrow his vehicle to use in the commission of this felony.

And he stated, no. However, he would then assist them in [showing them] how to hot-wire a vehicle. Then they could gain possession of a vehicle to use. . . . The named individuals then approached him, as he stated, two days later and asked him if he wanted to have sex with a little girl. . . .

He stated that the little girl was at the residence of one of the named individuals.

Would any juror, Hanlon asked himself, doubt that the "named individuals" were Hernandez and Buckley—even though in the original disclosure statement it actually said Cruz had said they were Hernandez and Ray Ortega?

Throughout the trial, Knight had been driving home the point that "friends" or "partners" had committed the crime together and that Buckley, Cruz, and Hernandez were friends who lived near each other in Aurora.

When Dan Fowler was on the stand, he'd quoted Cruz as saying he knew who had committed the crime.

"He said they were friends of his," Fowler had said.

"Did he say where they were from?" Fowler was asked.

"Aurora."

Then Hanlon read the testimony of Ramon "Chuck" Mares as he was questioned by Tom Knight.

Q: Just without mentioning any names of anybody, just mentioning whether he [Cruz] said anything else about she was molested [sic] other than the fact he didn't rape her?

MR. JOHNSON: Your Honor, I am going to ask to be heard, not at this time.

THE COURT: All right.

BY THE WITNESS:

A: That a friend was there and that he knew—he also knew.

MR. JOHNSON: Objection, Your Honor. Now I ask to be
heard, right now.
THE COURT: Objection sustained and the last answer will be
stricken. The jury is instructed to disregard it.
MR. KNIGHT: I believe that is all I have of the witness.

Not only had Knight repeatedly hinted that the defendants
had accused each other, he'd encouraged the jury to think so,
Hanlon thought.

At one point in closing arguments, Knight had said: "[T]he evidence is clear that Cruz and Hernandez are both acquainted with
Buckley. If Buckley kicked the door in, all right. What does that tell
you about those admissions they made? Not only are they friends—"

"Objection, Your Honor," Gary Johnson had said. "I object to
that as contrary to law."

Laz joined in the objection. Judge Kowal, however, had let
Knight continue.

"You've seen that they're friends," Knight had said. "They live
in the same neighborhood. They're all in the same proximity with
respect to the victim's home. And I'm using it only in the direction
of Cruz and Hernandez because the fact is they've made statements which are directed as admissions against them.

"Okay. But they're also friends of Buckley's."

Johnson had objected again, and Judge Kowal again had let
Knight continue after reminding him to confine his remarks to the
evidence.

"This is only to Cruz and Hernandez I'm talking about,"
Knight had said. "Okay. They're friends. They're neighbors.
Therefore, when they make admissions that they've committed
this crime, it's much more—"

"Objection," Johnson had said.

"Objection sustained," Kowal had said.

Kowal had finally stopped Knight, but the meaning was already clear, Hanlon thought. Hernandez had said he'd been with "friends" or "partners" who actually had committed the crime. Cruz had quoted Donatlan as saying Hernandez was involved. All three men were friends or partners, Knight had reminded the jurors. He'd also told them that the names in the statements were being changed, that there were blanks that needed to be filled in. Could any jury have missed the point?

Hanlon didn't think so. Moreover, he didn't think the Illinois Supreme Court would think so, either.

Meanwhile, juror Michael Callahan was uneasy. The more he thought about the case, the more he worried that the jury was wrong, that his vote had been wrong. It seemed likely that if they were guilty, Cruz or Hernandez would have avoided the death penalty by testifying against the other. Even after they received the death penalty, however, they didn't do so.

During the trial, Callahan had taken reams of notes. It bothered him that three of the other jurors never took any at all. How could they listen to more than sixty witnesses and keep track of the cases against three separate defendants during seven weeks without taking any notes? Were their minds already made up?

Another thing that occurred to him after the trial was that none of the defendants owned a car. Did they steal a car? Where did the car come from? Two or three months after the trial, Callahan called up Tom Knight and asked to meet him for lunch. Callahan was looking for reassurance, hoping Knight, whom he considered "a real quality guy," could persuade him the right thing had been done.

"I told him where I was coming from," Callahan said later. "I told him I wasn't all that comfortable with putting these two guys away, that I still wasn't totally satisfied that these two guys did it.

"I wanted to see if there were more things that he could tell me about the case. Maybe he could tell me some other things that didn't surface at the trial."

Knight, however, didn't have any additional information that could salve Callahan's concerns. Instead, he just disagreed with Callahan's conclusions.

"I remember him telling me he just couldn't believe my thought process on Buckley," Callahan said. "I told him I thought that the anthropologist was awful, and he thought that was real good stuff."

10

MELISSA ACKERMAN

While there are certainly cases of wealthy criminals who
spend their money to beat the rap, it is often too easy to
convict innocent but poor people of murder.

Bill Kurtis, *American Justice,*
Arts & Entertainment Network, 1997

O N SUNDAY, JUNE 2, 1985, the killer was smoking a few
joints and driving aimlessly in a blue Gremlin shortly
before noon. He'd spent some time driving around
Aurora, parking near a ball field and getting stoned. Now he was
cruising along U.S. Route 34 through the small town of Somonauk,
a rural village of thirteen hundred about twenty-five miles southwest of Aurora. He saw two young girls riding their bicycles on a
gravel road near Route 34 on the southern edge of town. He passed
by them and pulled over to the side of the road.

According to his own admission later, he decided to abduct
the two girls. He took the knobs off the interior passenger-side
door locks so that when he managed to get the girls into the car,
they could not open the doors. Then he drove back to where he
had seen the girls.

He stopped and asked the girls for directions to Somonauk's
downtown, and as they stopped riding, he got out of the car and
grabbed the closer girl and threw her roughly through the driver's-
side window into the passenger side of the car.

The eight-year-old girl tried vainly to unlock the car door as the young man chased her seven-year-old friend and second-grade classmate, Melissa Ackerman. Melissa struggled with the young man just long enough to allow her friend to escape from the car. The eight-year-old had the presence of mind to give up on the door and instead crawled through the open driver's-side window. She ran toward farm machinery across the street in a John Deere Company parking lot and hid behind a tractor. She peeked out and saw the young man drive away with her friend. Melissa was pounding on the passenger window and screaming.

The terrified eight-year-old, her clothes torn, ran a half mile to the rural home of Chuck Hickey, a high school mathematics teacher she knew. She knocked on the door and tried to tell the occupants what had happened. She was so hysterical that the family could hardly figure out what she was talking about. All they knew for sure was that she was telling them that a man had taken her friend Melissa and had driven away in a car. That was enough for them to call the police. All the police departments near Somonauk responded immediately and started looking for a small, beat-up blue car driven by an unshaven man with brown hair and a mustache. Chuck Hickey also called Melissa's parents.

The lone killer later said he calmed Melissa by talking to her while she was in the car. He kept her covered with a dark-colored sleeping bag on the passenger-side floor as he chatted to her about school and other things. She told him that she liked gymnastics. He drove her out to a small creek near the town of Mendota, seventeen miles away, and made Melissa get out of the car with him. He sexually assaulted her and drowned her, leaving her body covered with rocks and brush in an irrigation ditch. A short time later, he got back into the car and drove off.

After the killer had driven about three miles back toward Aurora on Route 34, he saw a Village of Mendota police car following him. The young man pulled into a gas station. The patrol car followed. The killer went into the station and bought a Pepsi. Returning to the car, he encountered the cop. The officer pointed out that the car lacked a current vehicle identification sticker and asked for identification. The young man could produce only an expired fishing license. The name on the fishing license was Brian Dugan.

The police officer examined the car, but he did not notice the unattached door-lock knobs, which still were sitting in the ashtray. He did not see the marijuana joints or the hunting knife that the young man kept in the glove compartment. He made a note of the name on the fishing license and let the young man go.

Meanwhile, sheriff's officers had rushed to the scene of the abduction. They found the bicycles on the side of the road, but they could find no distinctive auto tire tracks. Several squad cars were sent west down Route 34, the direction the eight-year-old said the young man had gone. Bulletins were issued to state police and police in neighboring counties to look for a battered blue car. Eventually, reports of a battered blue car came from as far away as Michigan and Indiana.

Police didn't expect a ransom demand; Melissa's father was unemployed, and the family had little money. They concluded they were looking for a sex criminal.

The county and village police set up a command post at a volunteer fire station in Somonauk. The FBI set up a post in the rectory at St. John the Baptist Catholic Church, which Melissa attended. Searchers in aircraft and on horses, dog trainers and their dogs, and volunteers began combing the area. They found nothing.

Later that evening, when the county sheriff's police learned that a man named Brian Dugan had been driving a car that matched the eight-year-old's description, they contacted the Aurora Police Department and the sheriff in Kane County, where Dugan lived. They asked that Dugan be picked up and held for questioning.

When Kane authorities got the request and checked Dugan's records, they realized that he was the same person whose license plate number had been reported five days earlier by the nineteen-year-old Geneva woman who had escaped when he tried to pull her into his Gremlin. The following day at about 6:45 A.M., a virtual SWAT team of Geneva and Kane County police officers in unmarked cars waited for Brian Dugan to return to his job as a stock handler at Midwest Hydraulics after a one-week vacation. As Dugan stepped from his car, he was met by a very large group of angry men who had quickly surrounded his car. Each had a loaded gun aimed directly at Dugan's chest. Eleven years before, when he'd been arrested by Aurora police, he had tried to fight them off with karate kicks. This time he did not try any.

Official reaction was quick. First, Dugan was charged with the attack on the nineteen-year-old Geneva woman, because police already had her statement, which included the license plate number of the car and a description of him. Then he was charged with the attack on the twenty-one-year-old North Aurora woman, who was able to pick him out of a lineup. Eventually, he also was charged with the attack on the sixteen-year-old Aurora woman.

Kane County detective Thomas Atchison questioned Dugan about some unsolved crimes, but Dugan was not cooperative.

"He was tough for me to interview," Atchison said later. "He was probably the worst guy I ever interviewed, and I've interviewed a lot of shitheads. It was just his attitude, his whole demeanor. He was real cocky, and I came real close to going over the table after the guy."

Meanwhile, Melissa still was missing, and most people did not know that Brian Dugan was a suspect in Melissa's disappearance. Police and volunteers had searched for a week throughout the county and adjoining counties. On the Friday after Melissa disappeared, more than 250 volunteers searched a twenty-five-square-mile area. The search teams also included state troopers and sheriff's police from surrounding counties. Every stream, wooded area, pond, barn, and silo in the area were inspected.

Searchers found a bag of clothing and other items, but none of it turned out to be Melissa's. Friends and neighbors distributed 10,000 posters to homes and businesses. In an unprecedented move, the Illinois State Toll Highway Authority began distributing 130,000 flyers about Melissa's abduction to motorists. The flyers included a photo of Melissa and a description of the abductor.

On June 5, the FBI added twenty agents to its force of forty already investigating Melissa's disappearance. Later that day, county police called off the foot search for her. A reward for information leading to Melissa's safe return climbed to $50,000. Although it was summer vacation, children in Somonauk stayed off the streets.

Authorities speculated that the abductor might have left the state. DeKalb County sheriff Roger Scott, who was coordinating the investigation because the Village of Somonauk had only two police officers, said a psychic called in by the family had told them Melissa was still alive.

Melissa's parents, Thomas and Sheree Ackerman, clung to hopes that their only child would return. June 11, her birthday, was heartbreaking. The Ackermans had always had a big family party to celebrate, and some of her presents already had been purchased. A big balloon with the words "Happy Birthday" and a bouquet of red roses were delivered by one of Melissa's friends who knew roses were her favorite flowers.

One evening two weeks after Melissa disappeared, LaSalle County deputy sheriff Gregory Jacobsen and recent recruit Deputy Timothy Graham were standing by an irrigation ditch near a cornfield and a clump of trees outside Mendota. Jacobsen was explaining that the area was a hot spot where local teenagers came to drink. As he was talking, he caught a glimpse of some clothing near the ditch and looked down. Partly submerged in the water and partly hidden by rocks was a corpse that had become decayed, bloated, and unrecognizable.

By the time other officers responded to Jacobsen's call, it was dark. Police left the area undisturbed until morning and then combed through it meticulously for evidence. They gathered clothing that was strewn nearby. The body eventually was identified as Melissa Ackerman's from dental charts. Later, tests at the FBI crime laboratory in Washington, D.C., showed that fibers found on Melissa's clothing were the same type as those from Dugan's sleeping bag. The lab also established that dirt Dugan was believed to have tracked into his boardinghouse matched the type of dirt in the area where Melissa's body was found.

The coroners from DeKalb and LaSalle counties said Melissa had met a "violent death" within an hour or so of her abduction.

"The tragic death of Melissa Ackerman has shaken the entire Chicago area into a new awareness of the dark side of human behavior," read an editorial in the *Chicago Sun-Times*. "None of the Ackermans' neighbors can rest easily until Melissa's abductor is found."

Dugan was still locked up in the Kane County Jail on $350,000 bond. He was getting lots of visitors as investigators tried to determine which of several other attacks Dugan also had been involved in.

Kane County detectives Atchison and Robert Cannon met with him to discuss the Donna Schnorr murder. Dugan admitted to having gone on several occasions to the quarry where the body was found, but he denied any involvement in the crime. He stated that he drove a brown-and-gold Chevy during the summer of 1984 but said that it had been stolen, sometime around the time of the Schnorr murder. (In fact, records showed he'd filed the stolen-car report a month afterward.) He also told the detectives that the car was later recovered and towed away and that he had gone to see the car. He said that the car's windows were broken out and he decided not to reclaim it, since it was not worth what he would have had to pay for the towing and storage.

"We substantiated through Aurora that in fact he had reported it stolen, but when we talked to Will County [police], we found out that he had lied to us about the recovery of the car," Atchison said. "They had located it, but he never came out to look at it."

Police towed the car and parked it behind the jail where Brian Dugan could see it from his cell window.

"It worked real well," Atchison said. "He immediately went to his attorney and wanted to cut a deal."

The next day, DeKalb sheriff's detective Glenn Gustafson searched the fifty-dollar-a-week room that Brian Dugan was renting in a ninety-eight-year-old yellow Aurora boardinghouse at 306 South LaSalle Street. The room had been searched previously with the permission of the landlady, but without a warrant. Now armed with a warrant, Gustafson confiscated several items, including a buck knife in a sheath and a single long hair found under Dugan's sleeping bag. Later it was determined that the strand of hair under the sleeping bag was similar to the head hair of Melissa Ackerman.

Two days later, the sixteen-year-old Aurora woman who had been raped was driven to the Aurora Police Department by her boyfriend. The Aurora woman had seen the name of Brian Dugan as being the person arrested in the attack on the Geneva woman, and she suspected it was the same man who had attacked her. With Dugan already in jail, the woman was not as frightened of him, and her boyfriend had finally talked her into going to the police station.

The boyfriend had also read about the abduction of Melissa Ackerman a few days before and thought that the description of the car sounded the same as the one that the attacker had driven in his girlfriend's case. He told Aurora police that he had even called DeKalb police and told them the name and initial, Brian D., of the man who attacked his girlfriend and that it could be the same guy who'd abducted the little girl.

The woman told Aurora police the story of her attack and the reason why she believed it had been committed by Dugan. She described the dirty blue Gremlin accurately, remembering a broken lock on the glove compartment (the glove box kept falling open, revealing a hunting knife), the black interior, the gearshift lever on the floor, a rip in the carpet by the gas pedal. There was little doubt that she was describing Dugan and his Gremlin.

Later that month, a friend who had recently lived with Brian Dugan rode his bicycle over to Denise's house, where he talked with her mother, Dianna, about the charges brought against Dugan. According to Dianna, the friend said that he and his girlfriend suspected that Dugan had molested their daughter. He said that Dugan used to babysit for their three-year-old daughter on occasion, and that one time he and his girlfriend had come home and noticed that she was "walking funny." They thought Dugan might have done something to her sexually.

The friend said he had become suspicious of Dugan after Dugan had borrowed the friend's car one night. The friend had found a pair of girl's underpants under the front seat when Dugan had brought the car back.

Now Kane County authorities were building a case against Dugan for the Schnorr murder. A report from the Illinois state crime lab stated that a comparison of paints showed that Brian Dugan's Chevy might have been the vehicle that had knocked Donna Schnorr's car off the road in July 1984. Forensic scientist George Dabdoub found that the paint chips that were transferred onto Schnorr's car by the collision were "consistent with and indistinguishable from" paint samples taken from Dugan's 1974 Impala in color, layer sequence, and chemical composition.

The cause of Melissa's death eventually would be established as asphyxiation, although decomposition made it impossible to determine whether she had been strangled, suffocated, or drowned. It was also impossible to determine whether she had been sexually assaulted, although later analysis of swabs taken from the mouth and anal canal indicated the presence of sperm, leading authorities to believe that the little girl was raped both orally and anally. No semen was found on a vaginal swab, but vaginal rape could not be ruled out.

On June 21, Melissa's funeral was held at the stucco St. John the Baptist Church. Many of the Somonauk businesses displayed window signs reading "Closed Friday from 10:00 A.M. to noon in memory of Melissa Ackerman." Many of the five hundred mourners at the church were children. Adults and children wore buttons that said "Pray for Missy." Outside the church, flags waved in honor of Melissa along the village's sunny streets.

On June 25, Dugan was officially charged by LaSalle County police with the abduction and murder of Melissa Ackerman of Somonauk. He was arrested by a group consisting of members of the LaSalle and DeKalb county sheriff's departments and special agents of the FBI while he was still incarcerated in the Kane County Jail. He was transported to the LaSalle County Jail under very tight security, and he was held without bond. A court appearance was scheduled for the following day.

The next day, he was brought to court in LaSalle County under extremely tight security. Police put him in a lineup, but Melissa's eight-year-old friend was unable to identify him. Dugan stated in court that he could not afford an attorney, and he was assigned public defender George Mueller, who was vacationing in Germany. Another attorney from the public defender's office was allowed to speak with Dugan after a complaint was made that Dugan was without any counsel until Mueller returned.

Dugan was charged with five counts of murder, three counts of kidnapping, and six counts of aggravated sexual assault. LaSalle County chief circuit judge Alexander T. Bower ordered him held without bond. Dugan, shackled and wearing a prison jumpsuit, did not speak and turned his eyes away as the prosecutor outlined the charges against him. LaSalle County state's attorney Gary Peterlin said he would ask for the death penalty.

Later, during plea bargaining, Dugan admitted that he had undressed Melissa, tied her hands, raped her anally, and drowned her. The police officer conducting the interview asked him why he had killed Melissa.

"I wish I knew," he answered. "I wish I knew why I did a lot of things, but I don't."

Later in the interview, he added, "I don't understand why it happened, and saying I'm sorry doesn't really change anything, does it? But I am. I'd like to understand, if I ever could find out, why I did those things."

Brian Dugan was behind bars. His long string of violent crimes had finally come to an end.

PART TWO

———————

JUSTICE

11

BRIAN DUGAN

---

*The violent end to Cheryl Ferguson's young life is both
senseless and tragic. . . . Our outrage over her murder,
however, cannot justify the subversion of justice that took
place during the investigation, which ultimately affected
the trial of her accused perpetrator.*

David A. Berchelman, Texas judge, ordering
a new trial for Clarence Brandley, 1989

A LTHOUGH BY JUNE 1985, John Sam was no longer a
sheriff's detective, he still wanted to do what he could to
capture Jeanine Nicarico's killer. He started by meeting
with a new ally, Randy Garrett.

Garrett, age twenty-six, was a security guard on the midnight
shift at George Williams College in DuPage County, where he was
also a student taking classes in psychology. He had an affinity for
puzzles and mysteries, and press accounts of the Jeanine Nicarico
murder trial had intrigued him. He thought the prosecution
theory seemed awfully vague and inconsistent. Why, if there was
no solid evidence, were these men being prosecuted? Garrett
thought it was a case that would be interesting to dig into and
write about.

He started by reading through back issues of newspapers, and
he attended a day of the trial. He also called J. Michael Fitzsimmons,
the DuPage County state's attorney, whom he'd met as a senior in

high school while participating in an extra-credit program called Government in Action. Fitzsimmons had let the students watch him prepare a witness before she had testified.

Fitzsimmons remembered the class when Garrett called. He said he didn't know the details of the Nicarico case and suggested that Garrett call lead prosecutor Tom Knight, although he cautioned that Knight probably wouldn't have time to talk until the trial was over. Garrett did call, and Knight was cordial, but as Fitzsimmons had predicted, Knight was too busy to discuss the case.

The more Garrett learned, the more intrigued he became. The only evidence against Cruz and Hernandez seemed to be based on statements by witnesses who had little credibility. The statements attributed to Cruz and Hernandez, for the most part, everyone accepted as false. There was no corroborating evidence. There was a shoeprint tying Buckley to the case, but the defense was arguing it didn't match. To Garrett, the case was a bigger puzzle than ever.

When the trial ground to a close and Cruz and Hernandez were convicted, Garrett was shocked. It seemed very clear that no one was sure what really had happened. When a date was set for a death penalty hearing, he decided to attend that, too.

The line outside the courtroom was very long. Later, Garrett learned that Cruz had allegedly threatened to have some type of weapon brought into the courtroom so he could kill Tom Knight. No one was admitted until the entire courtroom was checked.

While waiting in line, Garrett talked to a man behind him who turned out to be a juror from the trial. The jurors were no longer needed because the judge would decide the sentence, but the juror had decided to show up anyway. Garrett asked the juror whether Buckley might have been convicted along with Cruz and Hernandez had the jury known that Buckley was an acquaintance of John Ruiz, the son of the Nicaricos' cleaning woman. Judge Kowal had ruled that evidence about Ruiz was not relevant and wouldn't be allowed in front of the jury. The juror, however, said that the jury had known all about it. He pointed to a tall man near the head of the line and said that he too was a juror. The second juror's wife, the first juror said, had been in the courtroom while the jury had been excused, and through her, the jurors had learned about Ruiz being the son of the cleaning woman. The jurors also learned that Ruiz knew Buckley.

Although he was new to the legal arena, Garrett knew he had heard significant information. Garrett called Frank Wesolowski, the chief public defender, who agreed to meet. Tom Laz asked to sit in on the meeting.

Garrett hadn't known what to think of Frank Wesolowski the day he had seen him during the trial. Wesolowski had come in late, and then everyone in court had had to wait while he went to retrieve something he had forgotten. During the proceedings, he hadn't asked many questions. But when Garrett met Wesolowski at the public defender's office, he was impressed. Wesolowski, he realized quickly, knew the case pretty well.

Wesolowski showed Garrett a photo of the shoeprint on the door. Garrett could easily see that it didn't match the photo of Buckley's shoeprint. This, Wesolowski told Garrett, was a case that was wrong from the beginning.

Wesolowski thought it had been a big mistake to conduct the investigation through a grand jury. The twenty-three people on the panel thought it was up to them to solve the crime, he said. And the prosecutors kept calling witnesses back and badgering them until they gave the testimony that the prosecutors wanted.

Wesolowski gave Garrett the phone numbers of former

detective John Sam and Phil Gilman, the chief of the DuPage crime lab—people, Wesolowski said, who were worth talking to.

Garrett called Sam and arranged a meeting on June 28, 1985, at a lounge in a Hyatt Hotel in Oak Brook, a posh suburb between Chicago and Naperville. Actually, the two men almost didn't meet, because unknown to Garrett, there were two lounges in the hotel, and Garrett was in the wrong one. He waited and waited until someone finally told him there was another lounge. Garrett went to the other lounge, but Sam had just left. A waitress ran out and caught Sam just before he got into his car.

Sam came back and sat down with Garrett. Sam had had a couple of drinks, and he talked freely about the problems with the case. Garrett was amazed at Sam's openness. Here was a former cop—who hadn't asked for any verification of Garrett's identity—plunging right in and discussing all kinds of details. Sam said the case was bigger than either him or Garrett and that Garrett would have to get the backing of a newspaper or another independent institution if the real story was ever to come out.

"They have the wrong guys," Sam said.

It was the first of several meetings at which Sam explained his perspective on the case.

Sam told Garrett that the theory that John Ruiz was the mastermind who set up the crime as a burglary was ridiculous.

"John Ruiz tells Alex, Buckley, and Cruz to go rob the house with the boat because the mother cleans the house and they got a lot of nice shit," Sam would say, explaining the absurdity of the theory. "Okay. They come back and say, 'Well, John, we didn't rob the house, but we knocked off a ten-year-old girl who lived there, raped her brains out, and dumped her at the Prairie Path. How do you like that?' Is he really going to say, 'It's okay, guys.

The next house, you go get another one and do it right'?

"Now, here come the police, knocking on Ruiz's door, saying, 'We hear you killed a little girl in Naperville.' The police just wreck his life for the next week and a half. He's a possibility because his mother was the cleaning lady. I'm on his ass all day long. You think this Ruiz ain't going to give up these three assholes who just went out and snuffed a little ten-year-old? *And* make $10,000 and be the hero of Naperville and Aurora? He could run for political office.

"I go to see him one day, he's slitting rubber off some god-damned wire to take copper to the junkyard to get some money. You think he ain't ratting on three guys who just knocked off a ten-year-old? In a minute. In a heartbeat, he'd be over there."

Sam told Garrett he figured Buckley, Cruz, and Hernandez were indicted because the Fitzsimmons people wanted to solve their biggest case before the primary election. Then, in the remaining nine months of their administration, they were stuck with it. If they dropped the charges, it would be clear to everyone the indictments were politically motivated. That's why Knight needed the special grand jury, so he could tailor his case.

"It's easy," Sam said. "Do we need a witness to say such-and-such? I think we can find one of them. Bring them in front of the grand jury."

It was the same thing Wesolowski had complained about to Garrett. Knight, Wesolowski said, ignored the original testimony from the young men of East Aurora and just kept bringing them back to the grand jury until they told him what he wanted to hear.

"Why didn't I ever go to the grand jury?" Sam said. "Why didn't other policemen go to the grand jury? Here you got the fucking vision and all this other bullshit, how come they didn't go to the grand jury? But all these assholes who sniffed glue in Aurora, they're in the grand jury. What do they know that we don't?"

Sam was also bothered by the prosecution theory because it presumed that so many people would be involved in the killing of a little girl. Sam's experience had taught him that child molesters acted alone.

"If you listen to Tom Knight, he's got seven, eight guys at this goddamned scene," Sam would say. "They wouldn't have had room in the car for the victim. They would have to have had a bus."

Sam regretted the day authorities had first heard of Alex Hernandez. Nobody wanted to let go of his statement about holding Jeanine down. If he had turned out to be the killer, the police could have congratulated themselves on how clever they had been to trick him into admitting it. As it was, all that had happened was that they had focused on the wrong people.

"I think maybe we would have gone much farther if we had never come into contact with Alex," Sam said.

At their first meeting, Sam told Garrett that Jeanine's murder was the kind of crime a killer tends to repeat, and if they didn't catch the criminal, he was going to do it again. The arrest of Brian Dugan had been in the newspapers over the past two days. Sam told Garrett it sounded to him as though the killer he'd been looking for might have been caught. Melissa's murder had been very similar to Jeanine's. It was unlikely that there would be more than one predator killing little girls in the same area.

Sam told Garrett he had called his old boss at the DuPage sheriff's office, Sergeant James Montesano, and suggested that Montesano have someone check Dugan out for a connection to Jeanine's murder.

It later turned out that Detective Warren Wilkosz did investigate Dugan. Wilkosz got the time cards from the Art Tape & Label Corporation, establishing that Dugan was not at work on the day of the Nicarico crime. He learned that Dugan had owned a green Volare, a car that looked very much like the Ford Granada the tollway workers reported seeing on the Prairie Path. He went through the evidence locker in LaSalle County looking for hiking shoes. Dugan, however, refused to talk to Wilkosz. After that, Wilkosz said, he didn't take the investigation any farther because he was told to wait for further orders that never came. On January 15, 1986, he wrote a report summarizing his activities, and there the matter rested.

Sam asked Garrett what kind of car Dugan had been driving when he'd been stopped after the Melissa Ackerman killing. A blue Gremlin, Garrett said. Doesn't match, Sam said. But he told Garrett to find out what kind of car Dugan had been driving in February 1983, when Jeanine was murdered.

Next, Garrett called Phil Gilman. Gilman had been chief of the DuPage County Crime Laboratory. He'd been forced out, and he suspected the real reason was that he'd made it clear he didn't think Buckley, Cruz, and Hernandez were guilty. The investigators had brought a tremendous amount of material into the cramped crime lab, and none of it had matched the suspects to the crime. Gilman thought Tom Knight had made up his mind too quickly about the suspects and pushed too hard to get the lab to support his theory.

Expecting that indictments would come down right before the Fitzsimmons-Ryan election, the lab technicians had even run a cynical betting pool, trying to guess the date, he said.

Gilman told Garrett that Knight had pushed very hard to get the lab technicians to say that a pubic hair from a Puerto Rican was found in the victim's vaginal area. But the lab workers had no accurate way to identify a hair as Puerto Rican and, furthermore, it didn't show up in crime scene photos. Wherever it came from, it wasn't there at the time of the crime.

However, Knight wouldn't give up, Gilman said. Knight never asked anyone to fabricate evidence, but he pushed the technicians to keep looking again, to see if there was some way they could make the connection. Gilman thought Knight's actions were improper.

"A prosecutor is in a peculiar position because he doesn't represent the victim, he represents the state," said Gilman, who also was a lawyer in the Massachusetts bar. "His obligation is to do justice, rather than to represent a party. That is a tough distinction to work with sometimes. I think Tom lost sight of the fact that his responsibility was more to the people than to the victim of the crime."

Then in early December 1995, Randy Garrett heard one of the most dramatic news items of his life. He was at home, and a television news program was on. A bulletin about Brian Dugan was reported. Brian Dugan, the newscaster said, had admitted he'd murdered Melissa Ackerman. He'd admitted he'd murdered Donna Schnorr. And he'd said that he, alone, had murdered Jeanine Nicarico.

It sounded as though the killer John Sam had been looking for had been caught after all.

Stephen Buckley, sitting in his cell in the DuPage County Jail, was thrilled when he heard the news from Carol Anfinson, the public defender named to represent Buckley after Gary Johnson left the case. Others involved in the defense thought now it would be only a matter of a short time before the whole case was cleared up.

Meanwhile, as official investigators dug into Dugan's past, Garrett did his own research. He gathered all the police reports he could and put them into chronological order. Sam knew a salesman named Brad Ireland who knew the Dugan family. Sam gave the name to Garrett, who called Ireland's number. A woman he talked to said she didn't know the Dugans that well but suggested he call another couple, the McKennas.

Eventually, Garrett tracked down the McKennas' daughter, Sue McKenna, at the family's tile business in Naperville. Sue said her family had been neighbors of the Dugans when both families lived in the suburb of Lisle, just east of Naperville. Dugan's father was an abusive alcoholic, and she said she often would hear yelling and fighting. Sue described Dugan's mother as a sweet person who tried to work things out but couldn't. Sue said her father tried to help, getting Brian interested in baseball and taking him along on a family vacation, but Brian was clearly a troubled youth. He used illegal drugs at an early age and was caught setting fires several times, including one at his junior high school.

Next, Garrett heard about Bruce Bartimes, who had been a friend of Dugan's. Garrett called him, and the two men talked for almost an hour. Bartimes had multiple sclerosis, was legally blind, and talked with some difficulty, but he was friendly and cooperative.

Bartimes said he'd known Brian Dugan's brother and had gone with the brother to visit Brian at the state penitentiary at Pontiac. Brian didn't seem to have any trouble getting drugs in jail and had given his brother four or five joints to take home. Brian's only hobbies, Bartimes said, were drinking alcohol and smoking marijuana.

Bartimes said Dugan had dreamed of trying out for the Chicago Bears after getting out of prison. He'd played on a prison football team and apparently was pretty good. He never tried out, though, and it was clear his personality had deteriorated while he was imprisoned.

Bartimes also told Garrett about the stolen jewelry that Dugan had brought to his house and the subsequent harassment from Dugan after Bartimes gave the jewelry to the police.

After the interview with Bartimes, Garrett talked to Bernice Larson, who ran a boardinghouse where Dugan had rented a room on two separate occasions. Larson had kicked him out the first time because he'd never paid his rent, but she let him move back later when he said he'd reformed and gotten a job.

Larson said Dugan was pleasant to her but that she'd had a bad feeling when he told her he had a vacation coming up. With nothing to do, Dugan would get into trouble, she thought. She tried to get him involved in tearing down a barn next door, but the project wasn't ready to start.

On the morning of Melissa Ackerman's murder, Larson had been sure he was going to do something bad. He had sneaked out very early in the morning, taking a bag of clothes with him. After he had returned, she'd found the bathroom full of sand and mud. When she had confronted Dugan, he'd said he would clean it up.

Another piece of Brian Dugan's past came from a couple who had been in a bowling league with his parents. They said that when Dugan was sixteen, his mother had caught him undressed with a girl who was only twelve or thirteen.

The couple's daughter said she had sat next to Dugan in the fifth grade. Dugan, she said, had never been accepted by any group and didn't have many friends. Instead, he had seemed to hang around with his more popular younger brother and his brother's friends. When he had been in high school in Lisle, he'd kept nothing in his locker but a bottle of whiskey. The class's ten-year reunion had been in August 1985, right after his arrest for the murder of Melissa Ackerman. Dugan, of course, had been the big topic of conversation for the night.

Next, Garrett talked to Denise's mother, Dianna, in what turned out to be the first of many conversations. At first, she said that the family could not believe Dugan had murdered Melissa. Sooner or later, they thought, the police would realize they had the wrong man. Her son had gone to visit Brian, and Brian had said he was innocent.

By now, Denise had married someone else and had moved into a house on the west side of Aurora. Later, once she had finally concluded Dugan was guilty, Denise had worried whether she was somehow responsible for what Dugan had done. He had often said that she made him crazy. Denise's mother asked him whether that was true during a phone conversation while he was in jail. He said no, that nobody was responsible but him. He said it was something in his head and he wanted to find out why it happened, too, because he didn't know why he did those things.

Denise had first met Brian at her house. Denise's brother, Jack, had been having a party, and one of the friends he'd invited had brought Brian along. In the time he knew Denise, Brian had spent a lot of time talking to Denise's mother. When he had been kicked out of Bernice Larson's boardinghouse, Denise's mother had invited him to stay. By then, she had taken a liking to him, and the whole family had trusted him.

Garrett also talked to Denise. She said Brian would not talk about his past and that she had not known he had been in prison before they met.

Denise's sister, Debbie, said that she, Brian, and three others had gone to the Prairie Path on the evening that it was reported that Jeanine's body had been found there. Dugan had driven them there in his dark green Volare.

"We got out of the car [and] walked up to one of the police who asked us what we were doing in the area," Debbie said. "We told him that we lived pretty close and I wanted to see where it was."

Besides living with Denise's family and at Bernice Larson's boardinghouse, Dugan also had rented an apartment in 1984 from a woman named Marilyn Stadler. Eventually, Garrett got in touch with Stadler. She told him Brian Dugan had done no damage to his apartment and had been friendly with all the other tenants. Eventually, they had kicked him out, though. They'd evicted another tenant for punching holes in the walls, and Dugan had let the other tenant share his apartment. When the Stadlers had found out, they'd evicted Dugan, too. Although he hadn't damaged the apartment, he had left it a complete mess.

James Barry, who had bought the house that the Dugan family had rented in Lisle, said he'd found obscenities painted on the walls while the house was vacant in 1972. Neighbors later had speculated that the obscenities were painted by Brian, who had run away to Iowa before the family moved. When he had come back to the house, his family was gone.

A former friend of Brian Dugan's told how he and Dugan had hitchhiked on trips to California and Florida during which Dugan had then repeatedly committed burglaries. He said he had met Dugan just after Dugan got out of a juvenile facility in Dixon, Illinois. He said Dugan had said he was raped while he was incarcerated there. The friend said Dugan broke into an Aurora restaurant called the Twirly Top on April 1, 1974, by kicking in the door.

Dugan and the friend were caught right away. They both pleaded guilty to criminal damage to property and were sentenced to eighteen months of conditional discharge.

Garrett also tracked down a young woman named Barbara who had been attacked in Lisle by Dugan when she was ten years old, three weeks after the Twirly Top break-in. Barbara said he had approached her and asked for directions to the train station. He had walked with her a short way and then, from behind, had grabbed her by the face and hand and steered her off the sidewalk toward a small wooded area. Her nose had started to bleed, and she'd screamed. It had been enough to startle Dugan, and she'd gotten away. She'd run crying toward a field where a softball game had been under way, and Dugan had not tried to follow. Police arrested him a few blocks away with blood on his jacket, and Barbara identified him immediately. Barbara's father attended the hearings in the case, but Dugan did not show up. Eventually, the father was told that Dugan had been arrested in another county and was in jail, and nothing more happened in the case.

Patty Levi, a prostitute, related how Dugan had beaten her severely. She said he had paid her beforehand but had then tried to take the money back. She said she'd fought with him over the money, and he'd gone berserk, beating her with a thick piece of lumber and locking her in the bathroom of an unfinished building.

Gradually, a picture of Brian Dugan emerged. He was born Brian James Dugan to James and Genevieve Dugan on September 23, 1956, in Nashua, New Hampshire. He had an older sister, Hilary, and three younger brothers, Steven, Jeffrey, and John James. The family moved to the village of Lisle in DuPage County in 1967. As a teenager, Brian and his younger brother Steve were suspected of breaking into neighborhood schools. Brian's first arrest was January 23, 1972, for burglary when he was fifteen years old. He was put under court supervision.

Later in 1972, the Dugan family moved to Batavia, a western suburb on the border of DuPage and Kane counties. Brian enrolled in high school, and he was made a ward of the Kane County court. Neither change seemed to straighten him out. A juvenile complaint for trespass to land was filed against him, and his probation officer said he was suspected in a home burglary, so he was sent to the Kane County Youth Home in Batavia. While he was in the youth home, his family moved again, this time to the east side of Aurora. He was released on December 5, 1972.

Three days later, Dugan and a friend broke into a Kentucky Fried Chicken restaurant on Lake Street in Aurora. Police said $4,000 was stolen. A different friend said the two took the money to Florida to buy drugs. Later, they went to Iowa and started committing burglaries in the Dubuque area. Dubuque police arrested them on December 28, 1972, and the two confessed to the burglaries.

On February 19, 1973, officials discovered a break-in and extensive vandalism at K. D. Waldo Middle School in Aurora, a school Steven Dugan attended. Brian and Steve were found with walkie-talkies taken in the burglary, and Brian gave an imaginative description of a person from whom he said he had bought his walkie-talkie. But Steve said the two found the units in the snow. Pressed about the discrepancy, Brian admitted the burglary. A Kane County judge refused to grant him supervision and gave him a suspended jail sentence that he warned would start the minute Brian got into trouble again.

At age sixteen, Brian quit school for good on April 12, 1973. Within weeks, Brian and two friends went on an Aurora burglary spree at Aurora Central Catholic High School, Sacred Heart

School, and Antoine's Supper Club, where they were caught at the cash register by the owner of the club and another man. Dugan was sent to a prison evaluation unit on May 2, beginning a long stretch in which he would be in and out of prison.

After he left prison and committed the break-in at the Twirly Top in April 1974 and attacked the young girl in Lisle, Dugan was arrested twice in Aurora, first for theft of gasoline and then for home burglary. The gasoline theft charge was dropped because the witness and complainant did not show up in court, and he received probation for the home burglary.

On October 4, 1974, Dugan was arrested while sniffing paint in a field behind a store with the same friend who had been at the Twirly Top break-in. Dugan reportedly tried to fend off the police with karate moves he'd recently learned and, on the way to the police station, tried to kick out the windows of a police car. He was charged with resisting an officer, criminal damage to property, aggravated battery, and unlawful use of an intoxicating compound.

Before serving any time for those offenses, Dugan and a friend fled to California. There they both served thirty days in jail for stealing a backpack in a camping area, possession of cannabis, possession of fireworks, petty theft, and possession of narcotics paraphernalia. Shortly after they got out, they were arrested again for possession of Valium and marijuana and disorderly conduct. Dugan gave a false name and served no jail time, but the friend served a few days because his driver's license connected him to the earlier campground theft.

After returning to Illinois early in 1975, Dugan spent a couple of days in jail on a battery charge for attacking his sister and shortly afterward was arrested for bringing a hunting knife into a hospital where he was visiting a friend. Then he wound up facing more serious charges.

While living at his sister Hilary's apartment in the DuPage County town of Villa Park, Dugan started a fire in an elementary school and made off with coins and a roll of stamps. The next day, he threatened Hilary and her child and kicked out the headlights of her car. He was charged with criminal damage to property, assault, battery, burglary, and arson. He pleaded guilty to the arson, and the other charges were dropped. He served less than seven months of his sentence of one to three years.

While in prison, Dugan pleaded guilty to another burglary and the attack on the police officers, receiving concurrent six-month sentences, which meant in effect that he served no extra time for those crimes.

On January 30, 1977, Dugan and another friend broke into two Aurora churches. At the second church, Dugan kicked in an office door, stole some items, and ransacked some other offices before police came. Dugan and his friend climbed out a window and up onto the roof but were caught on an adjacent roof. Dugan pleaded guilty to one of the burglaries and served less than six months of a sentence of two to six years. He was paroled on September 19, 1977.

On September 30, 1978, Dugan was caught after breaking into the same Villa Park school he had broken into in 1975. He told police he saw an intruder and tried to make a citizen's arrest, but police found he had the same amount of money on him as was later reported missing from the school. After missing several court appearances while the case stretched on for nearly a year, Dugan pleaded guilty to burglary and received a seven-year sentence.

While the school-burglary case stretched on, Dugan was charged with harboring a fourteen-year-old runaway girl in his

Aurora apartment and with an Aurora home burglary. Dugan used a false name in both cases, but a detective investigating the burglary recognized him. He got a seven-year term for the school burglary and a concurrent four-year term for the home burglary. He served slightly more than three years and was paroled on August 13, 1982.

Ten days later, he attacked the young woman who was a service station employee in Aurora. The young woman struggled and escaped when he tripped over a curb. That case was dropped when Dugan's brother provided an alibi that the brother later admitted was false. Jeanine Nicarico was abducted six months later.

As Garrett researched Dugan's background, he spoke with Naperville police chief Jim Teal and other investigators. Teal had gathered lots of arrest reports on Dugan which he made available to Garrett, and he was interested in learning whether Dugan had committed other murders. Garrett started meeting regularly with Teal and Captain Jon Ripsky of the Naperville Police Department.

Teal's own experience at the Prairie Path had helped persuade him that Dugan was the real killer of Jeanine Nicarico. On March 17, 1983, Teal had driven down the Prairie Path to the spot where Jeanine was murdered, just as Dugan had said he had twenty-two days before Teal did it. Coincidentally, Teal's unmarked police car had been a 1980 Plymouth Volare, the same model that Dugan had owned. When Teal had been ready to leave, he had realized that he would have had to either back up all the way down the Prairie Path or turn around. He had chosen to turn around and had driven forward, looking for a suitable place. As he'd approached the spot where the path was cut off by the tollway, he had seen an open area beside the trail. He had turned off the embankment to make a three-point turn, but he had soon felt his car sinking into the soft ground.

Teal hadn't wanted to get stuck, so he'd gunned the engine to get back up the embankment. Later, he'd learned that Dugan had described making precisely the same maneuvers.

"The hair on my neck froze," Teal recalled later. "That convinced me that the guy knew, that he had been there. He had done exactly the same thing that I had done."

Time and again, Garrett noticed, Dugan could have been caught but wasn't.

Six months before the Nicarico murder, Dugan had been arrested and charged with the attack on the service station employee, but the charges were dropped when his brother provided a false alibi. Had he been convicted and found in violation of his parole, he would have been off the streets.

If Eloise Suk had realized the young man who came to her church on the day of Jeanine's murder was the killer, she could have given police his name. If police canvassing the area had asked questions at the rectory, they might have learned what Suk had seen.

Had authorities set up surveillance before Dugan, Denise's sister, and the others drove to the Prairie Path, they might have noticed that Dugan's car matched the description given by the tollway workers. No one, though, asked for identification or took down the license plate number of Dugan's car.

If the eyewitnesses had said they saw a Volare instead of a Granada, Dugan might have become an early suspect in the Nicarico murder. If DuPage authorities had looked for a green car that was similar to a Granada, they might have looked for Volares, and found Dugan that way.

If the farmer who had heard a scream when Dugan attacked Donna Schnorr had called in an alarm immediately, the police officer in the area might have caught Dugan and saved her. If police had arrested Dugan on the day the nineteen-year-old Geneva woman had reported her attempted abduction and his license plate number, he would have been in jail instead of at large, free to murder Melissa Ackerman a few days later.

Why had Dugan gotten early parole from his third prison term? After Jeanine's murder, authorities had checked the list of paroled criminals. Dugan's name hadn't been on the list any longer. If he'd served his full parole, authorities might have investigated him immediately after Jeanine's murder.

One of the more frustrating incidents was the burglary at the Art Tape & Label Corporation on March 18, 1983. On that date, about three weeks after Jeanine was murdered, someone broke into the company's offices. The intruder rifled a vending machine and took some petty cash. Dugan's fingerprints were found on the interior of the vending machine.

Police investigating the burglary inspected Dugan's time cards, which also showed that he was absent on the day of Jeanine's murder. Other records showed he drove a boxy green car similar to the description of the car on the Prairie Path. He had a history of burglary and battery arrests and convictions, as well as the attack on the ten-year-old girl in Lisle. Yet none of the authorities investigating and prosecuting the burglary suspected a connection to Jeanine's murder. Instead, the burglary case was dismissed. The charges were reinstated seven months later, but he was never brought to trial. Even as authorities were zealously pursuing convictions in the high-profile Jeanine Nicarico murder, the prosecution complex allowed Dugan for the most part to fly under their radar, carrying on what local police later called a "one-man crime wave."

Bit by bit, Garrett started piecing together information about Dugan's crimes, his relationships, his places of employment, and his residences, reporting his findings back to Sam and Teal. Dugan, Garrett found, was a quiet loner who was always in some kind of trouble. He was a habitual burglar with a record of kicking in doors and attacking a young girl the same age as Jeanine Nicarico.

This, Sam thought, is the investigation that should have been done all along.

"The sheriff used to give awards for solving a good case," Sam said later. "I remember getting my award for solving the Jeanine Nicarico murder case and thinking, I don't want this fucking thing. I don't want my name on it. I mean, it was so depressing. Usually, I really did enjoy getting them, because what else did you get? You didn't get raises, you didn't get bonuses. It was just a little certificate—you could put a little frame around it or show it to your grandkids someday. It was something nice. But I didn't want my name on that one."

12

EDWARD CISOWSKI

---

*The requirement of proof beyond a reasonable doubt in a
criminal case [is] bottomed on a fundamental value determination of our society that it is far worse to convict an
innocent man than to let a guilty man go free.*

John Harlan, former U.S. Supreme Court justice,
in re *Winship*, 1970

ILLINOIS STATE POLICE lieutenant Edward Cisowski wasn't
sure why he'd been ordered to interview Brian Dugan.

Cisowski was the commander of the state police's
investigation division for Zone 2—a four-county area northwest of
Chicago that included DuPage and Kane counties. On the evening
of November 15, 1985, a month before Dugan's confession to the
Nicarico murder was made public, Cisowski learned that the state
police director wanted him to talk to Dugan.

Cisowski knew who Dugan was; Cisowski had worked on
the task force investigating Melissa Ackerman's murder, and he'd
also directed the state police investigation into Donna Schnorr's
slaying. Dugan was a prime suspect in both cases.

Now, apparently, Dugan might be ready to talk about something else. Cisowski wanted to ask about the murder of Linda
White, a woman who was drowned north of DuPage County after
being abducted. The modus operandi of that crime was similar to

that of Melissa Ackerman's murder, although there were some differences, too.

Cisowski didn't mind getting an evening call; he was a veteran detective who enjoyed his job.

"Cisowski is a very straight-up guy," Naperville police chief Jim Teal recalled later. "Both Ed Cisowski and John Sam strike me as being similar—guys who dig and question and never bend the truth."

Cisowski had become interested in law enforcement as a teenager when he'd unwittingly been involved on the periphery of a crime. Someone had left an extortion note demanding that an elderly widow leave thousands of dollars in a vacant lot next to the meat market Cisowski's father ran in an industrial suburb south of Chicago.

The wording of the note indicated that a teenager had written it, and because Cisowski's family lived behind the meat market, Ed was the first suspect. FBI agents soon realized he had nothing to do with the note, however, and instead set a surveillance base in the Cisowskis' home.

"The cameras, the radios, it was quite a thing to see," Cisowski recalled later. "There had to be forty guys there when they arrested this kid for extortion."

The experience made Cisowski want to be an FBI agent, but he received a letter from J. Edgar Hoover saying his eyesight might not be good enough. He tried dental school, but that didn't work out. When Illinois created its so-called Little FBI—the Illinois Bureau of Investigation—in 1970, Cisowski got a job. Eight years later, the IBI was merged with the Illinois State Police, and Cisowski became commander of a district in the state police detective division. He was a tall, lean, reserved man with a deep voice and a fondness for fishing.

Now, his job as commander required him to go see Brian Dugan.

Cisowski called his case agent for the Donna Schnorr murder and the agent for Linda White. "Bring your case reports," he said, "and the three of us will interview him."

The three men arrived at the LaSalle County state's attorney's offices on Saturday morning, November 16. Dugan and his public defender were negotiating plea agreements. Dugan, Cisowski learned, had admitted that he had murdered Donna Schnorr and Melissa Ackerman.

By midafternoon, authorities had accepted Dugan's confession to the Schnorr and Ackerman murders in exchange for a life sentence without possibility of parole. Dugan was ready to talk about more Kane County crimes, but first he insisted on talking to his Kane County public defender, Judy Brawka. Brawka was running errands, so everyone had to wait until she got home. She didn't arrive at the courthouse until early in the evening. At that point, she helped negotiate plea agreements for the attacks on the two women Dugan had raped and the Geneva woman he had tried to abduct. Brian Dugan admitted that he was responsible for all three.

Finally, at about 9:00 P.M., Dugan and his LaSalle County public defender, George Mueller, were ready to talk to Cisowski. Dugan seemed like a mild-mannered young man, Cisowski thought, the kind you'd let your daughter date.

The first words out of George Mueller's mouth were: "Which one of you guys is from DuPage County?" Cisowski replied that he was there to talk about Linda White, who had been murdered in another county.

Dugan, however, said that he did not commit that crime.

Cisowski didn't know if Dugan had committed two murders or thirty, but Mueller quickly made it plain he wanted to talk about the Jeanine Nicarico murder.

By coincidence, Cisowski lived only about seven blocks from the Nicaricos. As a result, he was familiar with the crime. He knew there had been convictions. He also knew that Tom Knight had said a gang of burglars had committed the crime, so it was quite possible another suspect was still at large.

"Well," said Mueller, "since none of you is from DuPage County, we'll talk hypothetically."

Fine, Cisowski said.

As Dugan and his lawyer began to tell Dugan's story, Dugan repeatedly indicated that he had murdered Jeanine Nicarico and that he had acted alone. Cisowski figured there were a couple of possibilities. Maybe Dugan committed the crime together with Buckley, Cruz, and Hernandez. They never had ratted on him during their trial, so now—when he was going to prison for the rest of his life anyway—he had confessed, saying he acted alone and trying to get his buddies out of prison.

Another possibility was that Dugan was just playing with the system, trying to muck up the works for his own reasons.

Then there was a third alternative. Maybe Dugan was telling the truth. After all, here was a lawyer whom Cisowski respected, saying that his client did it alone.

Dugan said he had been driving aimlessly through Naperville on the day of the crime. He said he'd stopped at a house to borrow a screwdriver. Then he'd resumed driving. Next, he'd stopped at the Nicarico house, and when he'd realized Jeanine was home alone, he'd kicked in the door and abducted her. He took her to the Prairie Path, where he assaulted her and killed her.

Jeanine Nicarico, age ten, murdered in 1983

Donna Schnorr, age twenty-seven, murdered in 1984

Melissa Ackerman, age seven, murdered in 1985

Brian Dugan, 1984

Stephen Buckley, 1987

Alejandro Hernandez, 1984

Rolando Cruz (second from left) with defense team, 1995: Tom Breen, Larry Marshall, Nan Nolan, and Matt Kennelly

JOHN SAM

EDWARD CISOWSKI

*Former DuPage County
sheriff's detective John Sam*

*Illinois State Police commander
Edward Cisowski*

MICHAEL METNICK

*Hernandez defense team, 1990 and 1991: Jane Raley, Michael Metnick, and
Jeff Urdangen*

*Defense attorney
Gary Johnson*

*Defense attorney
Frank Wesolowski*

*Defense attorney
Jed Stone*

*Defense attorney and
author Scott Turow*

*Defense attorney
John Hanlon*

*William J. Kunkle Jr., special
state's attorney in DuPage
Seven case*

*First assistant DuPage
County state's attorney
Robert Kilander*

1976 Ford Granada

Brian Dugan's Plymouth Volare

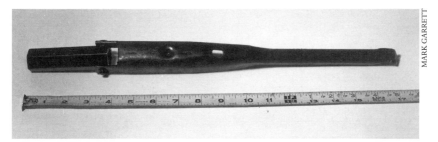

Standard issue tire iron from a 1980 Volare

Nicarico home, 1983

"Fayva" shoe similar to Brian Dugan's

Stephen Buckley's "Payless" shoe

Reversed image of shoeprint on the door of the Nicarico home

As Dugan and Mueller continued their story, Cisowski pointed out that Dugan could have gleaned his information from news media accounts. To test Dugan, Cisowski asked him what was in the Nicaricos' driveway.

Nothing, Dugan answered.

Now Cisowski figured the whole story was bogus. He'd gone by the Nicarico house on the day of the crime, so he knew that a twenty-two-foot yellow sailboat had been parked on the edge of the forty-foot-wide driveway.

"With all due respect," he said to Mueller, "your client is full of shit."

In reply, Dugan offered to take a polygraph test. He also said he could show Cisowski where the Nicaricos lived.

Fine, Cisowski said. We'll let you try.

On November 19, Dugan was sentenced as part of his plea agreement to life in prison for the rapes and murders of Melissa Ackerman and Donna Schnorr. Over the next couple of weeks, Cisowski talked to Dugan and his attorney several times. Dugan also talked to a state police psychologist and a hypnotist. On December 2, he passed a polygraph test. From Dugan's statements, which—although they varied on some minor points from statement to statement—were surprisingly consistent, the state police pieced together a rough version of what Dugan said had happened on the day of Jeanine Nicarico's murder:

Dugan had awakened at about 6:30 A.M. on the cot where he slept in Denise's unfinished basement. He got up, planning to go to his job at the Art Tape & Label Corporation, where he was scheduled to start at 7:00 A.M.

He went outside and drove off in his Plymouth Volare. As he cruised along North Avenue, however, smoking marijuana, he decided to blow off his job that day. Instead, dressed in shirtsleeves, ink-stained pants, and rubber-soled brown hiking shoes, he whiled away the morning driving aimlessly and smoking more marijuana. He tried to find a tavern in Elmhurst, where he had lived at one point, but he got lost. Instead, he headed back to Aurora.

He pulled into a gas station on Farnsworth Avenue in Aurora and called in sick. A clock on the wall showed it was 10:30 A.M. He bought a carton of chocolate milk and went on his way.

He stopped to play video games in a bowling alley called Gala Lanes West in Naperville, about three blocks from the Nicaricos' house. By now it was late morning, nearly the time when Patricia Nicarico would come home to make lunch for Jeanine.

Dugan got back into the Volare and started driving around. The car, though, wasn't running properly. He stopped at a home that he called red in one statement and brown in another. It was partly a single-story building but had a second story over part of it. He walked up the sidewalk. An older woman with a black-and-white print dress and granny glasses lived there. He asked her if he could borrow a screwdriver. She lent him a nine-inch yellow screwdriver.

He started cruising again, but the car still wasn't running right. He stopped again, this time in front of a house on Clover Court. He parked his car in the street and walked up the driveway. He noticed the wind blowing in a large fir tree.

A young girl came to the door. Dugan opened the screen door and talked to her, although she kept the wood door, which had a window in it, locked. She was wearing a nightshirt with a cartoon character on it. He told her he needed a screwdriver to fix his car and asked to use the phone. She told him to go to the neighbors' house.

He shut the door and started to walk away, but then stopped. He knew she was home alone. He turned around and walked back. He opened the screen door and kicked the wood door twice. On the second kick, it broke open, possibly snapping a chain. He walked in. He noticed the floor in the front hallway was wood. Just inside the door there were stairways. The one on the left led down to the basement family room, and the one on the right led upstairs. Beige carpeting covered the stairs leading down and the floor of the family room.

"Everything happened so fast," he told police.

He started to go down the stairs just as the girl started coming up. He saw a TV console in the basement family room and windows, possibly in patio doors, through which he could see outside. He grabbed her by the waist, picked her up, and covered her mouth with his hand. She grabbed at the staircase but wasn't strong enough to stop him.

He took the girl upstairs to her sisters' bedroom, noticing there was an unmade bed. He threw the girl onto the bed and told her not to move. She struggled at first but then stopped moving.

"She hadn't been hurt yet," he said.

At some point, he tied her hands and gagged her. He ran outside to his car and pulled it into the driveway. He returned to the house with a roll of medical tape. He also had a dry-rotted towel. On the towel, he said, was a picture of a "fool or joker." He had ripped the towel in half, and he used a strip to cover his victim's eyes. Then he used the tape, which he'd bought at a pharmacy on Farnsworth Avenue in Aurora, to hold the blindfold in place. The tape came in a metal can and was serrated on the edges. He wrapped it around her head four to six times.

He took a sheet from the unmade bed and wrapped her in it.

He carried her downstairs and outside, pausing to wipe away his fingerprints from the doorknob and the area around it. He carried her to his car, put her in the front seat, and drove off, looking for a lonely place. Eventually he wound up at the Prairie Path near Eola.

He drove his car down the path, veering to the right when it forked. He stopped and got into the backseat of his car with her and sexually assaulted her. At that point, he noticed that she had milky polish on her toenails.

Then he helped her out of the car, keeping one hand on her arm and carrying a tire iron. Wearing only a nightshirt in the cold February air, she walked barefoot on the gravel. He led her to the rear of the car.

"Where are we going?" she asked.

"Back home," he said.

He swung the tire iron onto her skull, and she fell forward, hitting her face on the car's bumper. He dragged her by her nightshirt into the brush at the side of the path until he reached a gully.

"I let go of her and I hit her again with a board, a piece of tree limb that didn't have any bark on it," he said. The reason he hit her again, he said, was that she made a noise that startled him.

He tossed aside the club and left her body lying faceup, hands untied and feet pointing down the gully toward the Prairie Path. He got back in his car and drove down the path away from Eola Road toward a point near the tollway. The area was marshy, though, and his wheels started spinning in the mud. He feared he might get stuck. He saw two maintenance workers about twenty-five feet away along the tollway shoulder. Their truck, he thought, was brown and the size of a pickup. He made a three-point turn and went back out the Prairie Path the way he had come in.

He tossed Jeanine's underpants, the sheet, and the tape in a trash container behind the Eagle Foods supermarket in Aurora. Later, he went back to Denise's house and walked down into the basement. At some point, he dropped the tire iron behind a hot-water heater or hot-water radiator. Later, when he learned authorities were looking for Cloud Climber hiking shoes, he threw his into a farmer's field as he drove along a road called Indian Trail.

He never mentioned stopping at the church where Eloise Suk saw him. Later, he said he did remember going to the church, but thought he had gone there on a different day.

It was a gruesome story. Now it was Cisowski's job to prove or disprove it.

His first step was to have state police detectives canvass the neighborhood to see if they could find the woman from whom Dugan had borrowed a screwdriver. Cisowski didn't want the Nicarico family to hear about the canvassing from neighbors instead of authorities, so he arranged to meet them at St. Raphael's rectory with Father Mike.

At the rectory, Cisowski told the Nicaricos what Dugan had been saying. Later, he accompanied them back to their house to compare the interior with Dugan's description. Generally, Dugan was correct, but he'd made mistakes. For example, he'd reversed the positions of the staircases going up and down, and he'd said there was a TV console in the basement family room. Actually, it had just been a TV on a stand. The floor by the front door was tile, not wood, but it was tile with a wood-grain pattern. There had been no chain on the front door or patio doors in the basement. Also, Dugan hadn't remembered seeing the small family dog.

Cisowski made several more trips to the Nicarico home to interview them, and Thomas Nicarico came to Cisowski's office to review some photos.

Next, the state police obtained the paperwork to have Dugan let out of jail briefly so they could see if he could lead them to the Nicaricos' house and the Prairie Path. By now, Dugan had a new lawyer—Thomas McCulloch of Kane County, who had agreed to represent Dugan for a fee of one dollar.

Because Cisowski knew where the Nicarico house was and might unconsciously tip Dugan, Cisowski didn't take part in the ride. Instead, he called Thomas Nicarico and explained the situation. Cisowski had told Dugan there was a sailboat in the Nicarico driveway, so the boat had to be moved. Thomas Nicarico helped Cisowski tow it to Cisowski's driveway. Now they were ready.

Two other police officers drove Dugan and McCulloch to an Aurora shopping mall and told Dugan to lead them from there. First, they wanted him to find the house where he had borrowed the screwdriver, which was in the same subdivision as the Nicarico home. The subdivision was one of 125 in Naperville at the time, but he led them there directly. He couldn't find the house where he had borrowed a screwdriver, however. Then they asked him to take them to the home where the girl had been abducted. Dugan found it easily. He then took them, after making some wrong turns, to the Prairie Path.

At the Prairie Path entrance, Dugan noticed some high-voltage power wires. He remarked that he didn't remember seeing them before. He knew the general area where the body had been left. He couldn't pinpoint it exactly, but neither could the county authorities who had been at the Prairie Path during the days after the body was found.

Over the next few weeks, state police continued to probe Dugan's story. Many of Dugan's statements were corroborated.

Time cards from the Art Tape & Label Corporation showed Dugan had skipped work on the day of the crime. His shoe size was the same as the print on the door. Records showed the B & R Pharmacy on Farnsworth Avenue in Aurora did sell the medical tape Dugan had described and that it had come in metal containers.

Dugan had accurately described the front door of the Nicaricos' house, saying it had one or more windows on the top and a handle on the right, although he'd mistakenly said it might have had a chain lock on the inside. He'd correctly said the glass in the door had not broken when he kicked it in. He'd accurately described the color of the basement recreation room carpeting, the wooden upstairs railing, and the home's general floor plan.

He'd correctly described the Disney figure on the victim's nightgown. He knew that the towel used as a blindfold was dry-rotted. He'd described a picture of a "fool or joker" on the towel, which did have a cartoonish drawing of Romeo and Juliet. He'd said the tape had a serrated edge, that it was three-quarters of an inch to an inch wide, and that it was wrapped four to six times around the victim's head, correct information that never had been made public. He'd incorrectly said there had been only one bed in the upstairs room where he had tied up Jeanine. In fact, there were two. He'd said he'd taken nothing from the house but a light-colored sheet in which he'd wrapped the victim. In fact, nothing was missing except a light tan sheet and a small security blanket.

Dugan fit the description of the man the tollway workers had seen at the Prairie Path on the day of the crime. His car matched the exterior color, interior color, and body shape of the car seen on the Prairie Path. The state investigators learned that when Dugan's car was repossessed in October 1983, it was missing a hubcap, just as had the car at the Prairie Path. It was missing its tire iron. And it also had a faulty carburetor or choke, which fit Dugan's story of engine trouble.

A farmhand who worked at the field where Dugan said he

had thrown his hiking shoes said he had seen such a shoe at the end of a row when he was turning over the soil that spring. State police hired a contractor to dig for the shoes, but the effort failed. The ground was frozen, and a tent they erected over the area quickly filled with fumes from the digging equipment.

Police checked with a local landfill operator, who was able to identify which area in the landfill contained the contents of the trash container in which Dugan said he'd tossed Jeanine's underpants, the tape, and the sheet. However, it would have cost $300,000 to excavate the seam, and there was no guarantee they would find anything. Cisowski did not have enough money to try.

With reluctant permission from the Nicaricos, police exhumed Jeanine's body to see if she was wearing the milky toe polish Dugan had described and to get hair samples to replace others that had been lost. She had polish on her fingernails but not her toes.

The tire iron was not behind the hot-water heater at Denise's house. Denise's mother, however, said there had been a flood recently, and that she'd tossed out many items that had been in the basement.

In Dugan's apartment, police had found an address book with about seventy-five names of Dugan's friends and relatives. The state police called them all, trying to find out if there was a link between Brian Dugan, Stephen Buckley, Rolando Cruz, and Alejandro Hernandez. Some of the people in the address book were helpful, giving the police names of additional people to call. But none of them ever had seen Dugan with the three men who actually were charged. There was no indication that Dugan, who was at least six years older than the others, ever had met any of them.

The state police also took all the police records associated with Dugan, Buckley, Cruz, and Hernandez and ran them through a computer to see if any links would pop up. None did.

Cisowski also tried to verify Dugan's explanation of where he got the towel he'd used as a blindfold. Dugan said he'd taken the towel from the trunk of a yellow Cadillac he'd bought at an earlier time from his mother's boyfriend, Larry Lord. When Cisowski interviewed Lord and Dugan's mother together, however, they said no such towel was in the trunk. Later, Dugan's lawyer, Thomas McCulloch, said Dugan's mother admitted that she and Lord were lying about the towel because it might have made trouble for her son. She wouldn't talk to Cisowski about the towel, though, and by then Lord was near death and mentally incapacitated.

During the investigation, Dugan told police of other crimes he'd committed. He said he'd raped a woman in her car in Elmhurst. The woman escaped when he'd threatened to kill her with a knife, running off naked between houses in the wintertime. Dugan himself had tried to flee the scene in her car but had crashed into a guardrail. Instead, he'd fled on foot.

Elmhurst police investigated Dugan's claim and eventually concluded such a crime had indeed occurred and that he was indeed the assailant.

Dugan also said he'd sexually assaulted a paperboy he'd abducted off the street and had anally raped a young relative. Police found no records of complaints in either of those incidents.

As the corroborating evidence piled up, Cisowski was surprised by the reaction of the Nicaricos and DuPage County authorities. Originally the Nicaricos had been supportive. It was Thomas Nicarico who noticed that photos of Dugan's Volare showed a missing hubcap, just as had been reported by the tollway workers. Now, though, the family was angry and resentful.

"Early on, the Nicaricos thought I was the greatest thing

since sliced bread because I was putting yet another guy on Death Row," Cisowski said later.

Soon, though, it became clear that if Dugan's story was accepted as part of a plea bargain in which Dugan would not get the death penalty, the original defendants would be freed and Dugan would get only a life term in prison, which he was serving anyway for the other murders. He would not be executed.

"Once the Nicaricos found out there was no Death Row, everything changed," Cisowski said.

As the investigation progressed, however, Cisowski became convinced Dugan was involved in the crime, although he wasn't certain of the extent. It puzzled him, though, that Dugan was confessing. Why? Had he hidden Jeanine's underpants where they might be found? What made Dugan think he might be a suspect in the case? Cisowski did not know that Dugan had a very good reason to seek a plea bargain: Detective Warren Wilkosz had questioned Dugan the previous summer about Jeanine's murder. Dugan had reason to think he was a suspect.

Cisowski also was puzzled by the reactions of Jim Ryan, the DuPage County state's attorney, and Sheriff Doria. Cisowski met with DuPage authorities two or three times a week and talked to First Assistant State's Attorney Robert Kilander every day.

The first time Cisowski met with Ryan, Sheriff Doria also was there.

"I don't like internal investigations," Doria said.

"This isn't an internal investigation," Cisowski said. "This is more information that you didn't have before."

"I don't like it," Doria said, getting up and walking out of the meeting.

Ryan was more polite, but he was no more helpful.

Ryan's aides had told Cisowski they wouldn't provide a case file or any information they already possessed because they wanted him to do an independent investigation. Their chilly reception of the evidence he was uncovering surprised him. Robert Kilander, who'd met with George Mueller, Dugan's public defender, three days before Cisowski first did, ridiculed the evidence and said Dugan was a liar.

Then police got an intriguing piece of new information. Eloise Suk, a church secretary, said a man named Brian Dugan had come to her church, which was less than a mile from the Nicarico home, on the afternoon of the crime. He'd inquired about a job and then left. Suk had written his name down on a piece of paper and put it in her desk. Although she'd lost the paper, she remembered the name because she thought the spelling was unusual; other people she'd known with the same name had spelled it "Duggan."

When Gary Johnson heard about Eloise Suk, he thought that was the clincher. Surely DuPage authorities would admit their mistake now, he thought. He was wrong.

Stories about Dugan's confession started appearing in the community newspapers, on local television reports, and in the *Chicago Sun-Times* and the *Chicago Tribune*. The new judge on the case, Robert A. Nolan, was annoyed. He hadn't been bothered when the defense had complained about pretrial publicity that hurt the defendants. But now stories were raising serious questions about the prosecution, which originally had been headed by his political ally, J. Michael Fitzsimmons. Like Fitzsimmons, Nolan had defeated a GOP-endorsed candidate when he'd won a full judgeship in 1978.

Judge Nolan issued a gag order. The case file was impounded.

No investigators or lawyers were to talk to reporters about any information in the case.

Nevertheless, in May 1986, Rob Warden, the editor of a legal investigative monthly called the *Chicago Lawyer,* printed a long article about the case. Warden was an unusual fixture in Chicago; he carefully scrutinized the criminal justice system and often uncovered surprising abuses by authorities. He had filed a lawsuit against the gag order, and, although he lost it (the Illinois Supreme Court upheld the gag order on May 5, 1986), Judge Nolan revised the order to be somewhat less restrictive.

The article, written by James Tuohy with help from Randy Garrett, was titled "The DuPage Cover-up." A secondary headline read: "The authorities know Brian Dugan killed Jeanine Nicarico. They know they've put the wrong men on Death Row. They don't care."

13

JIM RYAN

Forensic science can be the innocent suspect's best friend. Unfortunately, much of it is nothing more than mere quackery.

Rob Warden, coauthor of *A Promise of Justice* and other books and former editor and publisher of *Chicago Lawyer,* in the *Chicago Sun-Times,* March 8, 1987

JIM RYAN FACED A TOUGH CHOICE.

Until now, the boyish-looking Republican state's attorney had stayed carefully in the background while debate swirled around the Jeanine Nicarico murder case. A new FBI report, however, was going to change that. William Bodziak of the FBI, the nation's preeminent shoe expert, had looked at the Nicaricos' front door and had come to a conclusion: the shoeprint wasn't Buckley's. Bodziak also found that the door had been kicked more than once, just as Brian Dugan had said.

Should Ryan drop the charges against Buckley, who was awaiting a new trial? Should he say publicly that Cruz and Hernandez should be freed?

Ryan by nature was cautious. Although he'd been a Golden Gloves boxer as a teenager in the gyms of Chicago's West Side, his nose had never been broken. He was too careful for that. He didn't take unnecessary chances. Ryan had been taught that a boxer needs to keep his head while he's in the ring. Smart boxers go far. Boxers who fight from the heart get broken noses.

As a politician, Ryan followed the same rules. Don't follow your heart into the path of a nasty jab. Let someone else take the lumps. Although he was sometimes criticized for absorbing himself in task forces and ruling by committee, his political future looked bright. Just a year after Ryan was elected DuPage County state's attorney, James R. Thompson, then the governor of Illinois, tried to talk him into running for Illinois attorney general. Ever prudent, Ryan had decided it wasn't time yet.

Ryan had moved to DuPage County as a child when his father, Edward, a builder of modest homes, had relocated the family from Chicago. Jim Ryan and his wife, Marie, had six children. He earned a political science degree from Illinois Benedictine College in 1968 and a law degree from Chicago-Kent College of Law in 1971. He believed in the legal system and made a point of following the rules, even shunning the common practice of slipping off-the-record information about various cases to reporters. That was a good way for a prosecutor to make himself popular with the press, but Ryan thought it violated the prosecutors' canon of ethics.

Now, though, it wasn't clear even to a cautious politician which course was wisest.

If he decided to drop charges against Buckley, Ryan could call a press conference. He could have William Bodziak of the FBI assert that the shoeprint on the door was not Buckley's. Edward Cisowski, now a state police captain, could explain why the state police believed Dugan was the culprit. Ryan could say that he had relied on the work of the previous administration when he'd decided to proceed with the trial against Stephen Buckley,

Rolando Cruz, and Alejandro Hernandez. He'd even retained Fitzsimmons's top prosecutor to try the case. Ryan could let the news media draw the conclusion that it was Fitzsimmons's people who had sent the case in the wrong direction.

If there ever was going to be a time when he could walk away from the case, this was it.

That choice wasn't hazard-free, however. Ryan had carefully cultivated an image as a committed crime fighter. Opening the jail doors wouldn't fit that image; it was the sort of thing "liberals" would do. And even though he hadn't initiated the case, Ryan still would have some explaining to do. How could he defend the decision to use Louise Robbins and her novel shoeprint identification theories? And how could he explain the county's failure to imprison Dugan before he raped and killed more people?

There were the sheriff and the victim's family to consider, too. Ryan might get his own people off the hook by blaming his predecessor, but that wouldn't protect the sheriff's investigators. If Dugan's story were accepted as true, how could anyone explain Cruz's "vision" statement? How could Cruz have had "guilty knowledge" about the crime if he had nothing to do with it? To side with Dugan would create a rift with Sheriff Doria, who ran the county's biggest department.

As for the victim's family, the Nicaricos by now knew how the news media worked. They knew how to call a press conference, how to keep media interviews focused. They could create quite a splash if they ripped Ryan publicly for changing course. They could make him look like an inept politician who couldn't get a conviction in the county's biggest case. Dropping charges against Buckley and freeing Cruz and Hernandez without the Nicaricos on board would not be the path of caution, and the

Nicaricos were not about to get on board. If Ryan ever was going to drop the Buckley charges, he would need an excuse that didn't involve Brian Dugan.

The Nicaricos stoutly maintained that the original three defendants were guilty. For a whole year, they'd wanted to get the murderer or murderers of their daughter caught and indicted. For another whole year they had hoped that the young men who'd been indicted would be convicted. They'd attended meetings of Parents of Murdered Children, an organization that stresses, among other things, the importance of pushing authorities to solve crimes. They had attended every pretrial hearing, every day of the trial, every day of the death penalty hearings, and every day of the pretrial motions for Buckley's upcoming second trial.

They'd had to sit quietly at the trial while Cruz had smirked and winked at them. They'd heard the DuPage County prosecutors scoff at the Dugan evidence, picking it apart and calling Dugan a liar. They knew that jailhouse witnesses were saying Dugan admitted he was making up his story. The family was not about to give up without a fight. To do so would be to turn their backs on the sheriff's deputies and prosecutors who had worked so hard to secure convictions in the first trial.

"On numerous occasions, we have made known the reasons for our strong conviction that Brian Dugan did not murder our daughter," they would write the next year in a letter printed in a local publication called the *DuPage Profile*. "On the subject of Brian Dugan and the Illinois State Police Department of Criminal Investigation's (DCI) investigation into his possible involvement in our daughter's murder, we have been very vocal that based on our substantial involvement in that investigation, we do not believe he is the murderer."

Nevertheless, when Buckley's public defender, Carol Anfinson, talked to prosecutor Robert Kilander outside court one day in the spring of 1986, it sounded to her as though charges were about to be dropped. It made sense; the testimony of an FBI expert saying Buckley's shoe did not leave the print on the Nicaricos' door would be very powerful trial testimony. Anfinson was elated. Although there wasn't much evidence against Buckley, she knew it would be a tough case for her to win. Perhaps the prosecution complex was losing its grip.

Anfinson hurried to State's Attorney Jim Ryan's office and waited. While there, she saw the Nicaricos in the hallway. When Anfinson finally was called in, it was quickly clear that Ryan was not going to drop the charges. Instead, Kilander and assistant DuPage County state's attorney Patrick King shortly afterward offered a plea bargain: the charges against Buckley would be reduced to burglary with a prison sentence if he would plead guilty. Anfinson urged Buckley to consider the offer, but he dismissed it out of hand, saying he never would plead guilty to something he hadn't done. The trial was going to go forward.

The next step was to hold hearings on the Brian Dugan evidence. Carol Anfinson wanted to tell the jury at Buckley's second trial all about Dugan. That, she reasoned, was her client's best chance for an acquittal. The trick, though, was to find a way to let the jury hear about Dugan. Prosecutors didn't want all that information coming into Buckley's second trial. A hearing was scheduled at which the new judge, Robert A. Nolan, would decide whether a jury would be permitted to learn about Dugan's admissions.

From the prosecutors' point of view, the hearing would serve a second purpose as well. Ryan had taken plenty of blows to the chin in the news media as various parts of the Dugan story leaked out.

Some people seemed to think it was only a matter of time before Ryan would be forced to confess error. Others knew only that significant doubts hung over the case. The hearing offered Ryan and his aides a chance to defend their decision to retry Buckley, to get in a few licks of their own, and to publicly debunk Dugan.

"The murderer of Jeanine Nicarico is almost certainly behind bars," read a *Chicago Tribune* editorial on July 31, 1986. "But there is serious doubt whether any of the men convicted or formally accused of the crime actually did it. . . .

"The passions in Naperville run high over this case. It was a particularly horrible murder. And it evoked feelings of fear and anger. But it is still up to DuPage prosecutors to overcome whatever pressures there may be to disregard Dugan's story and undertake a fresh and open reexamination of the case. A prosecutor's responsibility goes beyond that of ordinary litigants. He represents the government, and it is his duty not only to win cases, but to do justice, even if that means losing a few."

Ryan needed to quash that line of thinking. The prosecutors thought they could blow Dugan's story out of the water. "Bring your wetsuit," one of Ryan's aides told reporters as the hearing into Dugan was about to begin.

The hearing, presided over by Judge Nolan, started on August 20, 1986. To win, Anfinson had to prove that Dugan's story had some corroboration, that it wasn't something he'd just made up. The legal term was "indicia of reliability." If Anfinson couldn't persuade Judge Nolan at the hearing that Dugan's story had indicia of reliability, she couldn't mention Dugan's admissions during the subsequent trial.

At the hearing, Illinois State Police captain Edward Cisowski was the star witness. He testified about the entire state police investigation. He admitted there were about two dozen inconsistencies between what Dugan had claimed and facts known about the murder. However, he also said that Dugan knew details about the case that had never been mentioned in the news media.

Then Anfinson played the videotape of Brian Dugan describing under hypnosis his attack on Jeanine Nicarico.

But prosecutor Robert Kilander poked holes in Dugan's story. Kilander, who was second-in-command to Jim Ryan, had taken on the Nicarico case after Tom Knight left the office.

Kilander pointed out that Dugan hadn't remembered the sailboat on the edge of the wide driveway. He had made mistakes describing the interior of the Nicaricos' house. He'd said Jeanine's nightshirt was white, when actually it was pink.

The most damaging weakness in Dugan's story, Anfinson thought, was that he described the truck the tollway workers had been driving as a brown vehicle the size of a pickup. Actually, it was a large orange-and-blue International Harvester 1800 state truck. Dugan's description, she thought, was so far off the mark that it undermined the impact of the many details he got right.

Kilander meanwhile seemed to be implying that Dugan had attended Aurora East High School together with Buckley, Cruz, and Hernandez. Cisowski was shocked. Kilander knew that Dugan had left the school years before the others arrived and that Hernandez had attended for only a matter of days. Cisowski thought Kilander was unfairly creating an impression that Dugan knew the others.

Kilander also implied that Dugan's description of the tape

used for the blindfold had been wrong because Dugan said it came in a metal container. A DuPage investigator had purchased Johnson & Johnson tape at the drugstore on Farnsworth in Aurora where Dugan said he bought his tape, but it came in a plastic container. Kilander argued that Dugan's story wasn't true. However, it turned out after the hearing that the store also had stocked Curity tape in metal containers in 1983 and that the tape used in the blindfold was Curity. Defense lawyers also learned that a store representative had told that to a DuPage investigator before the hearing.

Frank Cleveland, who had testified in the first trial in support of the theory that Jeanine was killed at the Prairie Path, now testified that she probably wasn't.

During Buckley's original trial, Cleveland had said scratches on the victim's body occurred as she was dying and dragged through underbrush, not afterward. He also had said she had a great quantity of hair, which could have prevented a rapid loss or scattering of blood.

At the hearing, however, he said that the scratches could only have been made several minutes after the victim's death, indicating she was dead before she was dragged to the spot where her body was discovered. He also said that she could not have been killed on the scene because there was too little blood.

In addition, investigators had exhumed Jeanine's body, which was dressed in her horse-riding outfit, to see if she was wearing the toenail polish Dugan had described. Although she had polish on her fingernails, there was none on her toes—another indication, Kilander said, that Dugan had fabricated his account.

On the last day of the hearing, Carol Anfinson was in a hurry to take a charter flight. Judge Nolan reprimanded her when she complained about his decision to end the morning session abruptly even though she said she needed only one more minute to finish questioning her witness. As Anfinson explained that she wanted to keep things moving because she had a flight to Europe later in the day, Nolan said: "I don't care for the tone of voice that you are using." Anfinson thought Judge Nolan was purposely setting her up to look bad.

Judge Nolan took a long lunch, attending a Republican Party event. Finally he resumed the hearing. As Anfinson gave her closing argument, with several glances at the courtroom clock, she said Dugan's knowledge of the murder was amazingly accurate. She pointed out that Jeanine's pink nightshirt was so faded that it looked white and that Dugan had called it white even though it always had been publicly described as pink. However, she allowed prosecutors, without challenge, to read into the record a statement by the hypnotist who had interviewed Dugan, indicating that individuals sometimes lie under hypnosis. They also put into the record the hypnotist's statement that people under hypnosis have admitted to crimes they did not commit and that Dugan reached only a medium level rather than a deep level of hypnosis.

Anfinson paced the courtroom as Robert Kilander gave his closing and at one point lingered behind him, causing him to stop for a moment.

As the day's session came to a close, Anfinson rushed off. To reporters, she said only, "I've got to get to my airplane!" as she sped away in a waiting car.

Buckley's parents, Marilyn and John, left the courthouse without a word. His sister, Carol, said, "What can we do about it?"

On September 5, 1986, Judge Nolan issued his ruling. Although no evidence had been presented during the hearing to support the idea that there was more than one intruder at the

Nicarico home, Nolan said the evidence was consistent with multiple assailants. He called Dugan's statements "totally unreliable."

"For a while, [Dugan] has been Mr. Big," Nolan said. "Maybe that's why he said what he did. He certainly has been the center of attention. Maybe if he could throw a monkey wrench into this case, he would be an even bigger Mr. Big.

"Whatever his motives, it is clear he was fabricating. I am not convinced he was in such a hypnotic state as that which, in my opinion, he pretended. He slipped in and out of his role like a bad actor on a stage. Perhaps he was gratifying some impulse or need he had. Perhaps this was his idea of fun."

Then Judge Nolan announced his decision. None of Brian Dugan's statements would be allowed in Stephen Buckley's second trial.

Stephen Buckley was discouraged. His jail experiences hadn't been good; another inmate had attacked him, seriously injuring him. He'd become so accustomed to living in a small cell that it made him nervous when he was brought into the open courtroom for various hearings. Privately, he said that if convicted of something he didn't do, he would rather be executed than spend the rest of his life in prison.

Gary Johnson was frustrated by the turn of events, and he decided to rejoin the defense team. He had left the law firm where he had been working and now was living on his severance pay and setting up his own firm. Working with Anfinson, Johnson would have access to the resources of the public defender's office and would not have to pay for transcripts and other expenses himself.

On September 19, 1986, Buckley's second trial was ready to

start. Potential jurors were called in, and the lawyers started asking them questions. Then the prosecutors produced another surprise. They had a new jailhouse snitch, James Byrnes, who would say that he'd heard Stephen Buckley admit to the killing. Another inmate, Eric Hook, would also testify that Buckley had admitted taking part in the crime.

The defense lawyers were astounded. All along, one of Stephen Buckley's advantages was that he had never tied himself to the crime in any way. While Cruz and Hernandez had made various statements claiming to have heard information about the murder, Buckley had said he knew nothing about it. He could argue that all he had done was cooperate with police.

The defense lawyers went into Judge Nolan's chambers and said they needed time to interview James Byrnes before the trial started. Judge Nolan agreed, and the trial was aborted. The potential jurors were sent home.

Johnson went to interview Byrnes, who was in prison in Indiana. It was immediately apparent Byrnes couldn't identify Buckley. His story implicating Buckley would not hold up. Byrnes was not going to be a problem after all.

When the next status hearing came up, Anfinson and Johnson said they were ready for trial. That surprised Judge Nolan, who had been expecting them to ask for more time. He was worried that the case might run afoul of the speedy-trial law.

In Illinois, the law requires that an imprisoned defendant be tried within 120 days or freed unless it is the defendant who seeks more time to prepare for trial. The law, however, isn't clear about what happens in a retrial, such as Buckley's. Judge Nolan wanted the prosecutors and defense to agree that there was no potential speedy-trial violation.

Anfinson and Johnson, however, felt the law did not require them to calculate whether there was a speedy-trial violation. To do so would waive an appeal issue at a later point. They refused to say whether they thought the speedy-trial rules were being met. Angrily, Judge Nolan ordered them to be shackled and jailed for contempt of court on bond of $1,000 each. Evidently, there was no room in his court for lawyers who did not want to play by the rules of the prosecution complex.

Sitting in jail, waiting for Carol Anfinson's husband to arrive and bail them out, was discouraging for Gary Johnson. He hoped to run someday for Kane County state's attorney, and he knew it wouldn't help his image to have been jailed by a judge. Still, he felt he had no choice. His first responsibility was to represent Stephen Buckley.

Despite the argument over the speedy-trial provisions, things moved slowly. Four months went by, and still there was no trial.

Meanwhile, Thomas Frisbie, a *Chicago Sun-Times* reporter who covered DuPage County, had started looking into Louise Robbins and her $1,000-a-day courtroom testimony. At least eight people were in prison for life in the United States and Canada after she had testified against them. Tom Knight had portrayed Robbins as the centerpiece of the case against Stephen Buckley. Frisbie wanted to find out whether Robbins's theories of shoeprint identification were valid.

First he called Russell Tuttle, an anthropologist at the University of Chicago who had written a soon-to-be-published criticism of a book by Robbins titled *Footprints: Collection, Analysis and Interpretation.*

Tuttle called Robbins's techniques "an utter travesty of science."

"There ain't nothing there," Tuttle said. "I feel very sorry for her. I don't think she is a total crook, just a person who has never known what science is all about because the courts keep sanctioning this."

Tuttle worried that some of the defendants Robbins had testified against might have been innocent.

"She doesn't have the beginning clue of how science works, how you do controlled studies, how you do blind tests," he said. "The courts cannot allow this kind of thing to go on."

Robbins's own data published in her book showed that her claim that she could determine the height of a person within one inch was wrong, Tuttle said. Only a third of the subjects she studied fit that prediction. Apparently, though, she had never noticed.

Next, Frisbie called Louise Robbins. She wouldn't respond to what Tuttle said because she hadn't had a chance to read his criticism. She said that her techniques would be debated the following February by a panel at the annual convention of the American Academy of Forensic Sciences. She said she expected the panel would be "less than objective." She suggested that Frisbie call Ellis Kerley, a professor of anthropology and forensic anthropology at the University of Maryland at College Park.

Kerley said he had taught with Robbins at the University of Kentucky and had testified at various trials that she was "a very qualified forensic anthropologist." He wouldn't, however, vouch for her shoeprint identification methods.

"I don't profess to be able to judge that," he said. "I can tell you that she is a very reputable scientist. She has developed this method, particularly footprint analysis, and presented it to the scientific community and it has been accepted—at least I'm not aware of sustained adverse comments against it—and she has extrapolated that to shoeprint wear, and I can't in all honesty comment on it."

Kerley said he didn't know of anyone offhand who would corroborate Robbins's shoeprint work.

Joseph Montjoy, chairman of Robbins's department in Greensboro, said the university did not monitor her courtroom work. He referred Frisbie to others in the field, including Jane Buikstra, a University of Chicago anthropology professor.

Buikstra, however, said she was not persuaded that Robbins could support her shoeprint identification claims. For example, Robbins had never done a scientific experiment to gauge how an individual's shoe wear patterns might change over a lifetime, Buikstra said.

Next, Frisbie talked to Timothy White, a professor of anthropology at the University of California at Berkeley. White had met Robbins in the late 1970s in Tanzania. His observations of her work in the field led him to believe that she would make statements that were poorly grounded.

Robbins, he said, should have done a blind test to check the accuracy of her shoeprint theory before she testified anywhere. He said someone should give her a hundred shoeprints of the same size and style and ask her to match them up with the people who'd made them. According to her theory, she should be able to match them perfectly.

"She makes one outrageous extrapolation after another," White said. "She sees that two physical skeletons are different, therefore the soft tissue must be different. Therefore, the way that is expressed through the sole of the shoe must be different.

Therefore, the shoeprint must be different. That is the reasoning she has come to believe, but it doesn't lie in the realm of science until it has been tested."

White said Robbins's courtroom experiences had taught her to drop some of her claims, such as identifying race or socioeconomic status from shoeprints. She still, however, insisted she could identify the unique wear pattern in a shoeprint.

Owen Lovejoy, who had testified against Robbins in Buckley's trial, said he'd testified against her at other trials, too, where she had given testimony he thought was bizarre.

Craig Tobin, a Chicago lawyer who'd had a case in which Robbins was an adverse witness, said Robbins had admitted under cross-examination that she never studied how shoes were made or how different surfaces, such as concrete and grass, wear away the bottoms of shoes.

During Tobin's cross-examination, Robbins also admitted that she never had devised a statistical test to determine if her students were representative of the general population. Instead, she just had checked random shoeprints of her students. It also had come out that Robbins had started testifying as the only expert in the nation who could identify unique shoe wear patterns in the same year, 1976, that she started her study of shoeprints. Moreover, she had not methodically examined particular shoes more than once to determine if the owner's wear pattern changes.

A Pennsylvania prosecutor who was the first to use Robbins vouched for her accuracy. In that case, Robbins had testified that the person who'd left two shoeprints probably would be a black man with a height of five feet ten to six feet two and a weight of 155 to 185 pounds. She hadn't yet started saying she could identify a suspect through a unique wear pattern.

"Dr. Robbins was able to describe the race, sex, and general physical characteristics of the suspect without being provided any information as to the focus and target of our investigation," the district attorney wrote in a letter to Frisbie.

Frisbie again called Robbins, who wouldn't talk about her courtroom testimony. She didn't hang up right away, though, so he asked her why she had never conducted a blind test.

"We're driving down two different roads," Robbins said. "One is the doing, collecting of shoes and then doing the blind test and matching up—this is a scientific test. Now taking that same kind of information and applying it to a particular case, and analysis of case evidence, now that's something entirely different."

Frisbie wasn't sure what that meant.

"How long does a person have to wear a shoe before the [unique] wear pattern gets on there?" he asked.

"Oh, it can be as much as, say, walking a hundred feet or walking for a day or wearing the shoes for a week," she said. "It doesn't take very long."

"If you put on a brand-new pair of shoes and walked a hundred feet, theoretically that would be enough to—"

"Yes."

"Does it matter what kind of surface you're walking on?"

"No, it doesn't really, because the wear on the bottom of the shoe is coming from the pressure points from the foot onto the shoe so the wear will start very quickly. . . . Even if you are walking on carpet or something like that, it will still show up."

"How about if you are walking on a mountain path that's all rocky and your shoes are getting turned every which way and slanting all around, how would that affect it?"

"Well," Robbins said, "it will still show your shoe wear pattern, because, though a rocky mountain path may cause you to twist your foot, you still are maintaining a stable support base for your body."

Frisbie tried to turn the conversation to the Buckley case, but Robbins refused to discuss it and got off the phone.

During an informal chat with prosecutor Robert Kilander in a hallway, Frisbie asked what he thought about Louise Robbins and some of her more extravagant claims.

"She's a very good witness who has been pushed too far by some prosecutors," Kilander said.

To Frisbie, that sounded like an admission that Robbins would say anything. He couldn't understand why the courts across the country would let her testify in cases where a defendant might be executed or imprisoned for life. He went to see Melvin B. Lewis, a professor at John Marshall Law School in Chicago who taught a class in scientific evidence. It was Lewis who had helped organize the panel that would examine Robbins's work. Lewis expressed contempt for Robbins and said she was just one example of a disgraceful pattern in which judges allow bogus "experts" to testify in trials.

"It seems that the only standard the courts are requiring of forensic science is that it be incriminating to the defendant," Lewis said.

Clearly, no one would want to be in the shoes of an innocent defendant against whom Louise Robbins was testifying.

On February 22, 1987, the panel met at the American Academy of Forensic Science's annual convention to debate Louise Robbins's techniques. The panel, which included three anthropologists, two criminologists, a judge, and a moderator, concluded that Robbins's methods were unsound.

"Much of what Louise does with wear patterns cannot be sustained," said panel member Richard Jantz, a University of Tennessee professor of anthropology. Louise Robbins, already beset by a recurring brain cancer, was finished as an expert witness.

Five days later, Randy Garrett, Ed Cisowski, and Gary Johnson went to see Brian Dugan in prison. They were accompanied by Dugan's lawyer, Thomas McCulloch. Johnson wanted to ask Dugan to testify at Buckley's second trial. Garrett was curious to learn more about Dugan. Dugan was quiet and polite, but he said he wouldn't testify because he didn't want to risk getting the death penalty. He didn't show any remorse about his crimes and said he never would have pleaded guilty to the murders if the evidence in one of the rape cases hadn't been so strong. Without his confessions, authorities lacked sufficient evidence in the murder cases to convict him, he said.

Meanwhile, Gary Johnson and Carol Anfinson had filed a motion to dismiss Buckley's case due to prosecutorial misconduct. In it, they argued that Ed German's notes and information about Donald Schmitt's and John Gorajczyk's shoeprint examinations had been withheld. They also said Stephen Buckley's car had been dusted for fingerprints without his permission and the results— presumably evidence in his favor—never had been given to the defense. The state also had withheld information about the type of tire iron with which Volares were equipped and the type of tape sold at the B&R Pharmacy, they said.

"The accumulation of the foregoing acts of misconduct, many of which alone are violative of due process and sense of fairness, indicate a pattern from the State that it will do whatever it takes, fair or unfair, to obtain a conviction in this matter," they wrote.

On March 5, 1987, the day that the motion was to be argued, the prosecutors dropped all charges against Buckley. After three years in prison, he was free to go home. Overcome by emotion, Anfinson found herself in tears for the first time in her career as a public defender.

The Buckley family was jubilant.

"I can't wait to get him in my arms," said Steve's sister, Carol. "I'm going to buy him a can of pop. He hasn't had a can of pop in three years."

Thomas and Patricia Nicarico, however, were angry and frustrated. At a press conference at their home, they made it clear they believed Buckley was guilty and that the state's attorney was incompetent.

"We're frustrated because after two agonizing years waiting for this retrial, to have it end the way it just did," Thomas said.

Patricia said, "I'm frustrated with the state's attorney's office. I just watched this case disintegrate in the last two years. . . . It didn't seem they were doing very much to make it stronger."

Judge Nolan was furious. He called the prosecutors and defense lawyers into his chamber and said he wanted an investigation. For a moment, Gary Johnson thought Nolan was angry about the alleged prosecutorial misconduct. Nolan, though, made it clear his concern strictly was about how Dugan's story had emerged, undermining the case against Buckley and violating the gag order.

Meanwhile, at a press conference, State's Attorney Jim Ryan implied that delays by the defense had let Buckley escape justice on a technicality.

"Within days [of the first trial], the People sought the retrial of Buckley," Ryan said in a statement to the news media. "The withdrawal of Buckley's attorney necessitated the appointment of new counsel and occasioned a lengthy delay, the first in a series of eighteen delays, attributable to the defendant Buckley."

Ryan said he was dropping the charges only because shoeprint expert Louise Robbins had become too ill from cancer to testify. Also, Eric Hook, the former DuPage County Jail inmate who was willing to testify he had heard Buckley admit to the crime, had fled the area.

"In the original trial, the testimony of Dr. Robbins, that the boot print found on the front door of the Nicarico home was that of the defendant Buckley, was critical to the state's case against him. Without that testimony, the evidence that remains is insufficient to proceed to trial," Ryan said.

"Today's action was in no way influenced by the statements attributed to Brian Dugan," Ryan said. "Those statements have been judicially determined to be unreliable, and I concur with that finding. Likewise, today's action has no bearing on the convictions of Cruz and Hernandez. Today's decision to *nolle prosse* the case against Stephen Buckley is necessitated by the current state of the evidence. In the absence of sufficient evidence, it is my duty to dismiss the prosecution."

Ryan did not mention that the "state of the evidence" against Buckley was exactly the same as it had been when Buckley first was brought to trial. The only difference was that Louise Robbins no longer was available to interpret it. Apparently, Ryan could find no other expert who would support Robbins's conclusions.

About a week after Buckley was released, it was time for oral arguments before the Illinois Supreme Court in Rolando Cruz's appeal. Thomas and Patricia Nicarico showed up carrying a doll, Supreme Court justice Seymour Simon recalled later, describing the sight as "heartbreaking."

State appellate defender Timothy Gabrielsen argued that Cruz's murder conviction should be reversed because he was not tried separately from Buckley and Hernandez. Codefendant Alejandro Hernandez made statements against Cruz but refused to take the witness stand and thus could not be cross-examined by Cruz's attorney, Gabrielsen said.

"Not a shred of physical evidence was adduced against Cruz at the trial," Gabrielsen argued. "He never made a single statement in which he admitted any illegal act."

But Scott Graham, an assistant attorney general, argued that the evidence against Cruz was "overwhelming."

"The trial court's conduct was exemplary," he said. "The judge could have done nothing more to guarantee him a fair trial."

Graham contended the dismissal of charges against Buckley was "absolutely irrelevant" to Cruz's conviction.

Trial testimony, he added, showed that Cruz knew details about the crime that could have been known only to the assailants.

In the week after Buckley was freed, an affidavit was filed in which Jackie Estremera admitted he had lied when he testified that Alejandro Hernandez had said he was present during Nicarico's abduction. At a hearing nine months later, he testified he concocted the account because of threats from a sheriff's investigator.

Also filed with the court were statements from two physicians who asserted that a tire iron could not be ruled out as the murder weapon.

Judge Nolan still was angry about the manner in which Buckley had been freed. He passed on his request for an investigation to DuPage County chief judge Carl Henninger.

"In my opinion, many things took place that should not have," Nolan said in a statement. "Some things did not take place that should have. Everything possible [should] be done to see that things that happened in this case never happen in this county again."

The following Sunday, an editorial appeared in the *Chicago Sun-Times* supporting Nolan's call for an investigation.

"Unusual circumstances fully justify the call by DuPage County Circuit Judge Robert A. Nolan for a special grand-jury investigation of the handling of the Jeanine Nicarico murder trial," the newspaper wrote. "The state's dropping of charges against defendant Stephen Buckley on March 5 cannot resolve all the loose ends in this bizarre case in which two codefendants have been sentenced to death."

Nolan's announcement forestalled a press conference by the Nicarico family scheduled for later the same day, at which they were to give their perspective of the case. Later that month, however, the Nicaricos decided to hold their press conference anyway.

At that press conference, on April 13, 1987, they charged that the evidence supporting Dugan's claim to be the real killer was fed to him through a conspiracy that might have included the state police or defense lawyers.

As the investigation progressed, Dugan revised his story to one that better matched the facts, the Nicaricos charged.

"It's a pretty darn good story that matches the facts pretty well," said Thomas Nicarico. "But for [the first] three weeks, it didn't match the facts."

"There were quite a few things we were told that were not in the reports [compiled by the state police]. In the middle of the second week, we began to complain that something wasn't right."

Among details that never were made public, the Nicaricos said, were that Dugan originally said the crime, which occurred in the early afternoon, took place at 11:00 A.M. However, no police reports recorded that statement, they said.

Dugan also said he saw a fireplace in the Nicaricos' house, which in fact did not have one, they said. The police reports also omitted mention of that, but Father Mike, who'd been present, was aware it had happened, Thomas Nicarico said.

"Somebody has been helping him fabricate a story," Thomas Nicarico said.

The state police defended the investigation.

"We believe it was conducted with the utmost professionalism," said Bob Fletcher, spokesman for the state police. However, Fletcher declined to discuss the Nicaricos' allegations in detail because of Judge Nolan's gag order.

Afterward, Randy Garrett asked Ed Cisowski whether he'd given the Nicaricos the information they said was not included in the state police reports. Cisowski replied that Dugan had never given that information to state police, and they had never provided it to the Nicaricos. Garrett suspected the information might have come from the prosecutors who met with Dugan's public defender, George Mueller, on November 13, 1985, two days before Cisowski was called into the case.

Thomas Nicarico had discouraged reporters from calling Father Mike to confirm that information was omitted from state police reports, but Garrett called anyway. Father Mike said he wouldn't discuss the matter without the Nicaricos' permission, which Thomas Nicarico declined to grant.

The DuPage County judges declined to appoint a special prosecutor and grand jury to investigate Nolan's complaint and instead passed his request to State's Attorney Jim Ryan, who, citing potential conflict of interest, passed it on to the Illinois attorney general's office two months later.

On July 8, 1987, the *Chicago Sun-Times* published a long article by Thomas Frisbie headlined "Unanswered Questions in the Nicarico Murder Case."

"There is no physical evidence linking Cruz or Hernandez to the murder," the article stated. "There are no eyewitnesses who saw them. There are no confessions in which either admits taking part in the slaying.

"In contrast to Cruz and Hernandez, who claim to be innocent, Dugan claims to be the real murderer."

The article raised questions about the "vision" statement, pointing out that the detectives who said they heard it didn't mention it again until nineteen months later.

Months went by again. On October 20, 1987, Illinois attorney general Neil Hartigan said his office would investigate the controversy surrounding the Dugan evidence. Judge Nolan called the decision "admirable." In January 1991, Hartigan's investigators would finally issue a report saying Ed Cisowski had accidentally fed information to Dugan via leading questions. The report also said that Judge Nolan's gag order had been violated but that Hartigan's investigators were unable to determine who was responsible.

The report angered Cisowski. During the height of news media interest in Brian Dugan's story, Cisowski had been careful not to let information leak from his office. He had tried not to let official information get back to Dugan. DuPage County investigators had been less meticulous, even showing photos of evidence to suspects, yet he was the one charged with imprudently leaking information.

At last, on January 19, 1988, the Illinois Supreme Court overturned the convictions of Rolando Cruz and Alejandro Hernandez.

Hearing the news on the radio was a moment that John Hanlon, who had worked on the appeal, never forgot.

"I can remember exactly where I was sitting," Hanlon recalled later. "It was about four blocks down from my office. I remember what parking meter I was sitting at. I remember what radio station I had on, and I remember—this was about three cars ago—I remember what car I was in. It's a moment that just kind of froze in time."

The court said prosecutors had deliberately tried to deny Rolando Cruz and Alex Hernandez a fair trial by prosecuting them together and using statements each made against the other.

The Illinois Supreme Court had not succumbed to the prosecution complex. Cruz and Hernandez were going to get new trials.

14

JED STONE

*When someone is charged with a crime as heinous as the
killing of a child, reasonable doubt goes right out the
window. Who's more innocent than a child? That brings
out all your passions.*

Ralph Meczyk, lawyer for David Dowaliby, whose Illinois
conviction in the murder of his seven-year-old
stepdaughter was reversed in 1991

JED STONE WAS WELL KNOWN in criminal defense circles as
a lawyer with solid experience in death penalty cases. Of
his ten clients who had faced the death penalty, all had
either been acquitted or received a lesser sentence.

Stone had a seductive personality and seemed to have a knack
for attracting high-profile cases. Other lawyers considered him
skilled and knowledgeable but also something of a publicity
hound. He had a reputation as a confrontational and brash lawyer
who tended to get under the skin of judges and opposing lawyers.

"Jed Stone is unreasonable," one DuPage County prosecutor
complained. "Jed believes prosecutors get jollies out of putting
innocent people in the penitentiary."

As appellate lawyers, John Hanlon and Tim Gabrielsen read
lots of trial records and had a chance to see who was an effective
trial lawyer. They thought Stone was the man Cruz needed for his
second trial.

Forty years old, Stone was a big, stocky man with an infectious laugh. He had grown up in Chicago's Far North Side neighborhood of Rogers Park and in the tony northern suburb of Northbrook. His parents, a car salesman and an English teacher, were New Deal Democrats. As a young law student, Stone had attended the famous Chicago Seven trial after the 1968 Democratic convention riots, and it taught him how the law can be twisted when powerful interests are at work. His childhood heroes were the TV lawyer Perry Mason, the real lawyer Clarence Darrow, and the Chicago Cubs shortstop Ernie Banks—and he didn't have the athletic skills to be Ernie Banks.

"I was groomed at an early age to be a lawyer for underdogs," he once told the *Chicago Sun-Times*. "The law is an instrument of keeping people under control. It has little to do with justice or fairness. When you represent poor people, pariahs [and] condemned men and women, the law is almost always against you."

The Cruz case intrigued Stone, so he traveled to Springfield to talk with the appellate defenders. Stone was convinced by the end of that meeting that prosecutorial misconduct had marred Cruz's trial, although he was not convinced that Rolando Cruz was innocent.

The next step was going to the prison at Menard in southern Illinois to talk to Cruz. Stone didn't often get interviewed by clients, and he felt somewhat taken aback. It was an odd feeling to be quizzed for the right to give a client free representation. But Stone liked Rolando instantly.

"He was a very bright, very well put-together kid for all that he had been through," Stone said later. Cruz, Stone thought, was smart, on top of his case, and a little cocky.

Cruz wanted to know who Stone was, what his background

was, and how many death penalty and non–death penalty murder cases he had handled. He wanted to know what Stone thought of him, what he had read, and why he was interested in the case. Stone's answers satisfied Cruz, and Stone became Cruz's new lawyer.

It was just the kind of case Stone relished. "There's two things I like about a case—the stink and the ink," he would say. The "stink"—an aura of impropriety—certainly enveloped Cruz's case. So did the "ink"—an opportunity to get news media coverage.

Stone's courtroom adversary in the case was first assistant DuPage County state's attorney Robert Kilander, who had represented the state in the Dugan evidentiary hearing.

Stone found Kilander to be a very smart, very capable lawyer, and he instantly respected and liked him. At the time, Stone was teaching a continuing education seminar at John Marshall Law School in Chicago. Over lunch, Kilander's name was mentioned, and some of the faculty members who had known Kilander for years assured Stone that Kilander was a straight shooter. Stone was pleased to know he was dealing with a legal adversary who was on the up-and-up.

After studying the case, Stone decided the evidence concerning Brian Dugan offered the best chance of winning Cruz's second trial. Point the finger at Dugan, Stone thought. Tell the jury that Dugan committed the crime and that he committed it alone. The meager amount of evidence against Cruz would look minuscule next to the huge amount of information implicating Dugan.

It was a strategy with some risk, Stone knew. When a lawyer tries to defend a client by claiming another person committed the crime, the jurors tend to forget about the reasonable-doubt standard. Instead, they ask themselves: Which one of these two did it? If a lawyer can't absolutely prove it was the other person who committed the crime, the jury will tend to convict the lawyer's client.

Moreover, the prosecutors could throw up legal barriers to keep the Dugan information from the jury. Dugan had consistently refused to testify in court without immunity from the death penalty, so his statements to police and his lawyers legally were considered hearsay. If a person who is not a defendant claims in out-of-court statements to be the real criminal, that information is prohibited from a trial unless there is some additional evidence to corroborate it.

Sure enough, prosecutor Robert Kilander promptly filed a motion to prohibit any mention of Dugan at the second trials for Cruz and Hernandez. So Stone knew his first step was to persuade Judge Kowal to the contrary. For if Judge Kowal prohibited the defense from putting on all or part of the Dugan evidence—as Judge Nolan had been prepared to do in Stephen Buckley's second trial—Cruz would be in trouble. Already the prosecution complex had pushed the prosecutors to retry the case. In all probability, the prosecution complex would affect the second jury, too, leading it to convict Rolando Cruz even though the state's evidence was scant.

The defense lawyers asked for a hearing at which they could show that information about Dugan should be permitted in the trial. They pointed out that more evidence had surfaced linking Dugan to the crime since Judge Nolan had called Dugan "a bad actor." For example, two forensic pathologists, Edmund R. Donoghue and Robert Kirschner, were ready to testify that wounds on the back of the victim's head could have been caused by a tire iron from a Volare, the model that Dugan drove. The Volare tire iron had a clublike design with a thick end. At the previous hearing, Frank Cleveland had testified that the weapon could not have been a standard tire iron.

It was an interesting reversal of roles. The prosecutors, Robert Kilander and his assistant, Richard Stock, were calling Dugan unreliable and questioning his involvement, while the defense lawyers were trying to show his guilt.

Working with Stone was Michael Metnick, now the lead lawyer for Alejandro Hernandez. Although Cruz and Hernandez were to have separate trials, the pretrial hearings were being held on a joint basis. Metnick and his staff did the bulk of the preparation for the hearings.

In some ways, Stone and Metnick were alike. Both were sons of car salesmen who grew up in Chicago, both had attended the Chicago Seven trial as law students, and both felt being a defense lawyer was part of a larger calling. There were differences, too: Stone was more flamboyant, using grandiose gestures and flourishes and employing a wide vocal range to argue his points. Metnick was comparatively low-key.

The judge in the case again was Edward Kowal. Stone was favorably impressed by Judge Kowal, who seemed friendly and open. Here, Stone thought, is a judge who can give Rolando Cruz a fair trial.

In March 1989, another development favored Cruz.

A preliminary examination at a California laboratory detected DNA traces in a six-year-old semen sample taken from the victim's body. DNA testing was in its infant stages in 1989, but it held out hope that it could help identify the real killer of Jeanine Nicarico. At a hearing on April 17, lawyers for both sides agreed to get blood samples from Dugan, Buckley, Cruz, and Hernandez to see if any of their DNA matched the semen sample.

"If the test points to Dugan and indicates he might be or is the person, and if it is negative for Cruz and Hernandez, I cannot imagine how DuPage County could continue to prosecute Cruz and Hernandez," Hernandez lawyer Michael Metnick told reporters.

However, the results were not that clear-cut. The test available at that time could say only whether a DNA specimen fell into a particular category. Dugan's fell into the same category as the semen sample, a category that included 10.5 percent of the nation's population. Buckley and Hernandez were excluded. But Cruz's DNA, though not a perfect match, was close enough that he could not be excluded because of possible contamination by a combination of cells.

Stone was excited by the results. Here was another confirmation of Dugan's story, another piece of evidence that showed Dugan was telling the truth. Dugan had claimed to be the killer and rapist before anyone had heard of DNA tests. It was unfortunate that the test didn't exclude Cruz, but then the prosecutors never had claimed that Cruz was the rapist anyway, only that he was involved in the crime.

Things seemed to be going Cruz's way. In April 1989, Rob Warden published an editorial in the *Chicago Lawyer* saying Ryan's handling of the Nicarico case had rendered him unfit for public office. On June 2, Judge Kowal sided with the defense and said there would be hearings into the Dugan evidence. Stone was elated and thought the prosecutors might wind up just dropping the charges. But Kilander and Ryan had no such intentions, and on August 8, the evidentiary hearing began.

This hearing was significantly different from the hearing in Buckley's case three years earlier. At the earlier hearing, public defender Carol Anfinson labored alone before the openly hostile

Judge Robert A. Nolan. This time, the defense team led by Metnick and Stone had enough investigators, aides, and lawyers to fill an entire row of seats in the courtroom.

On the first day, Dugan was called to the stand. He was refused immunity from the death penalty, however, so he took the Fifth Amendment and declined to testify.

The defense lawyers went on to argue that a significant amount of evidence corroborated Dugan's statements. The two tollway workers who were near the Prairie Path on the day of the crime had described seeing a person and a car who fit the description of Dugan and his car. Jeanine, the lawyers said, was killed in a manner similar to Dugan's two known murder victims. Dugan's foot size matched the print on the kicked-in door, and his DNA was in the same category as the semen taken from the victim.

Former LaSalle County assistant state's attorney Gary Garretson testified that there were so many similarities between the murders of Melissa Ackerman and Jeanine Nicarico that he had independently guessed Dugan would be a suspect in Jeanine's murder.

Michael J. Kreiser, an evidence expert with the Illinois State Police, testified that a plaster cast of tire tracks at the murder scene showed the tracks were made by a Goodyear Viva glass-belted tire, the type of tire sold on Dugan's Plymouth Volare.

Ed Cisowski again testified about what the state police had found.

Next, it was the prosecutors' turn, and they tried to discredit Dugan. They listed the inconsistencies in his story. They cited a May 1984 letter Dugan wrote to his girlfriend's mother while he was in the DuPage County Jail. Dugan had written: "Guess what we got in here. We have . . . Hernandez and Cruz, that infamous

[pair] from Aurora who we all know are sick baby killers."

They put on the stand a fellow inmate of Dugan's, Milton Burns, to testify that Dugan had boasted he was going to "clear out Death Row and make history" by confessing to crimes he didn't commit.

After twelve days of testimony spanning nearly four weeks, Judge Kowal ruled that the Dugan evidence would be admitted into Cruz's second trial.

Jed Stone was ecstatic; he thought the case was won. Exuding confidence, almost arrogance, he started talking about getting Cruz out of prison in time for Christmas. The case was beginning to look like a slam dunk.

"We thought it was extremely gutsy of Judge Kowal to do that," Stone recalled later. "He was following the law . . . both in terms of the evidence that we presented and in terms of the relevant case law. But still we didn't really expect that he would follow the law, and when he did, we were elated."

Bill Clutter, an investigator who worked on the Hernandez case, shared Stone's delight.

"At the end of the evidentiary hearing, we all felt we were going to win," Clutter said. "Jed made the comment, 'If this isn't reasonable doubt, I don't know what is.' "

More doubt about the prosecutors' case emerged when Jed Stone filed a motion claiming prosecutorial misconduct in part because no notes of the November 13, 1985, conversation among Robert Kilander, Patrick King, and Dugan's public defender, George Mueller, had been turned over to the defense. Ever since he'd heard the Nicaricos mention specific facts that Ed Cisowski had denied giving them, Randy Garrett had suspected there might have been notes of the meeting with Mueller that defense lawyers had never seen. He had suggested to Stone that Stone demand copies of the notes from the Mueller meeting.

When Stone filed the motion, Kilander said he'd already turned over the notes to Bill Clutter. Clutter shook his head. Then Metnick said that the defense would withdraw the motion if Kilander would turn over the notes.

"Well, when he produced them and we gave them to Cisowski, it was as if Christmas had come early for Ed," Stone said.

The notes showed that Dugan had provided information about the crime to Kilander and King on November 13, 1985, two days before Cisowski was called into the case. Dugan had given fifty-one facts about the case to the DuPage County lawyers. Many of them were the same facts Cisowski had been accused of leaking to Dugan. Now it was clear that Cisowski could not have provided the information in the notes to Dugan because Dugan already knew it.

The Nicaricos had charged authorities with purposely leaking information, and the attorney general's office had accused Cisowski of doing so inadvertently, yet the notes showed there had been no leak at all. The prosecutors had known all along that Dugan had inside information about the crime, yet the prosecution complex kept them from saying a word in Cisowski's defense. They had forwarded the request for an investigation—but not the notes—to the attorney general's office even though they knew that the accusations were groundless.

The defense didn't fare as well in subsequent pretrial motions. On October 27, Judge Kowal denied a motion for a separate sentencing jury, a long-shot request routinely rejected by Illinois judges at that time. On November 18, he rejected a request that the court appoint a forensic social worker and a forensic psychologist for the defense. On December 15, he denied a motion for an opinion survey. Also on December 15, State's Attorney Ryan rejected a request that Brian Dugan be granted immunity from the death penalty in exchange for his testimony.

Kowal also changed his ruling from the first trial and said he would allow the prosecutors to tell the jury that John Ruiz's mother had been hired by the Nicaricos just before the crime and that John Ruiz might have known Rolando Cruz.

For his trial team, Stone brought aboard Isaiah "Skip" Gant, a lawyer with a lot of capital experience, and Susan Valentine, an attorney who worked in Stone's office. Stone also had the services of Jeffrey Winick and Anne D. "Andi" Samuels, two young volunteer lawyers from the big Chicago law firm of Sidley & Austin, and of Marlene Kamish, a law student. And he hired John Rea, a private investigator who had worked for federal prosecutors, to dig into the case.

The trial started on January 11, 1990, in Rockford, the seat of Winnebago County in northwestern Illinois. The trial had been moved out of DuPage County because there had been so much publicity, it seemed unlikely that jurors could be found who didn't already know about the case. It was five years to the week after the first trial had begun.

In his opening statement, Kilander said that a death row inmate named Robert Turner would testify that Cruz, Hernandez, and Dugan all were present when Jeanine was slain. It was the first time in open court that prosecutors said Dugan and Cruz could have been involved together. Jurors no longer had to free Cruz if they believed Dugan was guilty. Now they could decide that Dugan and Cruz both played a role.

"For the first time, the state was dragging Dugan in," said Antoine "Tripp" Baltz III, a reporter who covered the case for the

DuPage Press Service. "We were all really surprised by that. Kilander even looked at the defense table before he said it. I think that the argument really shocked Jed Stone, and it was something that he never fully recovered from."

Kilander also changed the state's theory in other ways. He suggested that the lack of any substantial amount of blood at the Prairie Path showed Jeanine was killed elsewhere and then brought there.

Stone was shocked at that, too.

"I thought at a minimum the judge should have reacted to that," he said later. "He's been asked in the first trial to sentence a defendant to death by lethal injection, the ultimate penalty, because the state said: We swear to you, judge, she was killed on the Prairie Path and there was a mass of blood on the Prairie Path.

"At the second trial, the only thing that has changed is that Brian Dugan says, 'I killed her, and I killed her alone on the Prairie Path.' They now maintain she was not killed on the Prairie Path and that there was an absence of blood. Had I been the trial judge, I would have said to the state, 'What are you doing? Did you lie to me at the first trial, or are you lying to me now?' "

Instead, Judge Kowal ruled that Stone would not be permitted to tell the jury about the change in theories.

In his opening statement, Stone said DuPage County was interested in scapegoats, not justice.

"This case is so flawed, it stinks," Stone told the jury. He called the police officers and others about to testify against Cruz "a pack of liars."

Stone told the jurors he would prove to them that the crime was committed by Dugan and Dugan alone.

Then the witnesses started to testify.

Patricia Nicarico again recounted the story of her daughter's disappearance. Other witnesses were called to set the scene and describe the investigation. The evidence about the shoeprints on the door and in the dirt by the dining room window was admitted. Then, a week into the trial, Erma Rodriguez was called to the stand.

Rodriguez was Cruz's cousin, and about seventeen months after the crime, Dugan had moved to her neighborhood. Detective Warren Wilkosz quoted her as saying that on the night of the crime, Cruz came alone to her Aurora home, weeping and saying he was in trouble. Wilkosz also quoted her as saying that she had seen Dugan and Cruz together before the murder. Just as with the "vision" statement, no report had been written at the time, and the information surfaced just days before the trial.

When interviewed by a defense investigator, Rodriguez had denied ever making such statements. She repeated her denials on the witness stand.

In response, the prosecutors called Wilkosz to testify about what he said she told him, a legal technique called impeaching a witness.

Stone objected. He submitted a memorandum of law arguing that it was not permissible to call a witness solely for the purpose of getting another witness on the stand to provide hearsay. Kowal overruled him.

The dog handlers, Lori Towns-end and Lieutenant E. Stephen Tornfeather Towns-end of the Lake County, Illinois, sheriff's department, testified about the activities of the bloodhound at the Nicarico home. Stone submitted a memorandum of law arguing that bloodhound evidence is not permissible in Illinois courts. Kowal overruled him on that, too.

Stone was stunned.

"What I saw at trial was a judge and a prosecutor acting as if it was so important that the state prevail at trial that they were going to let stuff in that never should come in under any circumstance in any trial," Stone said later. "They were going to do it—even if it ultimately would mean reversal—because a conviction was so important."

Meanwhile, the trial continued with testimony from Ramon "Chuck" Mares.

At the first trial, Mares had said Cruz had admitted being present when Jeanine was beaten to death. Now he recanted that testimony. Instead, he said Cruz claimed only that he knew who committed the crime, not that he was present or involved. He said he had lied at the grand jury because prosecutors had threatened to imprison him for perjury if he didn't tell them what they wanted to hear.

Detectives Thomas Vosburgh and Dennis Kurzawa repeated their description of Cruz's "vision" statement. During his testimony, Vosburgh added a significant new detail. He said he and Vosburgh called Sheriff's Sergeant James Montesano on the evening of May 9, 1983, and told him about the "vision" statement. Under questioning by assistant prosecutor Richard Stock, he agreed, inaccurately, that May 9 was a Friday. Actually, it was a Monday, a fact that would take on significance later.

Next, Daniel Fowler and Stephen Ford repeated their stories from the 1985 trial. Fowler said Cruz admitted being involved in the crime but said he hadn't killed the girl. Ford, Cruz's former cellmate, repeated his story about Cruz saying that next time he would kill the witnesses.

Then Steven Pecoraro testified. Pecoraro had testified at the death penalty phase of the first trial only. Now he took the stand to say that Cruz, while still in the DuPage County Jail, had said, "I'm going to write a book when I get to the penitentiary on 'How to Kill a Little Girl, or Five Ways to Crush a Skull.' "

He said Cruz knew that his shoeprints were in back of the Nicaricos' house but that investigators never had confiscated his shoes, taking only Buckley's.

While testifying, Pecoraro muttered to himself on the stand and made noises that made no sense. When Stone asked Pecoraro if he was all right, he said he was praying. Later, he told defense lawyers he had ingested so much Valium before testifying that he had momentarily fallen asleep on the stand. Stone let him mumble away so the jury could see how nutty he looked. It was unlikely the jury would put much stock in Pecoraro's story, Stone thought.

On the same day that Pecoraro testified, Sheriff's Lieutenant Robert Winkler took the stand. Winkler had testified against both Hernandez and Cruz in the first trial. At that trial, he'd provided key details in his testimony about Hernandez that had not appeared in his report of their conversation.

Now Winkler added significant details again, this time about Cruz. At the first trial, Winkler had testified that Cruz had admitted offering to hot-wire a car for two friends. Now Winkler testified that Cruz had admitted he himself had actually hot-wired a car for them, a boxy green Lincoln Continental.

At the first trial, Winkler gave no explanation for not writing a report. Now he said Tom Knight told him not to write a report because Knight would put the information in a discovery disclosure. (Knight, however, did not put the information in the two succeeding discovery disclosures and in fact did not notify the defense of the statement until the third disclosure statement, dated July 10, 1984.)

Winkler also changed the date on which Cruz supposedly made the admissions. At the first trial, he'd said Cruz made the statement in late May, a week or ten days before Hernandez's statement on June 6. Now Winkler said the statement took place on March 13, 1984, which agreed with a report filed by Sheriff's Lieutenant James Montesano the next day.

Prosecutors now had two inculpatory statements that Cruz supposedly had given to authorities. Surprisingly, the days on which both of those statements were supposedly made had changed between trials, and even more startling, no police officer had ever bothered to write a report about either one. In each instance, the sheriff's officers testified that the reason they didn't write a report was that prosecutor Tom Knight told them not to. Later, Assistant State's Attorney Patrick King admitted he could not recall any case during his career as a DuPage County prosecutor in which he told a detective not to write a report. Yet the statements still could be used to argue that Cruz had inside knowledge of the crime and had actually hot-wired a car for the killers.

Then the new star witness took the stand, death row inmate Robert Turner.

Turner was on death row for murdering Bridget Drobney of Downers Grove, another DuPage County town. Turner had used flashing lights on his car to impersonate a highway patrolman at night in a rural area, and when Drobney had pulled her car over, he had abducted, raped, and killed her. Now Turner was hoping to avoid the death penalty. He had written a letter to authorities offering to testify against seven other inmates on death row but didn't mention Cruz. Later, when he did, DuPage County decided to take him up on it.

Turner testified that Cruz, while in the prison exercise yard, had admitted helping Brian Dugan and Alex Hernandez murder Jeanine Nicarico. In one of ten conversations that the two had during the "warm months" of 1987, Cruz told Turner that when they went into the house, they found the girl, Turner said.

"She wasn't supposed to be there," Turner testified. He said Cruz complained to Turner that Hernandez stupidly left a crowbar outside the Nicarico home but that Cruz remembered to pick it up. The three men then put the girl in the back seat of a car and drove off, Turner said.

"Once he got there, he told me they raped her, and after they got done, they drug her out of the car and Cruz told me that, you know, they beat her in the head and killed her with a crowbar," Turner testified. "I remember him telling me she didn't look too good, like she was sick, maybe."

Turner also said, "I remember him telling me it was a shame he had to kill her, because it was the tightest little white bitch [he'd] ever had," a phrase prosecutor Richard Stock hammered home to jurors more than once later in the trial.

The defense lawyers realized that Turner's testimony caused them lots of problems. First of all, he created a link between Dugan and Cruz. What was the use of proving that Dugan committed the crime if the state could use Turner's testimony to say: Sure, and Cruz helped out?

Second, if they wanted to use prison logs to show that Turner didn't have a chance to hear the story from Cruz, they would have to admit that Cruz had been on death row, which would tell the jury that Cruz already had been convicted for the crime, a big advantage for the prosecution.

Kilander, Stone decided, was a very bright lawyer.

Stone chose to counter Turner's testimony by introducing

prison logs that showed Turner and Cruz could not possibly have had as many conversations as Turner reported. The logs showed that Turner and Cruz were kept separate most of the time. The defense also put two other death row inmates on the stand, Richard Nitz and John Pecoraro (no relation to Steven Pecoraro), who testified that Turner had told them he was lying in an effort to avoid the death penalty.

Turner also testified he had made no deals in exchange for his testimony against Cruz. (Nine months later, though, Kilander testified on Turner's behalf at his resentencing. At that time, Kilander admitted that Turner wanted an assurance before he testified against Cruz that Kilander would testify at Turner's resentencing hearing.)

Cruz's defense lawyers were not permitted to tell the jury about the crimes for which Steven Pecoraro and Robert Turner were convicted. Nor were they allowed to tell jurors of a note Turner wrote encouraging his brother to lie during Turner's trial.

The prosecutors also called Michael Ryan, a mental patient and alcoholic, to the stand. Michael Ryan had claimed to have had a conversation with Rolando Cruz at an apartment building at a time when Cruz actually was in jail. Ryan was brought to the witness stand, where he shook, cried, and trembled for a few moments before he was escorted out of the courtroom, never to return.

Then it was the defense's turn.

First, Illinois State Police psychiatrist Nobel Harrison repeated the story he said Dugan, while hypnotized, had told him about the murder. State police investigator Thomas Petersik described the 1985 drive-around in which Dugan led police to the Nicarico home.

Then it was time to put Cisowski on the stand.

"The night before Cisowski's testimony, we put him through a two-and-a-half-hour direct examination, and he [had] everything down pat," Stone recalled later. "We had an outline of exactly where we wanted to go, and Cisowski was prepared to help us get there. And as I got maybe a third of the way into my examination of Cisowski, Kilander was popping up saying 'Objection,' and the judge was sustaining the objections. His ruling was a hundred and eighty degrees from his August pretrial ruling. It was shocking. It made no sense."

In opening arguments, Stone had promised the jury he would show them that Dugan alone was the killer. Now, however, Judge Kowal would not let him tell the jury that Dugan had always acted alone in his other sex crimes. The judge would not let Stone put on experts who would explain that this was a type of crime that generally is committed alone. What good was it to prove that Dugan was involved, if the prosecutors could argue that he and Cruz did it together?

"I believe in trying a case with a single theory of innocence," Stone said afterward. "I think that juries follow a bright line if you can give it to them. We had this clear, bright line for the jury to follow until we got this land mine that blew up and destroyed the continuity of the defense case."

Eloise Suk testified about Dugan's visit to the church where she worked. The prosecution, however, brought out that another unidentified Caucasian man and two others with darker skin had visited the church possibly on the same day and asked for a screwdriver. That made it seem more plausible that Dugan was acting with other people.

What had looked so good months before when Stone had

first come into the case was turning into another nightmare for Cruz. The closing arguments would offer little hope.

For the prosecution, Richard Stock focused on the brutality of the crime and the statements Cruz allegedly made to the witnesses who testified.

"They found Jeanine in the house," Stock said. "She wasn't supposed to be there, and they took her. You heard how Jeanine Nicarico clutched at the wall and grabbed at the door frame as they dragged her from the sanctity of her own home.

"Once they took her, it was too late to let her go. They had to kill her. She could identify them.

"But first, ladies and gentlemen, they beat Jeanine Nicarico, they raped her, and they sodomized her, and they deliberately beat her with a bat until her skull was crushed. And it was only then that Jeanine Nicarico's misery finally ended.

"They dumped her battered, naked body in the frozen woods, like it was a pile of garbage."

Then Stock talked about the shoeprints in the dirt outside the dining room window, implying that they were Cruz's.

"The only window that was not covered with drapes," he said. "The only window that provided a clear view into that home. The window that Ronnie Cruz stood at and looked into that home when he made a decision that the house was empty and they could go in."

Stock said Dugan was wrong when he said he was the only killer.

"We know that there's more than one person involved," Stock said. "We know that there's more than one burglar and we know that there's more than one killer.

"We have four different shoeprints found at the scene of the house. We have bloodhounds following different trails around the house. . . . Jeanine Nicarico was not killed on the Prairie Path."

Then Stock used Eloise Suk's testimony to discredit Dugan.

"Right about that same time, and she says it could have even been the same day, a male white and two male Hispanics come into her church. . . .

"Finally, she's starting to show them out, one of these guys, a male white, comes to Eloise Suk and says to her, hey, we are having some car trouble, can I borrow a screwdriver?

"Is this just a coincidence? Is it a coincidence that three years after Eloise Suk says she saw Brian Dugan, Brian Dugan is saying that [he] was out with car trouble trying to borrow a screwdriver?

"It is not a coincidence. Brian Dugan is lying to you, lying to his attorneys, and his attorneys are lying to you when they come in here and try and tell you Brian Dugan killed Jeanine Nicarico alone."

Stone gave his response, calling the evidence flimsy and saying Brian Dugan committed the crime alone.

"Ladies and gentlemen, we have now for the last hour and some minutes heard maybe for the first time the state's theory of this prosecution," Stone said, referring to Stock's closing argument. "But what we haven't heard yet is the evidence. Where is the proof, where is the evidence of this?"

Then Kilander gave the state's rebuttal. He suggested that Dugan was involved but that the mistakes in his story showed he didn't act alone.

"Isn't it logical to conclude that Dugan's involved . . . in those things about which he's right and he was absent from those things about which he's wrong?" he asked the jury.

Kilander also said that the shoeprints near the dining room window were different from the shoeprint on the door, proving there was more than one person committing the crime.

"Ladies and gentlemen, there is affirmative evidence that more than one person committed this crime," he said. "We have the footprints by the house that have already been discussed."

To Stone, Kilander's argument stung. Stone realized that he had let the photos of the shoeprints come into evidence without objection, without comment. He hadn't asked witnesses during cross-examination whether the shoeprints were Cruz's. It had never occurred to him that anybody would argue that they were Cruz's shoeprints. Now it was too late. The defense would not get another chance to address the jury.

"When Kilander stood up in his rebuttal closing argument and said: 'Those two shoeprints are different from each other and different from the boot print on the door, and that's evidence that three people committed this crime,' I thought that was effective," Stone said later. "Those words stung. I knew I had been had."

Kilander also inaccurately told the jury that Dugan had to confess to the Nicarico crime to avoid the death penalty for the Donna Schnorr and Melissa Ackerman murders. He told the jury that it was being shortchanged because it was being asked to judge Dugan's credibility without hearing directly from him. He didn't mention that his office refused to grant Dugan immunity from the death penalty in exchange for his testimony.

The case went to the jury, and on February 1, 1990, the jury returned with a verdict: guilty. Kilander slammed his fist on the table in triumph. The defense had brought in a flashy Chicago attorney who had called the case corrupt. The news media had trumpeted stories about the Brian Dugan evidence. The trial had been moved out of Kilander's home county. Yet he'd won. Twelve jurors had vindicated him.

Seated in the audience holding the hand of Cruz's mother, Dora, defense lawyer Andi Samuels felt physically ill.

"I was confident that there was no way that the jury could hear the Dugan testimony and come back saying Rolando Cruz was guilty beyond a reasonable doubt," Samuels said later. "It was inconceivable."

Samuels (who subsequently married and changed her surname to Kenney) said she thought Cruz was convicted because of the crime scene photos and the "vision" statement.

"If you looked at the crime scene photos, it made you want to find the bastard that did this and put him away for a very long time," she said. "Those photos were just outrageous, horrendous. I can still close my eyes and see them."

The "vision" statement gave jurors a basis for believing Cruz was the culprit, she said.

At the sentencing phase the next day, prosecutor Richard Stock told the jury Rolando Cruz had kicked in the Nicaricos' door. Until now, prosecutors had argued that Buckley had kicked in the door.

"[Jeanine] was in her own home, behind her own locked door, having a bowl of ice cream and watching TV when Rolando Cruz kicked in the door, went downstairs, and took her from her home, from the sanctity of her own home," Stock said. "I ask you once again to consider the evidence in this case, find that in fact this is exceptionally brutal and heinous behavior, and we ask that you return the verdict indicating that Rolando Cruz is eligible for the death penalty under both of those aggravating factors."

Two women on the jury openly cried while Stone gave the defense argument. Yet the jury voted to give Cruz the death penalty.

"The jury sat around in the jury room after the case was given to them," Stone said later. "They prayed, they thought they had to be spokespersons for Jeanine Nicarico, and I think they said to themselves, though never articulating it to each other, we don't know whether Cruz did this or not, but we cannot take the chance that he did. And they found him guilty.

"The crime is terrible. What happened to that child is unspeakable. And I think they said to themselves: We cannot take the chance that he did do this, and we will find him guilty.

"Now, that is a violation of their oath, and it is a terrible thing for a jury to do, but I am convinced that that's what they did."

During the trial, Stone had appeared to go into a deeper and deeper funk. When the verdict was announced, he paled. Afterward, he gave a news conference. It was uncharacteristically muted. Also unusual was its brevity. Normally, Stone answered every question; this time he cut the press conference short, saying, "And now, excuse me, we need to get on with the business of saving this young man's life."

The jurors had decided not to talk to the news media after the trial. But reporter Tripp Baltz caught up with one of them as he was about to get into his car. Baltz asked why the jury had voted to convict. The juror hesitated a moment and then said that the violence of the crime had been the decisive factor.

Later, in an interview with the *Chicago Sun-Times*, juror Rafael Diaz added that the jury also had relied on the integrity of the law enforcement authorities who testified.

After the trial, freelance community journalist Chana Bernstein aired a series of one-hour interviews on public-access cable TV stations in DuPage County suburbs. The programs were critical of the prosecution and irked DuPage authorities. On several occasions, Bernstein talked to Cruz, and she was surprised by his sense of humor. Bernstein thought that worked against him.

"When people saw him trying to smile, they misinterpreted that as an arrogant, callous attitude toward the crime he was accused of," Bernstein said.

In reality, Bernstein thought, Cruz was trying to keep his chin up and keep smiling despite the horrendous predicament he was in.

Four months after the trial, Judge Kowal formally authorized the death sentence the jury had signed in February.

"I know someday I will obtain my freedom because it has been proven that I'm innocent," Cruz said, before he was led away in shackles. "I will continue to fight. I don't want to die for something I didn't do."

When Judge Kowal read the sentence, law student Marlene Kamish, who had assisted Stone, noticed that Judge Kowal actually gave the death penalty to Alex Hernandez, not Cruz. Later, she checked to see if perhaps that technicality might help Cruz, but she learned that, if challenged, the judge would simply correct the error.

Stone filed a request for a new trial, citing 108 inconsistencies in the prosecutors' case.

"This is one of the saddest days of my career at the bar," Stone said. "An innocent man is sent to the gallows and a guilty man remains unpunished. I think this prosecution is a result of Mr. Ryan seeking statewide office and not being able to do the right thing."

Robert Kilander told the *Chicago Tribune* he considered Stone's statement "the most ludicrous, irresponsible statement I've ever heard in a courtroom. . . . He's lost, and he simply chooses to challenge and accuse others."

For defense team member Jeffrey Winick, the outcome was enough to give him nightmares for years.

"The troublesome thing about the criminal justice system I learned in this trial was that prosecutors who I thought were bound by the pursuit of truth and justice were allowed to treat their side of the case as a game in which they were pursuing victory," Winick said later. "Rolando was going to be killed on the basis of perjured testimony. I can't imagine a worse nightmare as an attorney than having an innocent client who you can't save from being killed."

Rolando Cruz was devastated. The chance for a second trial had given him so much hope, yet he'd been convicted again. By now, he'd been behind bars for almost seven years. During that time, life for the rest of the family had gone on without him. Cruz was frightened, yet determined not to give up.

Three days after the death sentence was formally handed down, Cruz discussed his emotions during a collect call to reporter Thomas Frisbie.

"I don't want to die for something I didn't do," Cruz said. "It's really right now. They've got a death warrant on me. It's not something I'm just thinking could happen. They're planning it."

Cruz talked a little about the case, saying he'd never made the "vision" statement. The witnesses against him had lied or changed their stories, he said. He was especially bitter about Robert Turner.

"I want my freedom," he said. "They can keep their justice. I don't know if they know what such a thing as justice is, but I know

I want my freedom. I want to be able to live, to work, to have a family, kids, be able to know I can go see my mom any time I want."

Cruz said he never would have talked to authorities if he'd known how the law worked. No one had read him his rights until the very last minute.

"They are going to kill me because they want a lie, and they don't want to admit it. I told the attorneys and my friends and family I am willing to sign an affidavit that they are not going to be sued. I just want to go home. I want to see my mom and sister and meet my two nephews that have been born since I was locked up.

"Sometimes, it's hard to deal with, but I keep pushing. I ain't going to give up for nothing. I don't know how to give up anymore. I don't think I am going to."

In a way, Jed Stone wasn't surprised how the trial had turned out. He'd known it was a must-win case with political overtones. The state's attorney, Jim Ryan, wanted to be Illinois attorney general, and Ryan couldn't afford to say he had left a killer on the loose while he prosecuted the wrong men.

"I left the courthouse one day in Wheaton, and I looked at the state's attorney's [parking spot]," Stone said. "I looked at [the] license plate and shook my head. The license plate told me everything I needed to know about the case and the prosecution and how it was going and where we were going to go."

The car belonged to a DuPage County Republican Party official. Parked in the spot reserved for Jim Ryan, who later would be elected attorney general, it had the license plate "AG 2B."

15

MICHAEL METNICK

---

*[T]he jury is at least entitled to know that the government
at one time believed, and stated, that its proof established
something different from what it currently claims.
Confidence in the jury system cannot be affirmed if any
party is free, wholly without explanation, to make a fundamental change in its version of facts between trials, and
then conceal this change from the final trier of the facts.*

United States v. Salerno, United States Court of Appeals for the
Second Circuit, 1991

MICHAEL METNICK KNEW there was almost no evidence against his client, Alex Hernandez. He also
knew that might not matter.

A jury had just convicted Rolando Cruz for a second time. Now
Metnick had to persuade a different jury to do the exact opposite.

True, there was a very weak case against Hernandez.
However, there also had been a very weak case against Cruz. Yes,
Hernandez had the Brian Dugan evidence in his favor, but then, so
had Cruz. In theory, Hernandez should be able to win an acquittal
even if he didn't put on a defense. So should have Cruz.

Michael Metnick had been recruited to represent Hernandez
after the big Chicago law firm of Jenner & Block decided not to
take the case. Some people thought he was the best criminal
defense lawyer in central Illinois. He was not a big man, but he had

an earnest, intent appearance, and he could put plenty of emotional wallop into his arguments.

Metnick was surprised to find that he was Alex Hernandez's attorney. He had been practicing law for ten years at the time, but he was only vaguely aware that the Jeanine Nicarico murder was a controversial case in the Chicago area, which many people around Springfield thought of as being practically in another state. He had grown up on Chicago's North Side and attended John Marshall Law School in the city. He was an average student with average grades. When he'd graduated, he'd hoped to get a job through Marshall Korshak, a colorful Democratic politician who was friendly with Metnick's father, a West Side Oldsmobile dealer. Metnick met with Korshak about ten times, but no job materialized. Finally, a friend told him there was an opening in Springfield's municipal legal department. He took it and made Springfield his home.

As a Chicago teenager driving new cars with dealer plates, Metnick on several occasions was stopped by police officers. Seeing the dealer plates, the police followed him home so they could take money in exchange for not writing a ticket. Such experiences left him somewhat cynical of police. As a law student, he, like Jed Stone, attended the Chicago Seven trial. The electricity in the courtroom amazed him.

"In the Sixties, I saw that the great social changes were often being fought in the courtrooms," he said. "I just always felt that I would be part of that."

When the appellate defender's office called, Metnick thought there would be no harm in looking over the materials to see if he was interested. One of the first things he noticed was that none of the defendants had testified against another, even though they were facing the death penalty.

"To me, that belied common sense," Metnick said. "It belied experience. They were all offered deals to testify against the others in exchange for light sentences. In Alex's case, it was twenty years. It just didn't make sense that they were not flipping on one another."

Perusing Alex's grand jury testimony also convinced Metnick that Alex was innocent.

"As I was reading it, I actually was feeling chills through my body," he said. "A person does not withstand this type of questioning hour after hour, page after page on the transcript, and not state something meaningful, not state something that is incriminating.

"I saw how desperate Tom Knight was in the grand jury questioning to get Alex to say something. I knew Alex didn't have the ability to play games with Knight. I saw the ramblings that were going on, the desperation with which Knight was practically pleading with Alex and threatening him. Knight used every tactic imaginable to get Alex to make an admission, to say something meaningful, to provide some detail about what happened. And it wasn't there."

Common sense seemed to say that the state would just drop the case. Perhaps, thought Metnick, his commitment to the case wouldn't be all that time-consuming. He agreed to take it.

Metnick knew that defense lawyers by nature have a difficult time representing innocent clients. Usually, defense lawyers won't cast about indiscriminately for new information because they don't want to turn up something damaging that can be used against their clients. Instead, defense lawyers focus on attacking the prosecution's evidence.

This case, however, needed as much probing as possible,

Metnick believed. The more information he uncovered, the better for Alex. Metnick turned to Springfield investigator Bill Clutter, with whom he worked on a regular basis, and asked him to dig into the record. He took Clutter into the law firm's conference room and showed him the case file.

"It was just unbelievably huge," Clutter recalled. "It was bigger than anything else we had ever done. Usually, when we get a case, it might take up an accordion file. If it is a really big case, it might take up two accordion files. But this was banker box after banker box. Just the newspaper clippings filled up one box."

Clutter started by combing through the files and soon found the report by Warren Wilkosz in which he documented having investigated Dugan after Dugan was arrested for Melissa Ackerman's murder. Prior to that, nobody on the defense side had realized that Wilkosz had investigated Dugan.

Clutter met with Gary Johnson, Thomas McCulloch, Randy Garrett, and Naperville police chief Jim Teal. He reinterviewed witnesses and talked to the prosecutors. He went to the Prairie Path and to the church where the secretary had seen Dugan. He also found out that plaster casts had been taken of tire tracks on the Prairie Path. Prosecutor Robert Kilander had told Ed Cisowski there was nothing of evidentiary value from the Prairie Path, so the state police had not examined the casts while they still had Brian Dugan's car. Now, in the summer of 1989, Clutter insisted on seeing them. Then he persuaded the state police to examine them. A test identified the tracks as coming from Goodyear Viva glass-belted tires, which were the original tires on Dugan's Volare. Clutter also found that the Viva tire was not the standard tire for a Ford Granada. The previous owner of Dugan's Volare said he had not changed the tires, except for putting on the spare when one of the tires went flat. The previous owner also said he hadn't put the hubcap back on after changing the tire, so the car was missing at least one hubcap then, as was the car the tollway workers saw at the Prairie Path later. The car itself, though, by now had been crushed and was no longer available for comparison.

When the joint hearing with Jed Stone was held on the Dugan statements, it was Clutter, working with Metnick, who did most of the investigating.

Meanwhile, Metnick was preparing for the trial, which was to be held in Bloomington in central Illinois, where it was judged there would be less pretrial publicity. To assist on the trial team, he recruited Chicago lawyer Jeffrey Urdangen and Jane Raley, a former appellate defender with lots of experience in capital cases.

It was on February 1, 1990, that the defense lawyers learned that Cruz had been convicted at his second trial. That was discouraging. But Metnick also knew that Hernandez had some advantages in his second trial that he had lacked in the first one.

First, Metnick could use the information about Brian Dugan to help cast doubt on the case against Alex. Second, some of the witnesses who had testified in the first trial no longer were available. Jackie Estremera had recanted his testimony, and Armindo "Penguino" Marquez had disappeared after telling his sister that he had lied on the stand. Third, Metnick already had seen the prosecutors spring a surprise on Jed Stone by changing theories at the last minute, so he knew he would have to be prepared for that.

Unfortunately for the defense lawyers, Judge Kowal had ruled against the defense on some key issues. He said they could not present psychologists' reports about Alex's habit of making up stories unless prosecutors also were permitted to tell jurors about his past criminal history. He also ruled that prosecutors could undermine Eloise Suk's testimony about Dugan's visit to her church by mentioning the visit of three other people she couldn't identify. The prosecutors could use that information to imply that Dugan had made a separate visit, possibly accompanied by Hernandez.

For all practical purposes, the defense lawyers realized, those rules meant they could use neither Alex's history of making up stories nor Eloise Suk's testimony. Metnick thought overall Suk had hurt Cruz at his second trial.

Then a new witness appeared.

Stephen Weimann, who had been in the DuPage County Jail with Hernandez, said Alex had talked about the crime. "I was there and I just went along with it because I was scared," Hernandez had said, according to Weimann.

Metnick was angry. Another jailhouse snitch was coming forward conveniently just when the prosecution could use another witness. Was there to be no end to the snitches who materialized at the exact moment that the state needed them? He tried to get Judge Kowal to bar Weimann from the trial, but Kowal refused.

Then it was time for the trial to start in a dark, small, modular courtroom in the McLean County courthouse. Michael Metnick, Jane Raley, and Jeffrey Urdangen were the defense lawyers. The prosecutors again were Robert Kilander and Richard Stock.

Jury selection started on April 17, 1990. Three days later came the opening statements.

Robert Kilander presented the prosecution's.

"The evidence will show that . . . a sequence of events occurred which, when taken as a whole, proved beyond reasonable doubt that Alex Hernandez is clearly responsible for and guilty of the charges against him," Kilander said.

Metnick responded that Hernandez had mental difficulties

and had told authorities stories that were known to be untrue. For example, Hernandez had said that Cruz and Buckley had stolen items from the Nicaricos' house even though evidence showed otherwise.

"There is no physical evidence that links Alex to this crime," Metnick said. "There is no eyewitness evidence and no circumstantial evidence that links Alex to this crime. . . . Alejandro Hernandez is not guilty of this horrendous, heinous, unspeakable crime that occurred to young Jeanine as she was taken from her ten-year-old world, over seven years ago."

Again, the first few days of the trial were devoted to setting the scene.

Patricia Nicarico told how a neighbor had called her at about 3:15 P.M. and told her Jeanine was missing. When Patricia got home, she thought Jeanine might be hiding. She went upstairs and looked in Jeanine's room, but everything looked as it had that morning.

"It was just so spooky," Patricia Nicarico said when she testified. "Everything was the same. The TV was on."

Unlike Stone, Metnick cross-examined Patricia and Jeanine's sisters. They testified they did not search the yard or step up to the window where the shoeprints were found in the dirt. Kathy Nicarico, the younger of Jeanine's two older sisters, and a friend said they did not know if other girls with Jeanine's other sister, Chris, had made the prints while searching for Jeanine.

Meanwhile, defense lawyers had learned more about Stephen Weimann, the newest jailhouse snitch. Prosecutors, they found out, had withheld information about Weimann, including that he had acted as an informant for the county. Kilander himself had authorized Weimann to wear an eavesdropping device as part of a different murder investigation.

Armed with this new information, defense lawyers argued that Weimann should not be allowed to testify. Before Judge Kowal could rule on their request, Kilander capitulated, saying he would not call Weimann to the stand.

Meanwhile, another new witness appeared, Detective Albert Bettilyon.

Bettilyon had not testified in the first trial. Now he said that he'd heard Hernandez admit to the crime in the room with Armindo "Penguino" Marquez and the box of money.

"I was in on it," Bettilyon said he'd heard Hernandez say. "All I did was hold that little girl down while they hit her on the head."

Bettilyon testified he was ten to twelve feet away from the cubicle where Marquez and Hernandez were talking. He also said Hernandez had said, "I was there that day. . . . I feel like I'm guilty, but all I did was hold that little girl down."

On cross-examination, defense lawyer Jeffrey Urdangen emphasized that Bettilyon heard only part of the forty-five-minute conversation. Moreover, part of the conversation was in Spanish, which Bettilyon did not understand. Bettilyon said he had no memory of the conversation other than what was in his report of one and one-third pages. The report was based on nonverbatim notes he had since destroyed.

Bettilyon testified that he heard Hernandez admit three or four times to holding down the victim. However, he also admitted that he had not put that information in his original report nor had he been called to testify about it at the first trial.

Then came another big surprise.

Deputy Sheriffs Thomas Bentcliff and Howard Keltner said they had heard Hernandez admit going to the Nicarico home to commit a burglary. Neither had filed a report at the time. Neither had testified at the first trial. Both had waited three years and nine months to come forward, even though they worked at the jail and knew how important the case was. They waited until December 1987. On December 14, Bentcliff filed a report. On December 22, Detective Warren Wilkosz testified in a postconviction proceeding against giving Hernandez a new trial. The next day, Wilkosz went to the jail to talk to Keltner in a private, closed-door meeting. And the day after that, Keltner filed a report.

Now on the stand in 1990, Bentcliff quoted Hernandez as sobbing, "Not me, not me" in the booking room of the DuPage County Jail as the charges in the indictment were read to him.

Although Alex had just stood up to more than three hours of intense questioning by seasoned detectives without making an admission, Bentcliff said he volunteered one as soon as the questioning was over.

"I didn't hurt anybody, I just went there to do a burglary," Bentcliff claimed Hernandez had said. Hernandez had also said something about drugs, Bentcliff said, adding that he hadn't heard that part clearly.

Keltner said he had heard Hernandez from the other side of a glass wall through an intercom. Keltner claimed Hernandez had said, "I went there to get money for drugs."

Next, Lieutenant Robert Winkler testified against Hernandez again. He said that on June 6, 1984, Hernandez had admitted checking out the Nicarico house with Cruz and Buckley to burglarize it.

"When they finally decided to go in for the burglary, he stated that he got nervous," Winkler testified. "He said he didn't want to go further."

According to Winkler, Hernandez had said that he asked the

two others to drop him off three blocks away. When they returned, Hernandez "immediately noticed a small girl in the back seat. The girl was crying. Her lip was cut and she was pleading to go home," Winkler said.

The two men dropped Hernandez off at his Aurora home and drove away with the girl, who was still alive.

On cross-examination, it was established that Alex was on a suicide watch at the time Winkler said the conversation took place and that Alex was taking psychotropic drugs prescribed by a jail psychiatrist.

Frank Cleveland, the Cincinnati pathologist, again testified. Metnick grilled him about his change in testimony that occurred just as the prosecutors changed their theory about where Jeanine was killed. He brought out that Cleveland had stopped doing autopsies at the time that he was called into the DuPage County case. Jeffrey Urdangen thought Metnick's cross-examination was just superlative and that Cleveland's credibility was destroyed.

Perhaps the highlight of the trial was the moment when Deputy Sheriff Paul Sahs testified. Prosecutor Robert Kilander was using Sahs to introduce the evidence about the two shoeprints in the dirt outside the Nicaricos' dining room window. Prosecutors repeatedly had used those shoeprints, which had different tread designs, to argue that there was more than one male assailant at the Nicarico home and that someone looking in the dining room window could see the house was worth burglarizing.

On cross-examination, Metnick asked Sahs what size the shoeprints were.

"The toe-to-heel measurements are relatively the same on both shoes, approximately nine and five-eighths. That is inches," Sahs said.

"And have you determined through your evaluation and research what shoe size a nine and five-eighths inch corresponds to?" Metnick asked.

Sahs said he had.

"And what size is that?"

"You are looking at about a size 6."

"About a size 6" sounded close to a size 7, and on the previous day, prosecutors had shown that Alex Hernandez admitted to the grand jury that he wore size 7 shoes.

"And when you say six, are you referring to a male's Size 6?" asked Metnick, who knew through research done by Bill Clutter that there was a difference between male and female tread designs.

"This would be a female's size 6," Sahs said.

A female's size 6 would be smaller than a male's, so it turned out that the prints near the dining room window were not close to Alex's shoe size after all. Instead, it suddenly appeared plausible that the prints were left by friends of Jeanine's sister, Chris, as they searched for Jeanine on the day of her disappearance.

Metnick was shocked. All along, prosecutors had argued that there were multiple assailants at the Nicarico home. All along, the only evidence had been the various shoeprints. In the first trial against all three defendants and in the second trial against Cruz, prosecutors brought up the shoeprints. Now Kilander had brought them up again, even though it turned out Sahs had told Kilander that morning that he had learned the prints were made by size 6 female shoes.

"The only window that provided a clear view into that home," Stock had argued at Cruz's second trial. "The window that Ronnie Cruz stood at and looked into that home when he made a decision that the house was empty and they could go in."

The difference in the shoeprints proved there were multiple assailants, so Dugan couldn't have acted alone, Kilander had argued in the rebuttal at Cruz's second trial.

Now, at Hernandez's second trial, the prosecutors again were using the shoeprints to argue that there were multiple assailants. And all along, the shoeprints had been those of female Nike shoes. Small female Nike shoes. All along, they had been too tiny to fit Rolando Cruz's feet. All along, they probably had been the prints of the teenage girls who had run around the house looking for Jeanine.

"Of all the egregious things that happened in this case, that was the most egregious," Metnick said later. "I think a really strong judge at that point would have given serious consideration to a motion for mistrial."

After Sahs revealed that the shoeprints had been made by female shoes, the prosecutors stopped mentioning them. But Metnick didn't think the testimony had had the impact it should have on the jury.

"The problem we have as defense attorneys is trying to convince the jury that attorneys—seemingly respectable career prosecutors—were concealing evidence," he said. "That is a hard sell to a jury, especially a central Illinois jury."

Meanwhile, the trial continued.

One of the tollway workers, Roger Seppi, testified that the car they saw at the Prairie Path could have been a Volare. But the other worker, Frank Kochanny, said the car was a Granada and that the driver was not Brian Dugan.

After six days of testimony, the prosecution rested, and the defense made its stand.

George Mueller, who had been Brian Dugan's public

defender in LaSalle County, testified that Dugan didn't have to make any statements about the Nicarico case to avoid the death penalty for his other crimes.

Brian Dugan, wearing shackles, was brought to the witness box.

"[On] February twenty-fifth, nineteen eighty-three, [in] Naperville, Illinois, did you enter a house at six-twenty Clover Court and at that time kidnap a girl named Jeanine Nicarico. . . . Did you take her to the Illinois Prairie Path and sodomize her?" Metnick asked.

"I'm not going to answer any questions at all in connection with the case," Dugan responded. Again he refused to testify without a grant of immunity from the death penalty.

State police Captain Edward Cisowski testified again about Dugan's version of Jeanine's murder.

Dr. Michael Baden, a New York pathologist, testified that a tire iron such as the standard one in a Volare could have been the weapon used to kill Jeanine. Baden's conclusion was different from that of medical examiner Frank Cleveland, who had ruled out a tire iron with a thinner design. Cleveland also again had testified that there was too little blood on the Prairie Path for Jeanine to have been killed there.

Until this point, the defense lawyers had considered putting Hernandez on the stand. Although a defendant has a right not to testify, juries often hold it against defendants if they don't. The lawyers thought Alex's agreeable nature might come through to the jury, which would be a benefit. On the other hand, he might say just about anything once prosecutors started cross-examining him.

It was Jane Raley's job to prepare Alex to testify, and she spent a lot of time working with him. As the time grew close, Raley spent an entire weekend helping him polish his testimony. Then

Michael Metnick and other defense team members arrived on Sunday night to hear how well Alex could do. Metnick was not impressed.

Although the lawyers knew Alex would deny participating in the crime and his manner seemed to exude innocence, he kept bringing up extraneous information that would hurt his case.

For example, when Raley asked about the first time Detectives John Sam and Dennis Kurzawa came to interview him, Alex launched into an explanation that would have been a catastrophe in the courtroom.

"Alex said, 'Well, I was in the back and I was smoking a joint [when they arrived],' " Raley said. "He was incriminating himself on many different levels just to answer a very simple question. It was a disaster. We felt he was just a loose cannon."

Putting Alex on the stand was a risk the defense decided it couldn't afford to take.

The defense rested, and Richard Stock gave the closing argument for the prosecution. He changed the theory back to the original one—that Buckley, Cruz, and Hernandez committed the crime.

"By holding Jeanine down when she was murdered, Alex Hernandez is just as guilty as if he had crushed her skull himself," Stock said. "If a low score on an IQ test ever becomes a legal defense to murder, to kidnapping, to burglary and to rape, all of us are in a lot of trouble."

Stock also said Brian Dugan was lying when he told his lawyers that he committed the crime alone.

"The evidence has proven that there is more than one burglar and killer in this case," Stock said.

He continued, "You heard of Lieutenant Towns-end's bloodhounds and how he followed different trails at the scene, at the home on Clover Court. . . . We also know that in March of 1983, shortly after the crime, Alex Hernandez told us that there was more than one burglar and killer—Buckley, Cruz, and Hernandez went to do the burglary and abducted the girl—and that he held her down while they beat her."

Stock pointed out several flaws in Dugan's story.

Dugan was wrong, Stock said, when he said Jeanine was wearing toenail polish. The previous owner of a yellow Cadillac from which Dugan said he got the towel used for a blindfold said there was no such towel in the car when he sold the car to Brian Dugan. The state police's scouring of the neighborhood showed there was no house where Dugan had borrowed a screwdriver. Dugan said there was only one bed in the room shared by Jeanine's sisters. Jeanine's hands couldn't have been tied in her home, as he'd said, because she'd left finger marks on the wall by the front door as she was carried out.

Moreover, Dugan changed his story, first saying he left her body with her hands tied but later saying he untied her hands when he sexually assaulted her, Stock argued. He said he'd left her faceup, although her body was found facedown.

Then Stock reminded the jury of Alex's own statements:

" 'Cruz, Buckley, and Alex Hernandez themselves planned a burglary in Naperville, east of Aurora, near Route 65 [the Nicaricos' neighborhood].'

" 'They drove to the house, and they cased the place.'

" 'I didn't hurt anybody. I just went there to do a burglary, to get money for drugs.' "

Stock was ready to finish his argument.

"When you retire to the jury room, use your God-given sense

in analyzing the evidence and applying the law," he said. "Return true and just verdicts in this case. Find Alex Hernandez guilty."

Then it was Metnick's turn to respond.

"Ladies and gentlemen, [Alex] can't be proven guilty, and he can't be proven guilty, ladies and gentlemen, because he is innocent, because he wasn't there," Metnick said.

"He never said, 'I did it. I was there. I did it. I confess. God help me. I did this terrible thing.' Nothing like that at all, ladies and gentlemen. . . .

"Don't you think that if [authorities] thought there was something there, he would be tailed, he would be followed, taps would be put on his phone, he would be trailed, his associates would be spoken to?" Metnick asked.

To some in the courtroom, Metnick's closing seemed far too long; it lasted for about three hours. To some reporters, he seemed nervous. At one point, he paused to fill a water glass from a pitcher and missed the glass, spilling water across the table.

During deliberations, jurors said they had reached a verdict on one count but had been unable to reach one on any of the others.

The defense lawyers asked that the verdict already reached be sealed so the jury couldn't change it. But the prosecutors argued against that, and Judge Kowal ruled in their favor.

The jury resumed its deliberations, and finally the lawyers were called back to the courtroom. Defense lawyer Jeffrey Urdangen got a ride there from Ed Cisowski. He noticed Cisowski take his gun out of his trunk and bring it into the courtroom. Cisowski did it in an offhand way, but to Urdangen, it seemed dramatic.

It turned out, however, that the jury was unable to reach a

decision. Originally, it had voted to convict on aggravated kidnapping. Had prosecutors agreed to seal the verdict, it would have been final. Instead, the jury rescinded it. In the end, ten jurors wanted to convict Alex, but two refused to do so. On May 11, 1990, in his second trial, Alex Hernandez had received a hung jury, just as Stephen Buckley had in the first.

"[The defense] appeared to grow a bit more nervous during each successive hour in the twenty that it took the jury to discover it could not agree on a verdict," wrote Hal Dardick, a columnist for several DuPage community newspapers. "Displaying less emotion but still looking haggard were prosecutors Robert Kilander and Rick Stock and the detective [Warren Wilkosz] who has worked on the case for seven years."

After Judge Kowal declared a mistrial, prosecutor Richard Stock walked up to the front of the courtroom and shuffled through the papers with the clerk. He wanted to look at the jury forms to see what the original verdicts were. When he saw that the jury had voted to convict Hernandez for aggravated kidnapping, he threw the forms down on the desk. Had the first verdict been sealed, Hernandez would have been convicted and probably sentenced to sixty years. The state wouldn't have had to retry him on the other charges, and the case could have been over.

"We all went out to breakfast the next day," Jeffrey Urdangen recalled later. "It was a very wonderful, expansive feeling. It was the best that Cruz or Hernandez had ever done in that case. We thought it was just going to get even better. Maybe they wouldn't try the case again."

At the same time, the defense lawyers were shocked at how close the case was. They felt that they had atomized the state's case so completely that even Lieutenant Towns-end's bloodhounds wouldn't have been able to find anything to sniff at, yet the jury had voted ten to two to convict. With all the evidence they'd presented, with all the holes they'd poked into the state's case, they had only barely overcome the prosecution complex.

Later, juror Cynthia Kraft said she wished the jury had known the full story about Brian Dugan.

"I think, if all of the evidence had come out, it would have changed a lot of minds," Kraft said. "Personally, I think we would have found him [Hernandez] innocent."

The jurors had written about nine unanswered questions on a chalkboard. The first vote was four for guilty, four for innocent, and four undecided. Some argued that Cruz's conviction indicated Hernandez was guilty, too. At one point, however, there were ten votes to acquit.

"That showed me that nobody was really sure about the way they felt," juror Robert McCrary said.

McCrary said Hernandez might have been acquitted had the jury known about his history of making up stories. As it was, McCrary could not persuade all eleven of the other jurors to acquit, even though they agreed the prosecution was misleading. He thought some of them were more focused on ending deliberations in time for Mother's Day.

"They just wanted to [reach a verdict and] go home," McCrary said. "If that is justice, that's sick."

16

JEFFREY URDANGEN

In a criminal case, the defense is not obligated to call any witnesses or introduce any evidence. It can simply try to disprove the prosecution's case by cross-examining its witnesses or by relying on the presumption of the defendant's innocence. Many, perhaps even most, defendants put on no case.

Alan M. Dershowitz, *Reversal of Fortune*

IT SOON WAS CLEAR THAT any hopes that prosecutors would not retry Alex Hernandez were futile. Jeffrey Urdangen knew it was going to take an incredible effort to win Hernandez's third trial. This time, the prosecutors wouldn't get caught using the misleading shoeprints by the dining room window. What could the defense do to win an acquittal this time?

Urdangen had grown up in Chicago and started working in poverty law while he was still at John Marshall Law School. He had tried to get a job as a public defender, but he'd lacked the necessary political connections. After working for a very small law firm for about a year, he'd decided to start his own practice in 1981.

Now, ten years later, he had put together a successful practice. Just before Alex Hernandez's third trial, Urdangen was the first lawyer in the country appointed to represent a defendant under the new federal death penalty act Congress had enacted in 1988. The defendant, Darnell Davis, eventually was convicted but was spared the death penalty. Urdangen also headed the death penalty committee for the Illinois Attorneys for Criminal Justice, the state's largest organization of criminal defense attorneys.

Urdangen had first met Michael Metnick through a drug-trafficking case. Urdangen had been hired by a woman who had been stopped by police with five hundred pounds of marijuana in her trunk. Metnick had been hired by her codefendant. Urdangen's client had been acquitted, and when the trial was over, Metnick had asked him to join Alex's defense team.

Reading over the case record, Urdangen came to believe that Tom Knight had made up his mind whom he was going to charge before the grand jury ever had started. Knight had called in Hernandez's alibi witnesses and picked apart their testimony, which meant they wouldn't be of much use in a trial later. Some of them didn't speak English or had bad memories. They were easily confused.

Knight's questioning was rambling. He was fishing, looking for leads, Urdangen thought. He thought it was Rolando Cruz's attitude that convinced Knight he was on the right track. Cruz was sort of flip and punk and clearly was telling lies, claiming that he knew who did it. When Knight learned about Buckley's hiking shoe, that was the clincher.

Urdangen had been thrilled to work with Metnick on Hernandez's second trial. Now it was time to prepare for the third. A month after the second trial ended in May 1990, the defense filed a motion asking for a new judge.

"The law was against us on this," Urdangen said later. "We filed a motion as soon as the case got put back on the call in Wheaton to substitute Judge Kowal. We thought we would try to send Kowal a signal. To our delight—although he denied the motion—he said he was recusing himself from the case. He never gave a real reason; he just said it was time for someone else to take this case."

John J. Nelligan replaced Kowal. Some local lawyers thought that, in general, Nelligan was the best DuPage judge for defendants. The defense lawyers thought Nelligan was a much more pleasant man than Kowal, and they hoped he would be the new ingredient that would give Alex a chance to win.

The defense team refiled many of the pretrial motions that Kowal already had rejected, hoping that Nelligan would give them better rulings. It turned out to be an unrealistic hope. Nelligan made a point of emphasizing early on that he respected Judge Kowal, and he made it clear he wasn't going to make a habit of overturning Kowal's earlier rulings.

As time passed, however, Judge Nelligan did rule differently on a couple of key issues, perhaps most significantly that of Eloise Suk, the church secretary who had seen Brian Dugan.

In Cruz's second trial and in Hernandez's second trial, Judge Kowal had ruled that if Suk took the stand, the prosecutors could ask her about the other people she had seen at the church. Although no one had ever identified them, the prosecutors had used that to imply that Cruz, Hernandez, or Buckley had been to the church, too. Now Judge Nelligan wasn't going to let them do that.

"He heard evidence about it, and basically you could tell he thought it distasteful that a prosecutor would even try to use that totally irrelevant evidence to neutralize Suk," Urdangen recalled later. "He wasn't going to let them do it. He also essentially took the substance out of the bloodhound evidence. We went through a lot on that in pretrial with Nelligan before the third trial, and he finally said, in effect, Look, there is no connection between these bloodhounds and the guys who are on trial. There is just not. And there's nothing here that I think demonstrates that they were following Jeanine's trail. It is just irrelevant."

The defense also filed motions asking that the trial be moved to Cook County, which includes Chicago, so that Hernandez could have a jury with a racial mix. A poll commissioned by the defense showed it would be a bad idea to keep the trial in DuPage County because the county's residents tended to believe Hernandez was guilty. In the end, the trial was moved to the Mississippi River city of Rock Island, Illinois, because Rock Island had an available courtroom.

It was an old courthouse that had a certain amount of charm, but the courtroom itself had no charm at all. It was stuffy and filled by two big tables. There was no room to walk around.

For this trial, the defense lawyers decided to have the judge set any sentence instead of the jury. Normally, lawyers don't waive the right to a jury sentence in a capital case because juries are less likely than judges to impose the death penalty. In Illinois, if just one of the twelve jurors refuses, there is no death penalty. However, a jury in a capital case must be "death qualified," which means each juror must agree he or she would impose the death penalty if the law requires it, thus liberal-minded jurors who oppose the death penalty are weeded out. That means a death-qualified jury tends to be more conservative and more likely to convict.

"It was one of the gutsiest moves ever to waive a jury sentencing," said Jane Raley, a member of the defense team. "You lose a lot of issues on appeal once you have a judge decide the issue. It made me very nervous. I was involved in a lot of death penalty cases, and that's just one thing you never do."

On the other hand, this case was different because the crime was so brutal, Raley said.

"If the jury thought [Alex] did it, or was involved, he was going to get the death penalty. There was going to be no way to persuade the jury that he should not get the death penalty if he was involved in the crime."

Raley was confident the defense could convince jurors that Alex was not the main perpetrator. The challenge was to convince them that Alex was not accountable at all. There was so much intimation that he was there, that he saw what had happened, and that he had previously committed burglaries with other people.

The weekend before the trial started, a long article on the case appeared on the front page of the *Chicago Sun-Times,* jumping onto three pages inside. Written by Thomas Frisbie, it detailed many of the changes in testimony, the missing reports, and the misrepresented and withheld evidence that had characterized the case. "The statements of law enforcement authorities continue to conflict," the article stated. "For example, in a pretrial hearing last week, former prosecutor Tom Knight denied having a significant role in a 1983 attempt to get a statement from Hernandez by tempting him with a box of money. But Sheriff's Deputy Warren Wilkosz testified that Knight 'orchestrated' the entire effort."

As the trial started, however, an article with a different approach appeared in the Rock Island newspaper. The Rock Island story stated that security would be extra tight at the courthouse because of concern that gangs would be present for the Hernandez trial. Urdangen wondered how a story that might bias a jury in favor of the prosecution happened to appear just as the trial was starting. It certainly wasn't based on facts; there had been no gang presence at the earlier trials.

The trial began on May 6, 1991, after a week of jury selection.

By now, the lawyers knew their opening arguments stone cold. The prosecutors contended that Alex Hernandez was a heartless killer. Robert Kilander, again the lead prosecutor, told the jury that the crime was committed by Hernandez, Cruz, and Buckley.

Metnick argued that Hernandez suffered from schizophrenia and delusional thinking.

"The only evidence against him will be the confused, out-of-context ramblings of a confused Alex Hernandez," Metnick said.

Deputy Sheriff Kurzawa again testified about Alex's original "Ricky" story. Detective Albert Bettilyon again testified he heard Alex say that all he had done was hold Jeanine down. The other prosecution witnesses also repeated their stories.

The last witness for the prosecution was Sheriff's Lieutenant Robert Winkler, who had added to his story again.

In the first trial, Winkler had added elements in his testimony that did not appear in his report. He testified that Alex told him Jeanine's lip was cut and that the house was near Aurora Avenue. When the convictions were overturned, Justice Seymour Simon had cited those facts as sufficient grounds for a new trial instead of overturning the case outright.

At Cruz's second trial, Winkler had changed his testimony about Cruz's statement, saying Cruz had admitted hot-wiring a car for friends. That gave prosecutors a second admission besides the "vision" statement that they could use to tie Cruz to the crime.

Now, just as he had at the first and second trials, Winkler added more information that was very important. He testified that

Alex might have said they had switched drivers at the Prairie Path. Now, Buckley, not Cruz, was driving the car. The testimony by the tollway workers—that they saw a Caucasian driving the car— would no longer conflict with Alex's claims.

Urdangen cross-examined Winkler and emphasized how Winkler had kept changing his story. When Urdangen was finished, he felt that he had neutralized Winkler.

In retrospect, Jane Raley wasn't so sure.

"Many times I think we overestimated the jury's ability to see how the prosecution was misleading us and how dishonest they were," she said. "And I think that they were, especially in Rock Island. I think there were more changes in people's testimony. We were outraged about this, but I think these sorts of things went right over the jury's head."

After court ended for the day, the lawyers went back to an old house that Metnick had rented for the duration of the trial. Metnick was euphoric; he thought the case was won. In his view, there was no need to put on a defense, even though some of his witnesses were already in Rock Island.

Less than a month earlier, Metnick had defended a case in federal court in which his client was charged with possession of a gun by a convicted felon. Metnick had rested without putting on a defense and won. He wanted to use the same strategy for Alex Hernandez.

Why should we let them have anything? Metnick asked. Why should we put on the psychological evidence? That's going to let the prosecutors talk about Alex's criminal history. Why let them argue that the murder started out as a burglary?

Moreover, Metnick continued, why should the defense put on Dugan evidence? Why give Kilander an opportunity to try to spin some story that Dugan and Hernandez committed the crime together, as he had done with Cruz?

Metnick knew it was a gamble. He knew he had promised in his opening argument to tell the jury about Brian Dugan. He knew he'd be criticized if the strategy backfired. But conservative lawyering would never win this case in front of a jury, he felt. A bold stroke was needed.

"He was intoxicated with confidence about this strategy," Urdangen recalled later. "He felt so good, it was contagious. We really did feel we had eviscerated their case."

If the strategy didn't work, the worst that could happen was a hung jury, Urdangen reasoned. A hung jury would be as good as an acquittal. There was no way the prosecutors would put Hernandez on trial a fourth time, he thought.

Bill Clutter, although he was not a lawyer, opposed the idea vigorously. He'd first heard Metnick mention the idea a short while before while the two men were driving through Rock Island. He hadn't liked the idea then, and he didn't like it now.

Clutter thought the defense team was under too much stress. Metnick, already an intense worker, had been working double time on Hernandez's case. In January, his wife had asked him for a divorce, and Metnick still was devastated. During his time working with Metnick, Clutter frequently had heard Metnick say that the things that mattered most to him were his family and the people he worked with. Now that was falling apart. His wife wanted a divorce and his partners had to be annoyed by the time he was pouring into the case—first as a pro bono lawyer and then as a court-appointed one—and the money he was spending on expert witnesses and other expenses.

Clutter was discouraged, too. He had lost his seat on the

Springfield City Council on April 5, just before the Rock Island trial had started. The previous November, Clutter had lost a race for the state legislature by less than one percentage point. Clutter's political career had come crashing down, and Metnick was the most depressed Clutter had ever seen anyone be. The defense team had worked together smoothly in Bloomington, but there had been friction between Urdangen and Metnick over how to proceed in Rock Island. It was not the right time to make a radical decision based on gut instincts.

It seemed Metnick had forgotten about the prosecution complex. Logically, Metnick's idea was perfectly sound. The state hadn't met its burden of proof of guilt beyond reasonable doubt, so the jury had no choice other than to free Hernandez. But in this case, that wasn't going to happen.

"The jurors are not going to take a chance of releasing somebody who is accused of a crime like this unless they are absolutely convinced that he didn't do it," Clutter said later. "There is no way they are going to do it. If this had been a driving-while-under-the-influence charge, the case would have been over. If the crime was a barroom fight, the jury is going to say, This isn't the kind of guy who is going to be stalking me and my family. But Alex Hernandez was accused of this monstrous crime. The jury was not going to take a chance."

After the Bloomington trial, Clutter had interviewed the jurors. One woman had said she at first thought Alex was innocent but voted to convict him because he knew that the suspect drove a green car. How would he have known that if he wasn't involved? she asked. Clutter told her that newspapers had repeatedly reported that police were looking for a suspect driving a green car.

"She said, 'Oh, my God, if I would have known that, I would

never have voted to convict,' " Clutter recalled later. "I thought, gee, that wasn't our burden to prove. But basically, what she was telling me was that it was really our burden to point out that fact to her; it was our burden to prove these facts. We couldn't present less than a full case."

Metnick clearly thought resting the case was the right decision, but everyone was very uneasy about it. During the night, members of the defense team telephoned each other to discuss it further.

The next day, Metnick argued a motion asking that the prosecutors be prohibited from introducing evidence of Alex's past brushes with the law if the defense informed jurors about Alex's history of telling tall tales. Judge Nelligan denied it. In evaluating Alex's statements, Nelligan said, the jury should know that Alex was not a "babe in the woods," that contact with the criminal justice system was part of his makeup.

That ruling stripped away a major part of Alex's defense. What was the point of telling the jury about Alex's history of tall tales if the prosecutors could then introduce records of his arrests? Almost nothing prejudices a jury against a defendant more than knowledge of past arrests, even though, technically, an arrest is an unproven charge. Yet Metnick had promised the jury in his opening argument that he would put on evidence of Alex's psychological makeup. What would the jury think if he put on a defense without including that evidence?

"The Court's ruling that our psychological defense would open the door to Alex's prior bad acts would have given the State the opportunity to argue that Alex is a burglar, he kicks in doors, and he commits crimes with others," the defense later wrote in a motion for a new trial. "These facts would have bolstered the State's theory that Dugan committed this crime in concert with Alex."

Metnick asked for a brief recess, and the lawyers had a final discussion in a small room adjoining the courtroom. Metnick still wanted to rest without putting on a defense. Urdangen wasn't enthusiastic, but he thought that the worst that could happen was a hung jury. Jane Raley didn't argue against it, although she wasn't enthusiastic, either. They could ask for a delay, but the whole effect of a bold stroke would be lost if jurors realized they were fretting about it first. Back in the courtroom Judge Nelligan was waiting for them to tell him what they had decided.

The lawyers entered the courtroom and told Judge Nelligan they were ready to proceed with closing arguments. No defense witnesses would be put on the stand.

Urdangen could tell that the prosecutors were happy with that decision, which made him nervous. But there was no time to worry.

In his closing argument, Kilander asked the jury to take an imaginary look inside Alex's head. It was an artful approach that wove a pattern of conduct and presented it as evidence. Kilander was arguing from notes, and at one point a piece of paper dropped out of his hand and floated to the floor. The courtroom was so cramped that the paper fell on the floor near Alex, who bent down, picked it up, and gave it to the man who was trying to have him executed.

The jury was out for a long time. Then they sent Judge Nelligan a note asking if a conviction on aggravated kidnapping required a conviction on murder as well. Nelligan sent back a message that simply told the jurors they already had been instructed about the relevant law. He wouldn't tell the defense lawyers what was in the jury's note.

Finally, on May 16, 1991, the jury came back and gave a verdict: guilty. The prosecutors earlier had convinced Cruz's second jury that Cruz, Dugan, and Hernandez had committed the crime; now they had convinced Hernandez's third jury that Buckley, not Dugan, was the third participant. Haydee Hernandez, Alex's mother, started wailing in the courtroom. It was a long, sustained wail. Sitting in that cramped courtroom listening to Haydee sobbing, hearing the verdicts and knowing that the defense strategy had failed was the lowest point of Urdangen's professional life.

Later, Bill Clutter questioned the jurors. They had voted to convict because they believed Sheriff's Lieutenant Winkler.

It was an oppressively hot day as the lawyers crossed the parking lot to talk to Alex. It was difficult to explain why they had done what they did. Then there was nothing else to do but pack up and go home. The sentencing hearing would be held back in DuPage County in the Wheaton courthouse.

The flaw with the decision now was clear to Urdangen; he never really had considered that the defense might lose. He never had stopped to ask how he could live with the decision if the defense strategy backfired.

On August 13, 1991, it was time for the sentencing hearing. Metnick was demoralized, and without any discussion it suddenly seemed to be agreed that Urdangen would give the defense's arguments. Urdangen asked Gary Johnson, former Naperville police chief Jim Teal, and former state police director Jeremy Margolis to write letters to Judge Nelligan on Alex's behalf, which they did. All the other lawyers who had been involved in the case also wrote to Nelligan.

"Someday, sooner or later, the public will realize what has happened in *Nicarico*," Gary Johnson wrote in his letter. "Unfortunately, when the public does understand what has occurred, the prestige and credibility of prosecutors everywhere will be adversely affected. The Nicarico case will do to prosecutors what the Rodney King police beating tapes have done to the police."

Margolis wrote: "On the one hand, I believe in the death penalty. On the other hand, I know that the system makes mistakes. The certainty, the singular resolve, the unshakable philosophical and factual conviction that should be present before it is ordered that a man be bound, blindfolded and killed by poison are, in my opinion, not present here."

The defense put on a few mitigation witnesses and then called Margolis as a witness. As soon as Urdangen started asking Margolis questions, the prosecutors objected. An odd, almost surreal, debate followed on whether Alex's possible innocence was relevant to whether he should get the death penalty. Judge Nelligan ruled that Margolis could not testify. Neither could Teal nor Gary Johnson.

Then Alex's parents testified. Their obvious belief in their son's innocence was very moving, Jane Raley thought.

On the second day of the hearing, Urdangen gave his final argument, which was all about innocence. He read off names of innocent people who had been executed. After the argument, Urdangen was feeling very upbeat. He went to the Viking restaurant and ordered a drink. Judge Nelligan walked in and went to the corner of the bar. Nelligan ordered a drink and sat by himself, quietly drinking, just a couple of hours after the hearing. Urdangen wondered how Nelligan would rule.

Two days later, on August 16, 1991, the hearing resumed in a different courtroom. Nelligan said he was troubled by the paucity of evidence, that the case was too weak to sentence Hernandez to death.

"[There] was no direct evidence presented in the trial of this case with respect to the physical evidence or circumstantial evidence, fingerprints, hairs or anything of that nature that would tie the defendant in with either the Nicarico home . . . or at the Prairie Path scene where the body was recovered, or any other place," Judge Nelligan said. "It was just a complete lack of evidence of that type in this case."

Nelligan said the most damaging testimony was that of Detective Bettilyon, who had overheard the conversation between Alex and Penguino. Even that, though, was far from clear-cut.

"It is impossible to determine the context within which the statements the defendant made were made, not to mention the obvious meaning of the language that Bettilyon recorded," Judge Nelligan said.

Instead of the death penalty, Judge Nelligan sentenced Hernandez to eighty years in prison. It wasn't a victory, Urdangen thought, but it was a start. Finally, a judge had publicly admitted that the evidence against Alex was weak.

Looking back, Metnick reviewed the defense team's two major strategies: to waive a jury sentence and to waive defense witnesses. Judge Nelligan's comments made it clear the first gamble had worked, but the second had failed badly.

"In retrospect, I wish I would have put on the evidence," Metnick said later. "I don't think they would have found him guilty in Rock Island."

Juror Frederick Riportella also said he wished the defense had put on witnesses.

"I am sure that if information was presented about Dugan, it would have at least raised some questions in some of our minds," Riportella said later. "If there was one thing we all shared on that jury, it was a feeling that we didn't have enough information to make a good decision."

During the trial, while Urdangen was still helping to prepare a defense, he had called Randy Garrett to get Eloise Suk's phone number because the defense team was planning to use her as a witness. Now that Nelligan had barred the prosecutors from asking her about the other people she had seen in the church, the defense lawyers had been very excited about using her. They thought her testimony would be very powerful.

As Urdangen cleaned out his hotel room when the trial was over, he checked one last time to make sure he had collected everything. He opened up the drawer in the nightstand and he saw a piece of paper. He pulled it out. On it were Eloise Suk's name and phone number.

"I practically started to cry," Urdangen recalled later. "To think about what had just happened, and to see that note. And to think about what we gave up, what we didn't do. It was devastating."

17

LAWRENCE MARSHALL

Prosecutors, with virtually unbridled discretion to seek the death penalty, may pursue a death sentence even when the evidence is weak, and they may be reluctant to change course when contradictory evidence later arises. Even judges, many of whom also are subject to elections, can be influenced in their decisions to ignore evidence of innocence unless it is absolutely irrefutable. And recent changes to the appeals process, especially in federal courts, have made it more likely that executions will proceed even in the face of evidence raising doubts about a defendant's guilt.

Richard Dieter, executive director, Death Penalty Information Center, "Innocence and the Death Penalty: The Increasing Danger of Executing the Innocent," July 1977

LAWRENCE MARSHALL, A Northwestern University law professor, was standing by the elevator in a big Chicago law firm where he did some consulting work when one of the firm's partners came over with an interesting offer.

Rolando Cruz, the partner said, was looking for a lawyer to do the appeal after Cruz's second conviction. His legal team wanted someone who had appellate experience but wasn't always in front of the court on behalf of death row defendants. They wanted someone whose very presence told the court: This case is different. It requires careful examination.

Marshall, a bearded, heavyset man, had heard a little about Rolando Cruz; he knew Cruz had been sentenced to death for a second time. He also knew that no one had ever had two death penalty convictions reversed in Illinois. The court seemed to follow a practical rule: If you get convicted and the court gives you another trial, that's your remedy. If the second trial doesn't turn out the way you wish, then the court is not going to be very sympathetic to errors in the trial. The justices are not going to believe that two different juries made a mistake.

Marshall, who grew up in Boston, didn't know much about the Rolando Cruz case. He had been at Northwestern University School of Law when Jeanine Nicarico was murdered, but he wasn't very focused on community news. Before he made a decision, he decided, he ought to do some reading about the case.

Marshall returned to his office at Northwestern, logged onto an electronic news retrieval service, and ordered it to search for "Nicarico" and "Rolando Cruz." Without checking how many stories were found, he ordered all of them to be sent to the law library's printer. A couple of hours later he got a call from a library staff member saying, "What in the world have you done here? We are getting these reams and reams of paper." The printer was churning out hundreds of articles about the case.

Marshall started reading the articles, and the enormity of the case started to dawn on him. He had never seen anything like it. It seemed clear that Cruz was innocent and Dugan was guilty. Still, he wasn't sure whether he should take the case. He was thirty-one years old and was just a few years out of law school. He had just been promoted from assistant professor to associate professor, and his responsibilities as a teacher were increasing. On the other hand, how could he teach legal ethics if he turned his back on a call like this?

That year during Yom Kippur, the Jewish Day of Atonement, Marshall continued to ponder his decision. Around him, people were talking about the day of judgment and of who should live and who should die and who by fire and who by stoning. Marshall, who had studied the Talmud at a Jerusalem yeshiva, started to wonder if perhaps part of the reason that he was put on this earth was to take this case. He decided to look into it further.

First, he had a meeting with the lawyers. Attending were the original appellate defenders: John Hanlon, who was spearheading the effort to find new counsel, and Tim Gabrielsen. Also present were two of the lawyers from Cruz's second trial: Jed Stone and Susan Valentine. Then Marshall went to southern Illinois to see Rolando Cruz. Cruz was living in an eight-by-ten-foot cell with no window in the century-old Menard Correctional Center, the largest prison in Illinois.

It was Marshall's first trip to death row. It was an emotional meeting; Cruz spent a good part of it talking about his life. He also showed that he was very frightened. It was only several months since he had been convicted for a second time, and he was devastated. After the first conviction, he'd had hope that the appeal process would correct the error. Then Brian Dugan had made his admission, and the state police had uncovered all sorts of corroborating evidence. Cruz's legal team for the second trial had seemed sure they would win, talking about getting him home in time for Christmas. Yet he'd been convicted again. What could he hope for now? No one in Illinois had ever been granted a third trial in a capital case.

Marshall also knew the odds were long. He knew that he and the other lawyers were going to have to write the absolutely best-researched, best-written, best-reasoned, best-documented brief that they would ever write in their lives, and that they would have to put everything else in their lives aside for months and months. The brief, he knew, would have to tell the story of what had happened in a way that would capture the court's attention.

Although he was a law school professor and had clerked for U.S. Supreme Court justice John Paul Stevens in 1986 and 1987, Marshall was worried that he might not be up to the task.

"We didn't know if we could do it," Marshall said later. "You live with the self-doubt—asking, Am I really the best person to be doing this? I was absolutely frightened by the prospect that I wasn't and that somehow I was an impostor who had gotten this by an accident. The only way to make up for that was to work as I had never worked before."

Working with Marshall were John Hanlon, the appellate defender who had helped win a reversal for Cruz after the first trial, and Jeffrey Winick and Susan Valentine, attorneys who helped defend Cruz at his second trial. There also were a number of volunteer law students who helped do legal research.

The first step was to read the transcripts of the entire second trial and to make a synopsis of every page. It also meant reading significant parts of the first trial. Then the lawyers started exploring the legal issues.

"At that point, notwithstanding it being the second conviction, I had to believe there was no way in the world the court was going to be able to uphold this conviction," Marshall said. "It was so tainted, the errors were so manifest, that I don't care if it was a tenth conviction. The court couldn't uphold it."

Then came a crushing blow. On May 16, 1991, Alejandro Hernandez was convicted in Rock Island. The issues had seemed so clear in his case, too, yet here was another jury returning a conviction. Nothing seemed capable of turning the case around. Still, there was nothing to do but to keep on working.

"We wanted to be able to say to ourselves if, God forbid, we lost, that there was nothing else we could have done," Marshall said. "The Chicago Bulls were in the playoffs, and no one on our team knew anything about it. We used to go out for lunch and we would see players for the Los Angeles Lakers walking by on Michigan Avenue, and we couldn't care less. We were absolutely focused."

In the final brief, the appellate team cited twenty-one issues as a basis for overturning the conviction. The most important was the fact that the jury was not permitted to hear all of the Brian Dugan information.

The prosecutors, Marshall saw, had effectively poked holes in Brian Dugan's confession, saying he didn't see the sailboat on the edge of the driveway, that he described the television incorrectly, that he said there might have been patio doors in the basement. Under normal circumstances, however, almost no one could accu rately describe everything in a building in which he or she had been for only a few minutes, especially if almost three years had elapsed. It was amazing that Brian Dugan remembered as much as he did. But the jurors couldn't make a sensible decision if they didn't know that Brian Dugan had confessed to six other known crimes and was accurate about all of them.

"The state wanted to make this sound as though Brian Dugan came in and said: 'I killed JFK. I was the lone gunman, I was on the grassy knoll,' " Marshall said later. "If someone confesses to you, tells you a hundred facts and you are not sure about the hundredth because of some discrepancies, it has some credibility if the other ninety-nine were accurate. The jurors had to know about

Brian Dugan's confessions to all these crimes. They had to know about his modus operandi. They didn't. And they had to know that Brian Dugan always acted alone. That was the key."

In the closing arguments at the second trial, the prosecutors had argued that perhaps Dugan was involved in the crime but that he didn't do it alone. The defense needed to be permitted to show that Dugan did commit his crimes alone, Marshall felt. The jury needed to know that Dugan wrapped his victims in sheets or blankets, often blindfolded them, wielded tire irons as bludgeons, transported his victims in cars to secluded places, and sexually molested them, including raping them anally.

Other issues that Marshall thought were very clear included the use of Erma Rodriguez to link Cruz and Dugan and the testimony of the bloodhound handlers. Neither should have been permitted.

As the deadline for filing the brief approached, the legal team held all-nighters in the room across the hall from Marshall's office. The lawyers considered it ironic that their "war room" for fighting a case of legal injustice was Julius Hoffman Hall. Hoffman, who had presided over the landmark Chicago Seven trial, had gained a reputation as an imperious, pro-prosecution jurist with no sympathy for the defendants.

On the last night before filing, about fifteen people stayed up all night. They had charted every one of the brief's twenty-one sections. Every section went through multiple edits, repeated proofreading, and checking of the legal citations to make sure the page numbers and other details were correct. Finally, the brief was bound up, and John Hanlon drove it to Springfield and filed it.

While working as a consultant at the law firm of Mayer, Brown & Platt, Marshall had seen the meticulousness of the work done on briefs in cases that involved only money. There had been briefs in cases for which the firm had been paid $1 million. This brief, with a life at stake, had to be just as good. Marshall took it home and saw several typographical errors that had been introduced during last-minute changes, the point at which, as they used to say at Mayer, Brown & Platt, the gremlins get in. So Marshall and the others came back to the office, fixed the typos, redid the brief, rebound it, and filed an amended brief.

Then there was nothing to do but wait. The personnel on the Supreme Court had changed since 1988, when the court voted six to zero to order new trials for Cruz and Hernandez. Justice Seymour Simon, who wrote the opinion for Hernandez, had retired. So had Justice Howard C. Ryan, who wrote the opinion for Cruz. The new court was more conservative.

In December 1991, Marshall had lunch in Chicago with Jeff Urdangen, defense lawyer for Alejandro Hernandez at his second and third trials. They met in a food court in the basement of the State of Illinois Center, which was midway between their offices in Chicago's Loop. When they had finished eating, it occurred to them that it might be a good idea to go upstairs and introduce themselves to Marcia Friedl, who was writing the state's brief in response to the one Marshall had filed six months earlier. Friedl, who was working in the Illinois attorney general's appeal division, already had secured several extensions for completing the brief, so Marshall and Urdangen thought they would ask her if she intended to ask for any more.

They went up to the fourteenth floor and asked for Marcia Friedl. She came out with Mary Brigid Kenney, whom Marshall recognized as a student who had attended Northwestern University School of Law several years earlier.

Marshall greeted Kenney, who told him that she just had been assigned to take over the Cruz case from Friedl, who was about to go on maternity leave. Kenney had just started working on it. The attorney general would ask for much more time, perhaps three months, Kenney said.

Well, Marshall said, if you look at this case seriously, if you look at it honestly, you are going to come to believe there is something very wrong with it.

Then Marshall related a biblical story from the book of Esther, in which Esther becomes the queen of Persia and ultimately is put in a position where she can save her people. And when Mordecai, who had adopted her as his daughter, asks her to risk her life on her people's behalf, he says, "Who knows? Perhaps you have come to the throne for just such a time as this."

It wasn't, Marshall knew, typical talk between a defense lawyer and a prosecutor, but then, it wasn't a typical case. Later it would be rumored that Kenney was a disciple of Marshall's. Some people would even suggest that there had been a romantic relationship.

"Frivolous," Marshall retorted. "Absolutely frivolous. The spiritual level of the approach was what was unique. The idea that a defense lawyer was saying to a prosecutor, look at this case, and you'll see that there's nothing there—that wasn't unique. That's what defense lawyers say to prosecutors all the time."

A couple of months later, Marshall got some calls from Kenney asking for documents that were part of the record but that she didn't have. There was no indication what direction Kenney or her boss, Illinois attorney general Roland Burris, was taking. And then, suddenly, Rolando Cruz's case was a front-page story again.

On March 6, 1992, the banner headline in the *Chicago Sun-*

Times read, "Burris aide quits, hits Nicarico 'error.' " The secondary headline on the story read: "Wrong men convicted in girl's slaying."

"A deputy to Illinois attorney general Roland W. Burris quit Thursday because Burris refused to tell the Illinois Supreme Court that the wrong men might have been convicted for the 1983 murder of Jeanine Nicarico," read the story by reporters Michael Briggs and Thomas Frisbie.

"In an impassioned letter of resignation, Mary Brigid Kenney said Rolando Cruz and Alejandro Hernandez, both 28, were unfairly convicted of murdering the ten-year-old Naperville girl. Their trials, she said, were 'infected by many instances of prosecutorial misconduct.'

"Cruz is on Death Row, and Hernandez is serving an eighty-year prison term.

"Kenney said she is convinced the real murderer is convicted child-killer Brian Dugan, 35. Dugan has claimed since 1985 that he was the killer.

"Assigned by Burris to represent the state in Cruz's appeal, Kenney urged Burris to 'confess error.'

" 'I cannot sit idly as this office continues to pursue the unjust prosecution and execution of Rolando Cruz,' she wrote."

Mary Brigid Kenney had been assigned to write the Cruz brief the day she started working as an assistant attorney general. She was enthusiastic about her new job, partly because it would give her a chance to try cases in front of the Illinois Supreme Court and U.S. Court of Appeals. Her approach, which she had developed while working in the criminal appeals division of the Cook County state's attorney's office in Chicago, was to read the transcript first. As she read the record of Cruz's trial, she started to worry.

Alarm bells had gone off, Kenney said later, when Marcia Friedl, who had started work on the brief before it was assigned to Kenney, had said she didn't want her name on the brief when it was finished. Now Kenney thought she saw why. Cruz, it seemed clear to her, had not had a fair trial.

Kenney raised her concerns with other attorneys in the office, but they told her she had to press ahead. Just write a weak brief and hope you lose, they advised her, saying they had done that before.

"No prosecutor ever should do that," she said later.

Kenney thought Judge Edward Kowal had made a number of rulings that rendered it impossible for Cruz to get a fair trial. Most significantly, the jury didn't know enough about Brian Dugan. The evidence that Judge Kowal excluded was the evidence that convinced Kenney that Dugan was telling the truth.

"All that this jury knew was that Dugan had pleaded guilty to other murders," she said later. "They didn't know that Dugan's living victims had identified him in lineups. They didn't know that he had accurately described the known details of the murders and rapes and attempted rapes that he had committed."

Jailhouse snitch Robert Turner's testimony was extremely suspect because he never mentioned the evidence against Cruz in his original letter to the attorney general, even though the alleged conversations had already occurred, she said.

Kenney said she discussed the appeal with Richard Stock and

Robert Kilander after she had finished reading the transcripts. At the end of the meeting, she said, Stock had said, "We know you have problems with this case. We've got problems with this case, too. We don't know who killed this girl."

When Marshall heard about Kenney's resignation, he thought it would be enough to turn the case around. Nobody had ever heard of something like that happening before. It was unprecedented. Burris might very well confess error. If he did, the Illinois Supreme Court in all probability would accept his decision. The case would be over.

The next day, Attorney General Roland W. Burris called a press conference at the State of Illinois Center. Numerous members of the news media showed up. Burris was a Democrat and had no reason to protect Republican Jim Ryan, who was interested in winning Burris's job. Perhaps something dramatic was about to happen.

Burris, however, was not about to inject himself into the case. He avoided saying that he thought Cruz was guilty, but Burris didn't say Cruz was innocent, either.

"It is not for me to look at the record and make a ruling," Burris said. "[A] jury has found this individual guilty and given him the death penalty. It is my role to see to it that it is upheld. That's my job."

Later that day, DuPage County prosecutor Richard Stock told reporters that all the issues Kenney raised already had been heard and dismissed by judges or juries. Burris's aides implied that Kenney had resigned as a stunt to get attention, perhaps to run for political office.

Cruz, who already had spent eight years on death row, was not going to get out anytime soon.

Marshall was angered by Burris's response, which he considered political buck-passing.

"Everyone wanted to say, 'It's not my job,' " Marshall said later. "Everyone wanted to put it on the jury. But of course, the jury is only as good as the information it gets."

Several months later, the attorney general's office finally filed its brief asking that the conviction be upheld and Rolando Cruz be executed.

In the defense lawyers' reply brief, they followed the same philosophy they had followed for the original brief. Again, they had all-nighters. Again, they went through intense days of editing and reworking. Usually a reply brief is twenty to thirty pages. The Cruz reply brief was nearly sixty. It was filed in June 1992, and oral arguments were promptly scheduled.

Marshall knew that in a case like this, the oral arguments before the Illinois Supreme Court could make the difference. He knew he had to say the right thing, to make the right approach. The lawyers staged several moot courts, practicing their arguments, trying to anticipate what the attorney general's lawyers would say, what the justices might ask. Marshall was surprised to find that the various audiences at the moot courts had different reactions. The law professors wanted more focus on the legal issues. Practicing lawyers were more interested in bringing out key facts. People from outside the law profession thought there should be more emotion to get the court's attention.

Marshall believed that if he could get the justices to see that there was something really extraordinary about the case, to see that it was a case that needed careful study, Cruz would win. But if they just looked at Cruz as a defendant who had already been given a second chance, he was doomed.

Mary Brigid Kenney's resignation had put the Cruz case back in the public eye, but since then, that gaze had wandered. When Dugan had come forward, Cruz and Hernandez had been a cause célèbre, but that was long ago. Many people seemed to think that because neither of the original defendants had been freed, they must have committed the crime along with Dugan. As Cruz's case was building up to its legal climax, many people had lost interest.

Finally June 22 arrived, the day for oral arguments.

Marshall took his ten-year-old daughter with him to Springfield as he prepared to face the judges. The tension was high; so many people wanted to attend that each side was allotted passes to distribute. Marshall was very emotional during the arguments, covering a lot of points. Not one justice asked a question, however, which was extremely unusual. Typically, oral arguments are a time when justices probe each side's point of view. Marshall didn't know how to interpret their silence. He hoped, of course, that he'd already won.

Assistant Illinois attorney general Terence Madsen gave the prosecution argument, ending with the standard request for the court to "Set a date certain for the execution of Rolando Cruz." Then Madsen sat down, awaiting Marshall's rebuttal.

Madsen's closing words had stung. Marshall rushed to the podium and started by repeating the words: "Set a date certain for the execution of Rolando Cruz"? He couldn't believe it. The idea that anyone could suggest it was just too much for him. Then he responded to the points Madsen had made and sat down, again getting no questions.

Chief Justice Benjamin K. Miller announced that the court

would take the case under advisement, which was the usual procedure. People began to file out of the courtroom. As he walked out, Marshall saw Thomas and Patricia Nicarico standing there. He approached them and told them of the nightmares he'd had over what had happened to their daughter. He told them that it hurt him to know that they thought he was continuing to inflict pain on them. Please understand, he said, that he was trying to bring to justice the person who had really killed Jeanine. The Nicaricos looked at him in what Marshall thought was a hopeless kind of way and just shrugged, as if to say they didn't know what to think anymore.

Marshall continued to walk out of the courtroom. Right outside, there was a radiator, and he sat down, overcome by emotion. He cried, he said later, as he had never cried before. It was uncontrollable, hysterical weeping. His daughter panicked, thinking he was in trouble, perhaps cited for contempt of court. When Marshall realized why she was worried, he was able to assure her that he was all right.

Observers told Marshall that the argument had gone well. Some people told him it was magnificent, that there was no question that Cruz would win. Meanwhile, there was nothing to do but return to Chicago and wait.

The defense lawyers knew that three justices were retiring from the Supreme Court, so the decisions probably would be announced before the outgoing justices left the bench in December 1992. Each time it was announced that a batch of cases would be decided, the lawyers got more nervous. But weeks came and went, and still there was no decision.

Then came a bad sign. In late November, Marshall got a call from a television reporter asking him to respond to the affirmation of Cruz's conviction by the Supreme Court. Marshall didn't know what the reporter was talking about. It turned out that the decision was supposed to have been issued the previous week and then was delayed. A court spokesman had told the reporter that Cruz's conviction was affirmed. When the confusion about the timing became clear, the spokesman retracted his statement. The incident jacked up the tension for the defense lawyers. Was the spokesman wrong about the decision or only about the timing?

The court finally announced on December 1 that the decision would be issued December 4, a Friday. The defense lawyers gathered outside the Supreme Court offices in Chicago. The news media were out in force. Marshall noticed that some people were praying. Too late for that, he thought. Whatever has been decided has been written already. It was already sitting on a stack of papers inside.

Finally, the doors opened. Marshall walked inside and picked up a copy of the opinion. Immediately, he saw that it was written by Justice James D. Heiple, a bad sign. Heiple was an extreme conservative, the kind of justice who would decide that Cruz already had been given a second chance and ignore the rest of the issues. Marshall flipped to the end of the decision and saw that Cruz's conviction was, indeed, affirmed by a vote of four to three and that the state's prison warden was directed to execute Cruz by lethal injection.

Marshall glanced through the rest of the opinion. Heiple didn't just accept the evidence against Cruz at face value, he called it "overwhelming." He even claimed that the state had produced physical evidence to connect Cruz to the crime, although the state had not done so. Efforts to impeach the witnesses who testified against Cruz, Heiple wrote, were "ineffective."

Arguments that the jury didn't hear enough of the information about Dugan were irrelevant, Heiple said, because the jury never should have been told about Dugan in the first place. In Heiple's view, the state police investigation into Dugan turned up no corroborating evidence. The green car with the missing hubcap, the hiking shoe seen in the field, and the description of the tape used for the blindfold were irrelevant, he argued. "There is nothing to indicate the [Dugan] statements are trustworthy," he wrote.

Using Erma Rodriguez to introduce hearsay didn't amount to reversible error, he ruled. "We believe that facts of this case so overwhelmingly established the defendant's guilt that he would have been found guilty without the prosecutor's improper argument," he wrote.

Brushing aside all of the concerns about whether Cruz had a fair trial, Heiple made it clear he thought Cruz's conviction was proper.

"We have carefully considered all of the defendant's arguments, and cannot find merit in any of them," Heiple wrote. "The evidence provided by the State proved beyond a reasonable doubt that Jeanine Nicarico was brutally murdered at the hands of Rolando Cruz."

Marshall could hardly believe it. Of course, he would ask the Supreme Court to reconsider its decision; that was standard, but it almost never made a difference. Cruz didn't have any strong federal issues, and the federal courts seemed more intent on speeding up executions rather than worrying about whether the death rows across the country harbored innocent people.

Wearily, Marshall found a telephone and called his answering machine, leaving a message that the court had voted four to three to affirm. John Hanlon was at the Menard prison with Marlene Kamish, who now was a lawyer, and Rolando Cruz. Their plan called for Hanlon to dial Marshall's number to hear the message and relay the news to Cruz.

Hanlon could hardly believe it, either, when he got the message. There were two guards with him; both told him they were sorry, that they'd hoped Cruz was going to win. When he walked back into the prison to relay the news, he broke down and started to cry.

"Hey, what's wrong with you guys?" Cruz said. "Keep your chin up."

Turning to Hanlon, Cruz said, "I guess I am going to have to ask for a little more of Mrs. Hanlon's patience until we get this thing ironed out."

That stuck in Hanlon's mind. Hell, he thought, if Cruz can be that brave about it, that cool about it, then so can I.

Marshall, meanwhile, was in a daze.

"It was as if you just found your parents killed," he said. "It was that kind of shock, that kind of devastation. It was just unbelievable. People were hugging each other, people were crying. It was so hard to fathom. I never, ever had seen a case in which a judge had made up devastating lies like this."

It didn't matter that John Sam had quit his job, that state police Captain Ed Cisowski and Naperville police chief Jim Teal had put their careers on the line, that Mary Brigid Kenney had resigned. The years of work by the lawyers, investigators, and aides, the all-nighters, the efforts of some journalists, the hours spent away from families all had been wasted.

The prosecution complex was the law of the land.

18

MARY ANN G. MCMORROW

When innocence itself is brought to the bar and con-
demned, especially to die, the subject will exclaim, "It is
immaterial to me whether I behave well or ill, for virtue
itself is no security." And if such sentiment as this should
take place in the mind of the subject, there would be an
end to all security whatsoever.

John Adams, First Day Speech, 1770, in defense of British
soldiers accused of murders in the Boston Massacre

ROLANDO CRUZ NEEDED HELP from Justice Mary Ann G. McMorrow. McMorrow, it appeared, was the swing vote on the newly constituted Illinois Supreme Court, and Cruz needed the court to change its mind.

Cruz's lawyers knew time was running out. Yet there was hope. The claim that there was "overwhelming" evidence and the claim that physical evidence existed were so audacious, so without foundation, that perhaps the court could be brought to see its error.

The Cruz lawyers knew that it would take a phenomenal effort to get the court to reverse itself, a very rare occurrence. They made up their minds they would fight for a rehearing as no one had ever fought before.

"If there is one thing that we did in this case that was extraordinary, it is the effort that was put into mounting that petition for rehearing," Marshall recalled later. "We really felt that every word mattered. There was a strict page limit. We weren't going to exceed twenty-seven pages, and we had to both be respectful to the court and at the same time convince the court that it had made a terrible, inexcusable mistake."

There was a significant difference between this and most petitions for rehearing: the personnel of the court had changed. Three justices had retired on the very day of the Cruz decision. Of those three justices, two had been in the majority—voting to uphold Cruz's conviction—and one had been in the minority. The four remaining justices were split two to two.

Justices James D. Heiple and Michael Bilandic had voted to affirm Cruz's conviction. Justice Charles Freeman and Chief Justice Benjamin K. Miller had voted to overturn it. Miller, who was considered a very conservative law-and-order justice, had written a strong dissent. In 170 death penalty cases, Miller had never joined a dissent on behalf of a death penalty defendant, much less written a dissent. Now, he wrote: "Unlike the majority, I do not believe that the evidence of the defendant's guilt is overwhelming. . . . I believe that errors requiring a new trial occurred."

There were three new justices: Mary Ann G. McMorrow, John L. Nickels, and Moses W. Harrison. Harrison's past opinions indicated he was the most likely to vote for Cruz; Nickels, who had a conservative suburban background, appeared to be the least likely, even though Gary Johnson's job as state's attorney had led him to be Nickel's honorary campaign chairman. If there was a two-to-one split, it seemed probable that McMorrow, a Democrat from Chicago, would be the swing vote.

Marshall believed that the Cruz case was no longer just a legal battle, it was a political fight as well. Careers of such top Illinois politicians as Jim Ryan and Roland Burris were tied up in it.

To counterbalance that, to show the court that this was a case that needed very careful scrutiny, the Cruz lawyers decided to approach important Illinois figures to submit amicus curiae (friend of the court) briefs on Cruz's behalf. Although Marshall was a board member of the local chapter of the American Civil Liberties Union, he didn't want the ACLU to file an amicus curiae brief. That would be too easy to dismiss as another left-wing attack on the death penalty itself. Nor did he want Amnesty International's support. The Supreme Court justices would not be surprised by a brief from that organization, either.

Instead, Cruz's supporters approached the heads of the major religions and the deans of Illinois law schools. Chicago's Joseph Cardinal Bernardin of the Catholic archdiocese signed on. So did the head of virtually every other major religion. And six of the nine law school deans in the state filed a brief, the first time anything like that had ever happened.

"The specter of Rolando Cruz's execution on the basis of the court's current opinion cannot help but erode the moral force of the law and the public's confidence in our criminal justice system," wrote the twenty-four Christian, Jewish, and Islamic leaders. "The planned execution . . . is fundamentally inconsistent with the requirement that only the clearly guilty be subjected to the ultimate penalty."

Another amicus curiae brief was filed by two death penalty scholars, Hugo A. Bedau and Michael L. Radelet, who wrote that of twenty-seven hundred death row cases in the nation, there was not one in which the evidence of innocence was clearer. Fifteen former federal or state prosecutors, including former Illinois attorney general Tyrone C. Fahner and former Illinois State Police director Jeremy D. Margolis, agreed to submit a brief. So did several lawyers' groups. Film stars John Cusack, Edward James Olmos, Tim Robbins, and Susan Sarandon added their support by joining a fund-raising committee for Cruz's defense.

The defense prepared as they had before: the same all-nighters, the same meetings on end, the same drafts and edits. On the very last day before the petition for rehearing was filed, someone said a more passionate ending was required.

Marshall was so burned out he couldn't even think of getting to the word processor and trying to write another word. He went home to sleep, and then he woke up at three in the morning. He went to the word processor and wrote:

> The long and tortured history of the Nicarico prosecutions is well known to all members of this court. It seems safe to say, without exaggeration, that the continued prosecution of Rolando Cruz has engendered more controversy and anguish than any other criminal prosecution in modern Illinois history. The possibility that Rolando Cruz would be executed notwithstanding the very grave doubts so many reasonable people—including Justices of this very Court—share about his guilt and the fairness of the trial that he received is a frightening prospect to proponents and opponents of the death penalty alike.
>
> The jury that convicted Cruz did not share these doubts because it was not allowed to share in the information that so conclusively established Brian Dugan's lone responsibility for heinous acts that were carried out on Jeanine Nicarico. The jury that convicted Rolando Cruz did not share these doubts because it was led to believe falsely, through what the court concedes to be several impermissible means, that Dugan and Cruz could somehow have acted together.

Later that morning, Marshall added:

> There is, at this stage, only one possible way of begin-
> ning down the road toward a conclusion of this case that will
> instill public confidence in the criminal justice system: as the
> dissenting justices urged, this Court must remand this case
> for a new trial at which the jury is provided with a fair and
> thorough presentation of all relevant evidence. Only then
> can we possibly move to a broadly shared consensus that jus-
> tice has been done.

The amicus curiae briefs and the petition for rehearing were
filed on February 4, 1993. On February 9, the Nicarico case was the
topic of the television program *Unsolved Mysteries.* On April 1, the
judiciary panel of the Illinois House of Representatives endorsed a
resolution calling on the Illinois Supreme Court to order new trials
for Cruz and Hernandez.

And then, again, there was nothing to do but wait.

The defense lawyers were exhausted. They knew if they
didn't win a rehearing, there was little hope that Rolando Cruz
could avoid a lethal injection. The only hope would be the federal
courts, and Cruz's prospects there seemed bleak. As slight as their
chances seemed with the petition for rehearing, this was the only
realistic remaining opportunity.

Marshall had slipped into a clinical depression so deep that he
started seeing a psychiatrist and getting counseling. How could he
remain part of a profession that allowed this magnitude of injustice, a profession in which someone at the very top could create
lies like this? This wasn't about bad judgment, this wasn't simply
about reasonable minds differing. This was about the power of a
Supreme Court justice to make something up out of thin air.
Nobody could do anything about it.

The lawyers waited and waited. Finally, on May 28, 1993, Marshall got a voice mail message that he kept for years. Robert Schueler of the Illinois Supreme Court left word saying that the court had issued an order granting a rehearing in the case of Rolando Cruz. The attorney general's office was ordered to file its reply to the brief seeking a rehearing within two weeks. The defense lawyers were to reply within a week after that. And oral arguments were scheduled for June 22. Everything was to happen within the next three and a half weeks.

Where depression had reigned, ecstasy started shining. The lawyers knew that the court did not typically grant rehearings just to affirm a decision already made. The court had no reason to call for a new round of filings and arguments just to reach the same result. So in all probability, the court was leaning toward a new trial for Cruz. After all those depressing months of waiting, of feeling that the criminal justice system had coldly turned a deaf ear to Rolando Cruz's pleas, there was new hope. Probably too overconfident, Marshall went out and celebrated with a lovely dinner. He was elated.

Then it was time to get ready for the new oral arguments before the Illinois Supreme Court. The lawyers went through the same preparation they had for the first oral arguments. This time, the focus would be a little different, because it was now much more on the court's opinion. The defense lawyers knew how some of the justices had voted the first time around, so they knew where to direct their arguments. They needed to explain the audacity of the claim that there was overwhelming evidence—including physical evidence—against Cruz. They had to show that the court could not ignore the errors it had admitted occurred. Special attention had to be given to any questions from Justice McMorrow, whom the defense team still considered to be the swing vote.

The oral arguments were held on June 22, the same date as the previous oral arguments a year earlier. As Marshall made his arguments, Justice Heiple never looked at him. Instead, Heiple stared up at the ceiling the entire time. This time, however, Marshall did get questions, mostly from McMorrow. McMorrow seemed interested in mistakes that Dugan had made in telling his story. That was chilling; McMorrow was the key vote, and if she didn't believe the Dugan evidence was significant, she might very well seal Rolando Cruz's fate.

In a dramatic moment, Chief Justice Miller directly asked assistant attorney general Terence Madsen whether there was any physical evidence tying Rolando Cruz to the case. It was a direct confrontation by Miller of Heiple. Madsen paused and admitted that, no, there was no physical evidence that itself tied Cruz to the case. There was physical evidence, he said, to corroborate certain parts of Cruz's "vision" statement. But there was no physical evidence linking him to the crime.

And then, once again, the oral arguments were over, and there was nothing to do but wait.

In September, Marshall and John Hanlon met with DuPage County state's attorney Jim Ryan and offered a deal. Cruz would agree not to sue DuPage County for anything that had been done to him. He would agree never to talk publicly about the case. He would plead guilty to perjury and obstruction of justice for what he said before the grand jury. He would make a public statement accepting responsibility in some part for having lied to the police, for attracting attention to himself. He would be sentenced to the time he already had served in prison. The case would be over.

Ryan, however, refused to deal.

Then it was time to wait again. A piece about the case appeared on the CBS program *60 Minutes* on October 17, 1993, providing some distraction. The segment didn't draw a strong conclusion, however, and the defense team soon returned to wondering when the court would announce its decision.

The lawyers had assumed the court would take reasonably quick action, but they were wrong. Autumn slipped by, winter came and went.

In February 1994, *Chicago Tribune* columnist Eric Zorn wrote the first of what would be a long series of columns attacking the handling of the Jeanine Nicarico murder case. In his columns, Zorn cast doubt on the Cruz "vision" statement, the witnesses who testified against Cruz and Hernandez, and the attempt to discredit Brian Dugan's account.

Of the "vision" statement, he wrote, "Hey, it could have happened, right? The biggest break in the biggest murder case in DuPage County history could have slipped into the cracks for a year and a half."

Of the jailhouse testimony, he wrote, "Is there a jailhouse snitch out there so vile and nakedly opportunistic that DuPage prosecutors would be embarrassed to put him on the witness stand?

"And is there a representation of physical evidence so blatantly and demonstrably false that they would decline, in good conscience, to make it to a jury?"

In response, Anton R. Valukas, the former U.S. attorney for northern Illinois and a Ryan ally, wrote in a letter to the *Chicago Tribune*: "I was given access to the prosecutors' entire file to explore the retrial of Rolando Cruz. I concluded that there was no legal or ethical reason why this case should not be presented to a jury for determination."

In March, DuPage County state's attorney Jim Ryan won the Republican nomination to run for the post of Illinois attorney general, which Roland Burris was vacating so he could run for governor. The *Chicago Tribune,* despite Zorn's columns, endorsed Ryan.

The *Chicago Sun-Times* objected.

"Despite an otherwise effective record of performance as DuPage County state's attorney, charges that Ryan mishandled the notorious Jeanine Nicarico case are too troubling to ignore, especially since they involve questions of whether an innocent man might be executed for the murder of the ten-year-old girl," the *Sun-Times* wrote. "Because the charges relate directly to his performance as a chief prosecutor, they are enough for us to question whether he should now become the state's chief law enforcement officer."

After the primary election, which Ryan won easily, things quieted down. Spring swelled into summer, and there still was no word about Cruz's case.

Rolando Cruz was getting really depressed. In late June, he received a visit from Rubin "Hurricane" Carter. Carter had spent nineteen years in prison after he was convicted of shooting two patrons and a bartender at the Lafayette Bar & Grill in Paterson, New Jersey. Bob Dylan's 1975 song "Hurricane" made Carter's long ordeal a cause célèbre. Finally, Carter was freed in 1985 after a federal judge ruled his second conviction was based on "racial stereotypes" and errors by the prosecution.

Carter had been communicating with Rolando, and the two had become very close. Lazarus Martin, who lived with Carter and was the subject of the book *Lazarus and the Hurricane,* came along, and Marshall came, too.

At first, the men were not permitted in the same room and

had to remain separated by bars. In the course of their conversation, Carter stood up and shouted, "No! No!" It was, Marshall said later, as if he wanted to rip the bars out. He was a powerful man, and his emotion was genuine. Everyone broke down. Rolando said he couldn't deal with the waiting, the imprisonment anymore. Lazarus said, "Look, if I could learn to read when I was 16 years old, you can learn. You can get past this."

"It was an incredibly intense day," Marshall said.

And still there was nothing to do but wait. No one could figure out why it was taking so long. They had argued the case in June 1993, and now it was the summer of 1994. Finally, in July the lawyers received a call. A decision was going to be announced.

On July 14, Bastille Day, Marshall again made the trip to the Supreme Court office in Chicago. There was the same gathering of lawyers, although by now the Illinois Supreme Court had moved to new offices on 160 N. La Salle. There were the same prayers, the same debate about whether it did any good to pray at that point. And then the doors opened. How would Justice Mary Ann G. McMorrow have voted?

It didn't take long to get the answer. Justice McMorrow, whom the lawyers all along had seen as the swing vote, had voted to affirm Cruz's conviction.

"The record demonstrates that the defendant did receive a fair trial," she wrote. McMorrow admitted that the Erma Rodriguez and bloodhound testimonies were improper, but she didn't think they amounted to reversible error.

It didn't matter that Cruz's second jury convicted him based on a theory that was different from that at the first trial. It didn't matter that twelve jurors believed one thing and twelve other jurors believed something else.

"To date, 24 impartial jurors have found defendant Cruz guilty beyond a reasonable doubt," McMorrow wrote. "Considering all of the evidence in this case, I submit that it cannot be concluded that the jury's determination that defendant was guilty was palpably erroneous."

In a separate opinion, Justice Heiple dismissed Dugan's confession statements as "unquestionably false."

"It was an abuse of discretion to admit them into evidence," he wrote.

He called the law school deans who spoke on Cruz's behalf a "questionable cabal." Although he didn't apologize for his own errors in referring to overwhelming evidence and physical evidence, he assumed that the religious leaders hadn't done enough research.

"How many among them took the time to sift through the several thousand pages of transcripts and the numerous exhibits in order to form a knowledgeable judgment?" he wrote. "The 24 religious leaders who combined to use their names in a joint appeal to this court, even when considered collectively, do not have the knowledge of this case which is possessed by even one of the jurors who heard the testimony and received the evidence at the trial."

Yes, McMorrow and Heiple had voted against Cruz, but it didn't matter. McMorrow's was not the only surprising vote. Justice John L. Nickels, the law-and-order justice from Kane County, had voted to overturn Cruz's conviction, and his vote was enough. By a vote of four to three, Cruz was going to get a new trial.

"We are profoundly aware of the impact our decision will have upon Jeanine Nicarico's surviving family and friends," Justice Freeman wrote for the majority. "We are not insensitive to their personal anguish and tragedy. Not only have they suffered the unspeakable nightmare of her loss, but they are denied closure by our justice system, again and again. We deeply regret any role we play in prolonging their struggle and grief. Yet we are duty bound to play a larger role in preserving that very basic guarantee of our democratic society, that every person, however culpable, is entitled to a fair and impartial trial. We cannot deviate from the obligations of that role. The resulting loss to our entire society would be too great."

In his dissent—perhaps unintentionally commenting on the reliability of the criminal justice system—Heiple called a third trial for Cruz "another roll of the dice."

"Even an acquittal is a possibility," he worried.

Heiple was joined in his opinion by Bilandic, a former Chicago mayor who had succeeded Miller as the court's chief justice. Freeman and Nickels were joined in the majority by Justices Harrison and Miller.

Rolando Cruz, still on death row at the Menard Correctional Center, had mixed feelings. On the one hand, he was very excited that his death penalty conviction had been overturned a second time—the first instance of that in Illinois history. On the other, he'd had a conviction overturned before, and it had left him right where he'd begun—in a dark, dreary cell where he ate alone and was limited to one personal phone call a week and five visits a month. His lawyers seemed confident, but he'd seen that in the past as well. After all, Jed Stone had talked openly of getting him home for Christmas in 1989, more than four years before.

That night, the defense team had a party on Clark Street in Chicago. Many people who had been involved in the case stopped by. Ed Cisowski came. Mary Brigid Kenney arrived. Even as they celebrated a brief victory, however, they knew a hard road lay ahead. The Supreme Court had not ruled that the evidence was insufficient for a new trial. DuPage County state's attorney Jim Ryan already had told the news media that he would retry Cruz.

In reply, Marshall publicly asked Ryan to appoint an independent attorney to review the case.

"We need to get politics out of this picture," Marshall told reporters. "This case has been mired in politics from the beginning. . . . It's asking too much to think that he [Ryan] could be neutral."

In announcing that he would retry Cruz, Ryan had said the Supreme Court issued a mandate to try the case again, which enraged Marshall.

"When a court remands for a new trial, it is never telling you to retry, it is saying you *can* retry," Marshall said later. "Every first-year law student knows that. But he was just the same as Roland Burris. Everybody wants to pass the buck, to say: 'I'm not making any decisions. I'm just doing my job.' "

On July 17, 1994, the *Chicago Tribune* printed an editorial agreeing that Ryan should retry Cruz. "Ryan's decision to try Cruz again is also proper," it stated. "The high court found trial errors; it didn't find Cruz not guilty."

19

TOM BREEN

Sometimes in a crime of great viciousness, the jury gets carried away with the crime and doesn't look at the defendant's relationship to it.

Frederick R. Cohn, lawyer for Chicagoan Wilbur McDonald, exonerated two years after a 1971 conviction for a savage rape and murder, *Chicago Sun-Times*, August 16, 1973

Tom Breen was not a cause lawyer.

Breen, the son of an FBI agent and attorney, was a well-regarded Chicago defense lawyer who had previously been a prosecutor for ten years. Once, while prosecuting a rape case, he'd said to jurors, "If you don't think this man is dangerous, just remember he's an El ride and a transfer away from your door." Breen also had been a special prosecutor of seventeen Illinois prison inmates charged with starting a 1978 riot that killed three guards. Later, he would defend Illinois governor George Ryan's campaign organization against fraud charges.

For the most part, he thought, he had always represented his clients to the best of his ability. But a cause lawyer? One of those lawyers who took up crusades? Not Breen. For one thing, he thought the criminal justice system functioned fairly well.

When Breen had been a brand-new assistant state's attorney in 1973 in Chicago's Criminal Courts Building at Twenty-sixth Street and California Avenue, doubts had been raised about the conviction of a machinist named Wilbur McDonald. In 1971, McDonald had been sentenced to serve up to 150 years in prison for the 1970 rape and murder of a woman in Grant Park, on the city's lakefront.

In 1973, police had arrested a serial killer named Lester Harrison in the act of murdering another woman in Grant Park. Harrison had confessed not only to that murder but also to three others in the park, including the one for which McDonald had been convicted. Harrison had been able to tell prosecutors details of the 1970 murder that only the culprit would have known. Within twenty-four hours, Wilbur McDonald had been brought back from Stateville Prison and released on bond. Several weeks later, the case against him had been dropped, and the slightly built man had returned to his former job at Central Scientific Company, where he had been given the same salary raises and seniority that he would have received had he never gone to prison. To Breen, there had been nothing surprising about the state's attorney's actions. That was what you were supposed to do when you found out you had made a mistake.

Breen had had his faith in the system shaken later when he represented a man named Gary Dotson, who was convicted of rape in 1979. The victim, Cathleen Crowell Webb, recanted in 1985, admitting she was trying to cover up a sexual encounter with her boyfriend. The case wound up on national television. James R. Thompson, then the governor of Illinois, held a hearing and compromised. Thompson (who became known to the nation in 2004 as a member of the commission investigating the September 11, 2001, terrorist attacks) decided that Dotson was guilty but that he'd been in prison long enough and could go free with a commuted sentence.

Breen thought the jury never should have convicted Dotson in the first place. When Webb recanted, a judge should have granted Dotson a new trial. And when the case got to the governor, he should have ruled that Dotson was innocent.

Finally, a DNA test excluded Dotson as a suspect, and after much legal wrangling, Dotson won a new trial. Charges against him were dropped—four years after Webb recanted and twelve years after he was first accused. Even then, prosecutors wouldn't admit that Dotson was innocent. That case taught Breen about the prosecution complex, but he thought it was a rare phenomenon.

Breen had been brought into the Cruz case by Larry Marshall. When it came time to find trial lawyers for Cruz's third trial, Marshall had started out with several lawyers in mind. He'd decided, though, not to trust his own hunches. Instead, he'd called about thirty lawyers around the city and offered this scenario: Your son has just been arrested in DuPage County in a high-profile case. He's had his conviction overturned twice. Which lawyers, if you had enough money, are you going to go to for the retrial?

As the answers came back, certain names kept being repeated. They weren't necessarily the names Marshall expected. Many of the city's most prominent names didn't make it onto many lists. Some weren't thought to deserve their reputations. Others didn't work hard enough.

While traveling out West, Marshall stopped in to talk to Gerry Spence, the Wyoming "cowboy" lawyer who had successfully defended Imelda Marcos, won the Karen Silkwood nuclear contamination case, and gained an acquittal for Randy Weaver in the Ruby Ridge case. Spence expressed interest, but the two lawyers couldn't work out a way to handle the case with an out-of-town attorney.

Instead, Marshall selected ten of the top names on his list and started calling them.

Almost all of them said they would be interested, even though Marshall made it clear that there was no money up front, that there was only a slim hope of money from fund-raising, and that, in fact, there would be many out-of-pocket expenses.

Several of the final ten lawyers on Marshall's list dropped out because of schedule issues or other reasons. Six or seven visited Cruz, and the question of who would be Rolando Cruz's new lawyers became an item of public interest. The *Chicago Tribune* reported that Gerry Spence was "very interested." Ultimately, however, it became clear that three Chicago lawyers would be the choices: Tom Breen, age forty-seven; Matt Kennelly, thirty-seven; and Nan Nolan, fifty-one.

At first, Breen had misgivings about taking the case. He knew that it would mean long, heart-wrenching, rotten months. He knew it was the kind of case in which he was likely to get emotionally involved.

It sounded too much like a cause.

When Breen met Cruz, however, he wound up liking him immediately, and he decided to take the case.

"I was absolutely shocked that a guy who had been in prison so long could be so polite and that he could have such a good sense of humor," Breen said. "He was a complete and utter sports fanatic who knew every ballplayer on every baseball and every football team. He's a complete sports nut. I had a good time with him, and I just ended up walking out of there shaking my head."

To Breen, the first trial seemed to have been a farce, a sham. There was no way the three defendants should have been tried together.

In the second trial, it seemed the prosecution had just out-and-out cheated. The prosecutors had used a shifting theory: first, that Dugan didn't do it, then that Dugan might have done it together with Cruz. The state had taken advantage of a heinous crime that would impassion the jury. Testimony had been fabricated and a conviction secured, he concluded.

By this time, Rolando Cruz had been moved from the state prison to the DuPage County Jail. For some of the minor pretrial matters, Larry Marshall had represented Cruz by himself. One day, both men traveled through almost every criminal judge's courtroom as judge after judge recused himself or herself from the case. Edward Kowal, the original presiding judge who had since become chief judge, was not hearing criminal cases any longer. John J. Nelligan, who had presided over Alex Hernandez's third trial, recused himself. Finally, Marshall and Cruz ended up in the courtroom of Judge Ronald Mehling. Marshall was pleased; he had heard that Mehling was a fair-minded judge.

Once the trial team was put into place, the question became how to plan a strategy and organize the vast amount of material that had accumulated over the years. Tom Breen argued that the case had to be won witness by witness before the lawyers ever walked into court. It was too much to ask of a judge or jury to conclude that the jailhouse snitches and police officers were lying or mistaken unless there was overwhelming evidence. A huge effort was needed to uncover overlooked information. They had many facts in their favor already, but they needed more. They needed to dig into the Cruz case the way Bill Clutter and Michael Metnick had dug into the Hernandez case, only more so.

"To properly prepare this case you had to go back to square one, and you had to examine each and every piece of evidence,"

Breen said. "I started with this, that Rolando Cruz was innocent. I firmly, firmly believed it. If Rolando Cruz was innocent and I was right, then every piece of evidence that they used and pointed toward him had to be either a mistake or had to be a lie. Because evidence doesn't point to innocent people unless somebody twists it to point that way.

"So we went back to square one."

That meant the defense team would spend months focusing on the evidence against Cruz without even starting to look at anything relating to Brian Dugan. To begin, Breen met with John Sam in a little corner restaurant near Sam's new job in a heating business. Sam turned out to be a tough nut to crack. He didn't want to talk to Breen, didn't want to waste any more time in court. He told Breen that he sounded just like the other lawyers who had come into the case. None of them had been able to free Cruz or Hernandez, and almost everyone who tried to help had lost a job, put strain on their personal relationships or seen their lives swallowed up by a huge effort that seemed to gain nothing.

As the two men started on their second pot of coffee, Breen explained his plan to start reinvestigating everything from scratch. The defense had a great group of people, he said, but they needed Sam's help. By the third pot of coffee, Sam's resolve had weakened. He agreed to do what he could.

Much of that new investigative burden would fall on the shoulders of John Eierman, a former Chicago police officer who often had worked with Tom Breen in the past. One of Eierman's first assignments was to talk to a witness who had not testified at the earlier trials, Stephen Schmitt.

Schmitt had talked to authorities a couple of weeks after the Illinois Supreme Court decided to overturn Cruz's case for the

second time. A DuPage County detective and assistant DuPage
state's attorney Joseph Birkett had met with him and then written
up a report saying Schmitt had known Cruz in the DuPage County
Jail. Cruz, the report stated, had admitted that he'd murdered
Jeanine together with Brian Dugan and Alex Hernandez and that
Brian Dugan had raped her but that Cruz had killed her.

Breen didn't believe for a moment that Cruz actually had
made the statement. It was too much of an amazing coincidence
that the jailhouse snitches kept coming up with statements that
precisely matched the needs of the state at the moment. Why
would Cruz keep confessing to people in a way that supported the
prosecutors' changing theories?

At first, the prosecutors sought to show that Cruz,
Hernandez, and Stephen Buckley were the guilty parties. Steven
Pecoraro, Stephen Ford, and others backed up that theory with
quotes they claimed to have heard from Cruz. By the time of
Cruz's second trial, the prosecutors no longer could persuasively
deny that Dugan was involved, so they argued that he might have
been involved but that Cruz was the rapist. Robert Turner testified
in support of that theory. As Cruz's third trial approached, however, prosecutors knew that a new DNA test might show Dugan
was the rapist. Now Stephen Schmitt was ready to testify that
Cruz admitted to him that Dugan was the rapist but Cruz was the
one who killed Jeanine. It just defied belief.

In fact, Breen thought, it was almost laughable. Inmates consider a child-killer the lowest life form behind bars. For example, in
1985, when child-killer Brian Dugan was taken to the Joliet
Correctional Center, other convicts taunted him and dumped
feces and trash on him. On July 30, 1987, another inmate, saying he
was offended by the nature of Dugan's crimes, stabbed him nine

times. Since then, Dugan had spent much of his time in single-prisoner cells for his protection.

On top of that, Cruz was a Latino in a county jail populated mostly with white inmates. How could anyone believe that Cruz would freely admit to those inmates that he had brutally murdered a white girl? The other inmates would turn on him in a second. Even if he were guilty, someone in Cruz's position would not say anything to anyone.

Meanwhile, the defense tried an unusual legal tactic. The lawyers asked the judge to force the prosecutors to tell them exactly what theory the state would use this time—what's called a bill of particulars. The state's theories had changed several times over the past ten years about where the victim had been killed and who'd killed her. The defense lawyers argued they needed to know what theory would be used this time so that they could prepare themselves.

It was a difficult motion because in some sense judges had already rejected it in earlier trials. Judge Mehling, however, looked at the record and looked at some changes in the law. How can there be an effective defense, Judge Mehling agreed, when the defense doesn't know what their client is accused of doing? So Judge Mehling ordered the prosecutors to provide a bill of particulars. The prosecutors appealed, and the issue finally went up to the Illinois Supreme Court, which decided in Cruz's favor.

Breen and the other lawyers rented two small offices in the Monadnock Building, where Breen's offices were located in downtown Chicago. The lawyers called it their "war room." They bought shelving, rented a copier, and started assembling files. Much of the organizing was done by Jeanine Bell, who worked for Marshall at Northwestern University. She volunteered several hours each evening to catalog the thousands of police reports, investigators' reports, transcripts, and other documents. When she was finished, the lawyers had a file on each person who appeared in the case, and each file contained every report mentioning that person.

The lawyers also charted what the prosecution's case was and what their rebuttals would be. They prepared time lines to help organize the evidence. The entire system came to be flippantly referred to as CMS, or case management system.

Each Monday evening, the lawyers met to discuss the case. They also talked by phone or met with one another almost every day. Often the Monday meetings ran until nearly midnight. Sometimes the mood was lighthearted because everyone knew they had to maintain a sense of humor to keep going for the long run. At other times the meetings got tense. One of the things that always created tension in the room was the discussion of the death penalty. Lawyers in a capital case need to prepare for a death penalty hearing even as they prepare their case in chief, but it's hard to talk about for lawyers who are confident they will win.

At those meetings, the lawyers debated whether to have a jury or a bench trial. So far, no jury had acquitted any of the defendants. One school of thought said that an innocent defendant is better off with a judge deciding guilt or innocence because a judge usually will be less emotional. That strategy doesn't work with a judge who already has made up his or her mind that the defendant is guilty, but the lawyers thought Judge Mehling had not. They decided to waive Cruz's right to a jury.

Meanwhile, John Eierman, Breen's investigator, had started digging up more information. When Eierman went to talk to Stephen Schmitt, Schmitt admitted that his story was not true. He said authorities had told him he would get in trouble if he didn't go along with them. He was afraid he would be sent back to jail.

Schmitt then signed an affidavit saying that he had merely repeated what the police had told him to say.

The lawyers also noticed that Steven Pecoraro, who had been a jailhouse snitch in the first and second trials, had been represented by a lawyer with whom Breen had worked in the past. They called her and said they would like to talk to Steve Pecoraro about the case. She talked to Pecoraro, and he said that he did want to talk.

Eierman and one of the lawyers went to see him in a shop that he owned. Pecoraro said that his testimony had been coerced. He had testified against Cruz because the police had urged him to and because he was convinced that Cruz was guilty anyway. The next day, Eierman, Breen, Marshall, and one of the law students helping out on the case visited Pecoraro again. This time he gave them a signed statement. In the statement, Pecoraro said his testimony implicating Cruz had been false. In fact, he said, Cruz always said that he was innocent. As the lawyers prepared to leave, Pecoraro grabbed Marshall, hugged him, started crying, and said, as Marshall recalled later, "Please tell Rolando I am sorry. I didn't mean to hurt him."

Then Detective Warren Wilkosz paid a visit to Pecoraro. In his report of that visit, Wilkosz wrote, "Pecoraro advised that he met with the defense lawyers and they told him that if he testified again he would be charged in federal court with perjury."

Once again, Breen's team of defense lawyers suspected that a police report with false or misleading information had been filed. But this time it turned out they didn't have to guess. A surveillance camera had captured the entire conversation, making it clear that Wilkosz's statement was inaccurate.

On the videotape made by the surveillance camera, Wilkosz repeatedly asked Pecoraro whether the defense lawyers had influenced him.

"No, no, nothing like that," Pecoraro said.

"These guys pressure you or what?" Wilkosz said.

"No," Pecoraro responded.

"Did they bust your balls?"

"No."

In a sense, that surveillance camera was focused on the whole case. It was Wilkosz who had been the one who had gone to see jailer Howard Keltner right before Keltner suddenly came forward with his new story about Hernandez's admissions on the night he was jailed. Wilkosz had helped to secure the statement by Stephen Schmitt against Cruz. Wilkosz had filed the report that Erma Rodriguez said was untrue. It was Wilkosz who was accused of threatening to beat Jackie Estremera.

Now, here was a videotape that showed that Wilkosz had filed a report containing a misleading assertion. It was a sweet moment for the frustrated defense lawyers who had struggled with the case over the years.

At the same time, however, the defense lawyers realized that the most damaging element in the case against Rolando Cruz was the "vision" statement. Yet no one had put James Montesano, now a sheriff's lieutenant, on the stand and asked him whether Detectives Thomas Vosburgh and Dennis Kurzawa had really told him about it. During trial preparations, Randy Garrett had suggested that the defense do just that. The two detectives had claimed that after they'd heard the "vision" statement they'd made a telephone call to Montesano, who then was supervisor in the violent crimes section of the sheriff's detective bureau. Montesano, they said, had told them to call Tom Knight. They had called Knight, and he had told them not to write anything down.

Knight, Vosburgh, and Kurzawa had testified about the "vision" statement during the previous trials, but Montesano never had. Why not? His testimony would have helped establish that the "vision" statement had really taken place. Perhaps the reason he hadn't been asked to testify was that he wouldn't go along with the "vision" statement. Perhaps the defense lawyers should smoke him out—subpoena him in a pretrial hearing and hear what he had to say.

Moreover, Garrett said John Sam had always portrayed Montesano as dubious about the case from the beginning and as a straight shooter who wouldn't want to lie on the stand.

It was a tough decision, because the defense team didn't know what Montesano was going to say. They might create a witness who then would testify against them in the upcoming trial. He might have told prosecutors: Don't call me, but if push comes to shove, I'll stick with your story.

Despite the risks, the defense lawyers decided to do it.

Up until that point, the defense lawyers thought the pretrial maneuvers had gone very well. Stephen Schmitt and Steven Pecoraro had been neutralized. Things were gelling. Calling Lieutenant Montesano was a gamble.

A two-day hearing was held at the end of August 1995. On August 31, Montesano was called in to testify, and he looked awful. He obviously did not want to be there. The defense lawyers were excited. They could smell a huge breakthrough.

It didn't work out that way, though. Although Montesano said he didn't remember many specifics, he did recall Detectives Vosburgh and Kurzawa talking to him in May 1983 about statements that Cruz had made while at the sheriff's headquarters. Looking very uncomfortable as he testified, Montesano said he believed Vosburgh had called him at home and told him that Cruz had had a vision that included details the detectives thought he shouldn't have known.

The defense lawyers were sinking in their chairs. They'd created a monster. Here was a lieutenant—a man with credibility—now becoming the fourth person to support the story of the "vision" statement. Tom Breen called Randy Garrett, who had been so sure Montesano would not lie on the stand. "You're a fucking good judge of character," Breen snapped.

A day or two later, Nan Nolan discussed the outcome of the hearing with Garrett, who apologized for suggesting that they call Montesano. The witnesses at the hearing had said the initial conversation among Vosburgh, Kurzawa, and Montesano took place on May 9, 1983, a Friday night, and that they gave the details to Tom Knight the following Monday, right before a grand jury session. Garrett told Nolan that the days of the week in that account couldn't be correct; the special grand jury met only on Thursdays.

When he checked, Garrett saw that May 9, 1983, was a Monday. Why had the witnesses changed the day of the week? How could they mistake the day of the grand jury meetings when the panel had met on the same day every week for more than a year? Garrett suggested that Nolan check to see if any of those involved in testimony about the Cruz "vision" statement were not at work on Monday, May 9, 1983. Perhaps that would explain why the witnesses were changing the day.

Nolan brought up the point with the other defense lawyers, who said they already had noticed the change. However, no one checked to see if anyone was missing from work on the Monday in question.

All the defense team could do at that point was to keep trying to make their case stronger. Larry Marshall, Jeanine Bell, and a law student went to Georgia and North Carolina to look for prosecution witness Ramon Mares, although they never found him. John Eierman uncovered a new puzzle: Kerry Morrick—one of the men who'd found Jeanine's body—knew Brian Dugan well, according to longtime area resident Mark Benson, who knew both Morrick and Dugan. Benson said Morrick and Dugan regularly would play pool together at a bar after work on Fridays. Because Jeanine Nicarico was murdered on a Friday and Morrick was among the men who later told police where the body was, the defense team wondered whether Dugan might have told Morrick about the murder or even taken him to the Prairie Path to show him where the body was. A West Chicago man, John F. Symiwicz, had told the FBI that he saw an unattended, medium-size, dark-colored sedan that might have been a pre-1975 Ford product parked at 5:15 P.M. on Eola Road about five hundred feet from the Prairie Path entrance on the day of the crime. The description was similar to that of Dugan's car. Breen, Eierman, and Marshall went to Maine and interviewed Charles Bryant, Morrick's partner at the Prairie Path, but never established any proof that Dugan talked to Morrick about the body.

Eierman also found an ex-inmate who said he had been regularly raped in jail until Cruz had come to his aid. In apparent retaliation, the ex-inmate's assailant had later testified against Cruz.

The defense lawyers learned from Thomas McCulloch, Brian Dugan's lawyer, that Dugan had said prosecutors had offered him a deal if he would testify that he'd committed the crime with Cruz. The prosecutors, who earlier had kept saying Dugan's word was worthless, now apparently were willing to use his testimony. McCulloch was angry that they talked to Dugan without McCulloch present.

Meanwhile, the biggest pretrial question was about to be settled—the new DNA test.

An earlier test had established that Dugan's DNA was the same category as the DNA found in semen taken from Jeanine's body. That test, however, could not exclude Cruz. In August 1994, Marshall had met with Ed Blake, who had conducted that test. Now, Blake said, there was new technology that might be able to determine a much closer match. Blake tested some preliminary samples and said that there was enough DNA available for the new test. Finally, after several weeks of work, he told the lawyers he was almost finished and would have the results of the testing on the following Friday, September 21. He asked that the lawyers set up a conference call that included both prosecutors and defense lawyers.

At the appointed time, the lawyers called Blake, who said he wasn't ready yet. He said the results would be ready about four hours later, at about 3:00 P.M. Chicago time.

Marshall felt absolutely paralyzed; he didn't doubt Rolando, but so many things had gone wrong. He didn't know what to expect from the test. Perhaps the specimen had even been contaminated by some sinister people.

Finally it was time. A conference call was set up with DuPage County prosecutor Christopher Wheaton, the defense lawyers, and Blake. It was more frightening than waiting for a verdict. A verdict could always be appealed, but a DNA test could not.

Even as Blake started to talk, he kept the suspense mounting. He said that he had conclusive results and that they had identified one person and excluded another. Finally, he said who the results matched: Brian Dugan. There was a chance of only three in ten thousand that the sample could have come from someone else. Cruz was absolutely excluded.

On the phone, the defense lawyers were very reserved. In the office, however, they were thrusting their fists in the air, signaling triumph. There could be no more claiming that Dugan was just a liar who was making up his story. Dugan wasn't, as Judge Nolan had called him so long ago, just a bad actor. The new DNA test had established once and for all that Dugan was indeed the rapist, just as he had said ten years earlier.

20

SCOTT TUROW

On an almost unimaginable scale, evidence had been manufactured, witnesses coerced, facts twisted beyond recognition to fit government theories, evidence of innocence kept hidden from those accused and tried.

Edward Humes, *Mean Justice*

ALTHOUGH HE WAS KNOWN chiefly as the author of the book *Presumed Innocent* and other best-selling legal thrillers, Scott Turow also was a well-respected Chicago lawyer and former federal prosecutor. He'd heard something of the cases against Hernandez and Cruz and knew that another man, Dugan, had claimed to be the real killer.

The line among prosecutors was that Dugan was just a buddy of the others who was enjoying himself by screwing with the system. That sounded plausible to Turow. His impression was a prosecutor's impression: here are two defendants beefing, as usual.

Then Turow got a call from Jeremy Margolis, a former federal prosecutor and the former director of the Illinois State Police. Margolis said Hernandez was innocent, and he wanted Turow to take the case.

In Turow's opinion, Margolis was an avid lawman, the greatest gunslinger in the West. And yet Margolis also was unusually sensitive about innocent suspects getting caught up in the machinery of the law.

In 1975, Margolis had prosecuted a man named Darryl Biddings. Almost a dozen witnesses had identified Biddings as the man who had walked into the Queen of the Sea restaurant on Chicago's South Side, sprayed the restaurant with gunfire, abducted a father and son at gunpoint, shot them in a ditch in Indiana, and left them for dead. All the witnesses had good visibility, and none had a motive to lie.

Eventually, an FBI agent who had a hunch that the case was going in the wrong direction tracked down the real criminal, who by then was in an Indiana prison. Margolis had been mortified.

"When Jeremy said Hernandez was innocent, I knew he was really sensitive on the subject," Turow said. "Although he was a really zealous prosecutor and a very zealous police officer when he was chief of the state police, he also was somebody who never wanted to see the system misfire again. So when he said that, I figured, there may be something here."

Turow met with Margolis and Jeffrey Urdangen, but he wasn't optimistic about the case. Let's be realistic, Turow told them. It's hard to believe that the system is so screwed up that an innocent man would be convicted twice. That seems just about impossible. Moreover, Turow said, no one will ever get the appellate court to reverse the conviction. The Illinois Supreme Court already had given Hernandez his second bite at the apple. He'd had it, he'd lost, he was finished.

Margolis and Urdangen weren't surprised at Turow's reaction, and they didn't argue with him. Instead, they asked him to read Larry Marshall's brief in the Cruz case.

"I did that over the weekend, and my impression, my very

strong impression, was that the ruling excluding the evidence of Dugan and his other crimes was a legal outrage," Turow said later. "I have always felt that similar-act evidence is not treated correctly, that it should be much more frequently admissible. I knew there was absolutely no excuse in the world not to have let this evidence in. None. There was no prejudice. The state can't be prejudiced. And because Alex Hernandez had been the victim of the same ruling, I said, 'Okay, I'll take the case.'"

The case was legally meritorious, Turow told himself. But as for Hernandez really being innocent? There wasn't much chance of that, he thought.

Over the Thanksgiving weekend of 1991, Turow took all twenty thousand pages of the Hernandez trial record to a vacation home in southern Wisconsin to read it. Never before in his career as a lawyer had anything tormented and upset him so much. It was suddenly crystal clear what had happened. In the federal courts where he had worked, Turow had never seen prosecutorial over-reaching so wanton, committed with such abandon. By the time he got to the end of the second Hernandez trial and compared the overwhelming evidence of Dugan's guilt with the ridiculous, minuscule case against Alex Hernandez, it made him feel ashamed to be a lawyer. In Turow's opinion, it was clear that Hernandez had been railroaded.

"I had never seen anything like it. When I got to Robert Kilander and those shoeprints and the business of putting a witness on the stand to testify that they were size 6 shoes and never informing the defense that it was a women's size 6—I thought that stuff had gone out in the early nineteen thirties," Turow said. "I didn't think prosecutors in this country still did things like that. To try to put somebody to death with evidence that you knew was going to be misconstrued by the jury as probative of guilt when you knew in fact that it was probative of innocence? I'd never seen anything like that."

Turow's experience was in the federal courts. He knew that some prosecutors and police officers who worked in the state court system thought people in the federal system didn't understand the problems the state court lawyers faced. Federal prosecutors have the luxury of pursuing people who cheat on their taxes, bribe judges, pay off other people. Nobody is murdered because of those criminals. Nobody is raped. Nobody is beaten. If one of those criminals has to be freed because of an arcane legal principle, so what?

State courts, on the other hand, deal with some criminals who are a threat to the peace and security of the community. If a guilty defendant goes free, innocent citizens might very well be hurt. Moreover, there are so many burdens on the prosecution—so many loopholes, technicalities, and traps for the unwary—that prosecutors sometimes have to push the envelope if they are to ensure that criminals are sent to the penitentiary.

The problem with that line of thinking, Turow knew, is that prosecutors begin to lose their ability to recognize that the defendant is entitled to go free when the evidence isn't there. Then the prosecution complex sets in. Prosecutors start assuming that defendants are guilty and that the lack of evidence is merely another technicality. At that point, prosecutors are at risk of putting innocent people in prison or even on death row. If the jury is emotionally caught up in the case, it won't act as a check on the prosecutors.

That's what Turow suspected had happened to Hernandez.

"No crime is less likely to lead to rational deliberations than the abduction, rape, sodomization, and brutal murder of a ten-year-old child, especially when it is proven with gruesome photographic evidence presented daily in the presence of her grieving parents," Turow later wrote in his appeal.

Dugan, Turow thought, had an obvious motive to tell the truth: he was cutting a deal. If he could have named Cruz and Hernandez as two other guilty parties, he'd have done so in a heartbeat. The only reason he'd admitted the crime was that he'd done it. He'd get the same sentence no matter how many crimes he confessed to, and if he confessed to all those in which he was a suspect, he wouldn't have to worry about newly discovered evidence coming back to haunt him later.

Turow started meeting with Larry Marshall to discuss legal strategies. Tension grew somewhat between the Cruz and Hernandez lawyers because Marshall wanted to make use of Turow's fame to help Cruz. Although it was Marshall's job to do what was best for Cruz, Turow had to put Hernandez's interests first. Turow knew that the justices in the second appellate district were not going to appreciate having a celebrity lawyer-author strut into the courtroom with a coterie of television cameras in tow. He was determined to be completely low-key, to make sure that the court knew that he wasn't handling this case only so he could write a true-crime story or get material for another novel.

Turow's original assessment that there was no way in the world the appellate court would overturn the case quickly evolved into an advocate's position that there was no way the court could affirm it. Soon, an army of law clerks was working on the case. At one point, there were seventeen lawyers doing legal research. There was such an array of legal issues that it was hard to know where to start.

The clearest issue seemed to be the jury note. At the end of Hernandez's third trial, the jurors had sent a note to Judge John Nelligan asking if a guilty verdict for kidnapping meant they also had to find Hernandez guilty of murder. Without telling the defense what was in the note, Nelligan sent a message back saying: Read your instructions. It turned out later that the jury had been split seven to five in favor of an acquittal on the murder charge but voted to convict after Nelligan's response.

To Turow, the jury-note issue was a no-brainer. A defendant has the right to be present at his own trial. If the judge doesn't show the defense lawyers a note from the jury, the defendant is in effect not present. The judge is making decisions about how the jury is to be instructed without giving the defendant an opportunity to be heard. Turow couldn't understand why an experienced judge such as Nelligan had done that.

As strong as the jury-note issue was, though, Turow didn't want to lead with it. If the appellate court overturned Hernandez's conviction on the basis of the jury note, it would just order a new trial. Turow thought there was a good chance he could persuade the court to dismiss the case altogether because the evidence was so meager. Even Judge Nelligan had agreed the evidence was weak; that's why he'd refused to sentence Hernandez to death. Instead, he'd sent Hernandez to the medium-security Hill Correctional Center in Galesburg, Illinois, for an eighty-year term.

The sufficiency of the evidence, Turow decided, would be his lead issue.

Judge Nelligan had said the most damaging evidence was the testimony of Detective Albert Bettilyon, who claimed he heard Alex say, "All I did was hold her down." Bettilyon, however, admitted he did not know the context of the statement. He didn't know what Armindo "Penguino" Marquez was saying. For all he knew, Penguino could have said, "Repeat after me." Bettilyon's testimony was so weak that the prosecutors hadn't even used it at the first trial, when they'd still had Penguino as a witness. Turow argued that it was impossible to know whether Alex was quoting the imaginary "Ricky," repeating things Marquez suggested, discussing a ploy to get the reward, or engaging in a grisly bragging contest.

Moreover, it didn't make any sense. In the same alleged conversation with Penguino, Alex reportedly had said he didn't know what the victim was hit with. How could he not know if he was there holding her down? If the conversation was so incriminating, why wasn't Alex arrested or charged for almost a year?

"We didn't get to the jury note until the fourth issue in our brief," Turow recalled later. "And we spent a lot of time debating the tactics of that. Should we just slam it up front? No, we can't do that in a case where the sufficiency of the evidence is as doubtful as it is in this case. You've got to take your shot for a total victory first."

Turow also couldn't understand why Judge Nelligan had allowed Tom Knight to testify about Alex's grand jury testimony. He thought it was a patent violation of judicial discretion. If anyone wanted to know what Alex had said to the grand jury, there was a transcript available. And yet, Knight was allowed to take the witness stand over Metnick's objection and paraphrase things in a way that helped the prosecution. Cross-examination was almost impossible.

"The judge never should have let it happen, and it was symptomatic of his affiliation with the prosecutors in my mind," Turow said. "You don't let somebody paraphrase testimony when the record of the testimony is right there. Point me to the line, counsel, point me to the line, Mr. Witness, and read it. Did you ask him the following question? Yes I did. What was the answer that he gave? Read it from the transcript."

Next, it was important to get the justices to understand how Alex Hernandez could get convicted twice. This was a point that called for artful legal argument.

Turow asserted that the state had subjected Hernandez to double jeopardy. Under Illinois law, a defendant can't be tried a second time if the evidence at the first trial is ruled to be insufficient. Turow argued that Hernandez's third trial never should have been held because it was a violation of double jeopardy. The evidence at Hernandez's second trial, when Marquez and Estremera no longer were testifying against him, was too skimpy to make a third trial permissible, he said. That argument allowed him to bring up the Dugan evidence, which had been presented in the second trial but not the third. It was an inventive argument, and Turow didn't really expect to win on that issue. But it did help shed light on what he considered to be astounding prosecutorial misconduct.

"I thought there was a serious chance that there was just so much prosecutorial misconduct, so much stuff that was not just close to the line but way over it—flagrant, egregious prosecutorial misconduct—that the court would have reversed on that basis," Turow said.

DuPage County, meanwhile, argued that none of the issues relating to Dugan were pertinent. Barbara Preiner, who represented the county in the appeal, asserted that the Dugan information was irrelevant because the defense hadn't used it in the most recent trial.

Meanwhile, Turow was getting a taste of DuPage County's hard-nosed litigating style. When DuPage filed a motion, Turow would have five days to respond. DuPage, however, would put the motions in the mail on a Friday. Turow wouldn't get them until Tuesday, and then he would have only one day to answer. Turow would call and supply his Federal Express account number and fax number, but to no avail. DuPage kept mailing the motions on Friday, and Turow kept worrying that he wouldn't get a motion until it was too late to respond.

Turow thought the trial lawyers had been sandbagged on the issue of the psychological testing. How could the jurors understand Alex's actions if they didn't know about his limited mental abilities and his penchant for telling tall tales? Yet Judge Nelligan had in effect barred that information by ruling that if it came in, he would let the prosecutors talk about Alex's record of misbehavior. That, Turow thought, was clearly an erroneous ruling.

After the state filed its brief, which relied heavily on the Illinois Supreme Court's ruling upholding Cruz's conviction, Turow asked the appellate court to wait until Cruz's case was resolved.

"This was just pure dumb luck," Turow recalled. "Every decision I made turned out to be right. Obviously, one argument would be, Good God, they have just fixed an execution date for Cruz. Uncouple yourself from his fate as best as you can. Don't point that court at the Cruz case, for crying out loud.

"That was a very sensible argument. But I just felt that the decision was out there, and the appellate court was going to know that. They almost couldn't cut Hernandez loose or give him a new trial because the Supreme Court had set a day of execution for Cruz."

That would be almost as if the appellate court were reversing the Supreme Court. So although it struck him as hope against hope, Turow just didn't see that he had that much to lose by asking the appellate court to wait. The gamble paid off. On July 14, 1994, the Illinois Supreme Court changed its mind and granted Cruz a new trial. Now the Supreme Court's influence was working the other way. The appellate court would have reason to give Hernandez a new trial, too.

On January 4, 1995, oral arguments in the Hernandez case began in the old Fox River city of Elgin, northwest of Chicago.

Because Alex Hernandez had not received a death sentence at his third trial, his case was not automatically appealed to the Illinois Supreme Court. Instead it was sent to the appellate court. Unlike the Supreme Court, which had seven justices, the appellate court panel had three. The process, though, was similar. Lawyers filed briefs outlining their cases and then appeared in front of the justices to explain their positions.

Turow had never argued before the second district appellate court, and he hoped that he was not going to run into a conservative Republican buzz saw. One of the three justices, Robert D. McLaren, had been a DuPage County judge; it was his seat that Judge Nelligan had filled when McLaren had gone to the appellate court.

Turow knew the state had a rather appealing argument that Hernandez had waived all the issues about Dugan because his lawyers had not put on a defense, so he began by talking about the jury note. McLaren interrupted Turow and asked if he was conceding the issue of the sufficiency of the evidence. Turow replied that he certainly was not. Then he started discussing the jury note again. McLaren asked another question about the sufficiency of the evidence. Turow now realized that was what McLaren wanted to hear about.

It was music to Turow's ears. It meant, he thought, that the justices knew they were going to overturn the conviction and the only question was whether it was going to be totally reversed or sent back for a new trial.

Finally, after discussing the sufficiency of the evidence, Turow finished talking about the jury note. He was sure that Hernandez was going to win. Had he any remaining doubts, they were quickly dispelled when it was time for the state to argue.

Barbara Preiner, who represented the prosecution, stood up. Justice Lawrence D. Inglis asked why the state had not confessed error in the case.

"At that point I knew for certain," Turow recalled later. "The atmosphere of outrage and hostility from these three justices toward the state was really a dream come true [for me] as Alex's lawyer. I think that's exactly what their attitude should have been, and they did not treat the prosecutor kindly. They did not feel they should have treated the prosecutor kindly. I think they felt she failed in her obligation to the court to confess error in the case, and I think that they had the resentment that justices in a politically elected system often feel when the prosecutors are trying to shove onto them responsibilities that they should have shouldered on their own."

In addition, Turow thought, the justices were offended by what had happened in the case. They obviously had problems with Bettilyon's testimony. How could the authorities put a supposed $10,000 in a room with a man of Alex's limited mental capacities and pretend that the statement was reliable? How could they tell him to play the role of a junior G-man to get another guy to confess and then argue that what Alex said actually proved his own guilt? It was inherently unreliable, and it should have been suppressed long before.

Jeffrey Urdangen, who had helped bring Turow into the case, had come to watch the oral arguments. So had attorneys Larry Marshall and Jane Raley. Raley thought the justices went out of their way to grill Turow, possibly suspecting he was a celebrity lawyer who hadn't done much work and wouldn't know the case thoroughly. Turow, though, had worked overtime on the case and understood it down to the last detail.

"I thought the justices were out to get him," Raley said later. "He was able to handle their questions beautifully, though. He was extremely impressive during their questioning."

After the court session ended, Urdangen walked up to Turow. The two men gave each other an emotional bear hug. They were sure Turow had won.

On January 30, 1995, the Illinois Appellate Court issued its ruling, written by Justice Fred A. Geiger. Alex's conviction was overturned, and he was going to get a new trial. The justices based their decision on the jury note.

Chicago Tribune columnist Eric Zorn applauded the decree.

"And the shabby ball of string that is the prosecution of Rolando Cruz and Alex Hernandez continues to unravel. What a surprise," Zorn wrote. "Why not drop these cases now, accept Dugan's confession, and declare justice done, as it would be?"

Turow considered the appellate court's ruling a step in the right direction. Now it was time to hope that Cruz could win at his third trial.

21

MATT KENNELLY

Because I can no longer state with any confidence . . . that the federal judiciary will provide meaningful oversight to the state courts as they exercise their authority to inflict the penalty of death, I believe that the death penalty, as currently administered, is unconstitutional.

Harry Blackmun, former U.S. Supreme Court
justice, *Collins v. James*, 1994

MATT KENNELLY KNEW THAT Rolando Cruz had to win his third trial. Already Cruz was the first person in Illinois ever to get a third trial in a capital case after two convictions. There was no way he would get a fourth.

The other defense lawyers considered Kennelly a brilliant legal tactician. He'd grown up in Indiana and graduated near the top of his class at Harvard Law School. He'd been involved in a number of prominent court cases, but this was his first capital case on the trial level. Other lawyers thought he had an amazing ability to master complex records. The Cruz trial records, now some fifty thousand pages, would test that ability.

Kennelly didn't know much about the case when Larry Marshall first called him, but once he examined the material Marshall sent, he was hooked.

"It looked like a real interesting opportunity to work with

some really top people and try to help somebody out who was in a pretty desperate situation," Kennelly said.

To Kennelly, the case seemed to have gone in the wrong direction from the very beginning.

"It didn't seem as though they had done anything at the outset to look for people you would have expected to commit a crime like this," he said. "It was a sex offense. A violent sex offense. And they were looking for burglars. Burglars don't take little girls out of houses and rape them and kill them. [The authorities] never did anything, it seemed to us, to have looked for sex offenders. I think it began because there was a Latino maid in the place. All of a sudden, they were looking at Latino burglars."

Then the prosecutors took over, running their investigation by bringing Hispanics from Aurora in front of the special grand jury and asking about all kinds of things that had nothing to do with the case. It was an approach that defense investigator Bill Clutter criticized as the "Hispanic Inquisition."

"They seemed to start off completely wrong," Kennelly said. "And then, because of the early misdirection on the case, they dug a big hole, and then they were stuck there."

It was time to get the case unstuck. Some members of the defense team, however, didn't feel they were ready. Tom Breen agreed to ask Judge Ronald Mehling for another week. Mehling refused.

The defense team had decided not to ask that the trial be moved out of DuPage County, so it was to be held in the new DuPage County courthouse in Wheaton. The lawyers rented three town houses in nearby Naperville, which they started calling War Room West. They brought their files and the copier in rented trucks. They were ready to begin.

The trial opened on Tuesday, October 24, 1995, in the court-house's largest courtroom. Tension was high and security was very tight. Bailiffs checked everybody and everything that came into the courthouse. They opened up thermoses to make sure they didn't contain explosives. Rolando Cruz wore a belt with a 50,000-volt stunning device that a bailiff could trigger via remote control. For Cruz, it was frightening to have a bailiff sitting there ready to push a button on such a powerful device.

Again, the Nicaricos attended. Cruz's mother, Dora, came as well. Rubin "Hurricane" Carter showed up to support Cruz. Nicole Ballard Cruz, whom Cruz had married in 1993 while in prison, was working as a public-school sign language interpreter in St. Paul, Minnesota. She planned to come in for the end of the trial.

Judge Mehling, who was younger than the previous judges in the case, presided. To Randy Garrett, who now had joined the defense team and was paid a retainer to observe the trial, Judge Mehling looked a little bit like actor Harry Anderson, who had for-merly played Judge Harry T. Stone on the *Night Court* television program.

Heading the prosecution team was John Kinsella, who now was first assistant state's attorney. Assisting him were Robert Huiner, a veteran felony prosecutor, and Assistant State's Attorney Christopher Wheaton.

Kinsella gave a two-hour opening argument for the state. It wasn't easy; the case had begun falling apart. The snitch testimony was in disarray. Stephen Schmitt had recanted, as had Steven Pecoraro. Robert Turner wouldn't cooperate. Stephen Ford couldn't be found. Ramon "Chuck" Mares had changed his story several times and admitted to *Chicago Tribune* columnist Eric Zorn that much of what he'd said on the stand was not true. And now the DNA test had linked Dugan conclusively to the crime.

Kinsella constructed a new theory out of what remained, but he seemed disorganized. He said Cruz had watched as Jeanine was abducted from her home, then as Dugan raped her. Finally, he said, Cruz was present when Jeanine's body was dumped at the Prairie Path.

"If you find that Brian Dugan committed this crime by himself, this man is not guilty," Kinsella said, pointing at Cruz. However, there was evidence of more than one assailant, he said. DNA tests showed a hair found on the adhesive tape used to blindfold Jeanine could not have come from Cruz, Dugan, or Jeanine.

The lack of a significant amount of blood on the Prairie Path showed Jeanine was killed elsewhere, he added, thus attempting to discredit Dugan's story. He spent much more time arguing that Dugan did not do it alone than he did on the idea that Cruz was guilty.

In the opening argument for the defense, Kennelly ridiculed Kinsella's theory.

"If that's the way the crime occurred, it would be unique in the annals [of crime]," Kennelly said. "It defies logic. It lacks common sense. And the evidence is not going to bear it out."

Kennelly's opening was simple and direct: Dugan, not Cruz, was guilty. Kennelly said Cruz had fabricated stories to get attention.

"The stories he spun are baloney, and the police described them that way," he said.

On Wednesday, the second day of the trial, Sheriff's Deputy Ronald Benhart was the main witness. Benhart insisted there was very little blood at the Prairie Path where Jeanine's body was found. During cross-examination, Kennelly asked Benhart if he had testified in the first trial in 1985 that he had found "a large amount of blood."

Benhart said he had not. Then Kennelly pulled out the transcript from the 1985 trial and read it aloud, quoting Benhart as saying there was "a large quantity of blood."

Also on Wednesday, there was a debate over Stephen Schmitt, who had recanted his written statement that Cruz had made a self-incriminating admission. The prosecutors wanted to introduce that statement under a rule of evidence that allows the use of prior signed statements by eyewitnesses. Schmitt, though, wasn't an eyewitness, the defense argued. He hadn't personally observed an event. Judge Mehling agreed and barred Schmitt's written statement. It was a triumphant moment for Marshall, who had researched the law on the issue.

On Thursday, Sheriff's Deputy Lewis Stonehouse and the young men who had found Jeanine's body testified.

Stonehouse said there was very little blood on the Prairie Path scene. Again Kennelly confronted a witness with past statements. This time he produced 1985 testimony by Stonehouse saying there was "a great amount of blood," that blood had soaked into the ground, and that blood was "splattered" about the scene.

Breen cross-examined the men who had found the body, suggesting that they had turned it over. That would explain why the body was found facedown when Brian Dugan had said he'd left it faceup. Breen produced a statement from the previous July by one of the men, Gary Anderson, who had said that he could see the eye and the forehead of the victim. That would have been impossible if the body were in the same position as when police had first arrived. Anderson denied touching the body, but he couldn't explain how he could have seen the victim's face.

"I must have dreamed it," he had said at one point before the trial.

On Friday, Sheriff's Lieutenant Robert Winkler again testified about the statement he said he'd heard from Cruz about hot-wiring a car. Again he added to his courtroom account. At Cruz's first trial, he'd said Cruz had offered to show the others how to hot-wire a car. At the second trial, Cruz was said to have hot-wired the car himself. Now, Winkler said Cruz first offered to show the others how to hot-wire a car, but because they apparently could not understand how to do it, he offered to hot-wire it himself. Winkler also said Cruz admitted arranging to have the car junked and crushed at Kidde Car Crush, a business that in intervening years had gone bankrupt, leaving no records that could be checked to see if such a car really had been taken there, which would help explain why there was no trace of the car later.

Then, at long last, the defense attacked the Cruz "vision" statement.

Deputy Sheriff Thomas Vosburgh was cross-examined by Matt Kennelly. Kennelly asked why Vosburgh hadn't arrested Cruz on the spot when he'd made the "vision" statement. Vosburgh said he didn't think there was probable cause. That's what Kennelly wanted—he wanted to show that the state hoped to execute Cruz on the basis of the same evidence that didn't even amount to probable cause.

After the cross-examination, Judge Mehling said he had a few questions. He asked Vosburgh to define "probable cause." Vosburgh said probable cause was enough evidence to make a reasonable person believe someone had committed a crime.

So, Judge Mehling asked, after Cruz gave you the "vision" statement, police still did not believe they had probable cause to arrest him? Vosburgh agreed that was correct.

Then Tom Breen cross-examined Detective Dennis Kurzawa. Kennelly, during his cross-examination, had been cool and focused, standing behind the lectern and referring to notes and transcripts as he questioned Vosburgh. Breen was gruffer, sometimes yelling at Kurzawa, even about small points.

To Breen, the cross-examination showed that the momentum had changed from the prosecution to the defense. His questions were somewhat sarcastic, and he heard spectators laughing. He turned and saw that the people laughing weren't the handful associated with the defense. They were assistant state's attorneys and other DuPage County workers who had come into the courtroom to watch. "What this guy is saying is making no sense to anybody, and his own people are laughing at him as he is trying to explain it," Breen thought to himself.

Because Judge Mehling had set Mondays aside to deal with other cases, the second week of the trial didn't resume until Tuesday. On that day, Tom Knight started giving testimony that would stretch over two days. While on the stand, he gave an explanation for not asking for a report on the "vision" statement. The defense lawyers thought his explanation was just ridiculous. Knight said he was trying to avoid violating Cruz's rights because Cruz might not have been given a Miranda warning before he gave the "vision" statement. But the detectives could have given Cruz his Miranda warning and continued to ask questions. In addition, they asked him more questions the next morning even though they had not read him his rights. Over the next few days, they also had him fill out an affidavit for a search warrant and testify in front of the grand jury. A jury might have been persuaded by Knight's argument,

Marshall thought, but Judge Mehling wouldn't be. If there had been a Miranda problem, it certainly had evaporated quickly.

Also on Tuesday, medical examiner Frank Cleveland testified. As he had at the second trials for Cruz and Hernandez, Cleveland said he didn't think Jeanine was killed at the Prairie Path. When Kennelly cross-examined him, however, Cleveland admitted that he had testified at the first trial that the victim was killed at or near where her body was found.

On Wednesday, Knight finished his testimony. While Knight was on the stand, Breen asked him if he was aware that May 9, 1983, was a Monday, not a Friday. Knight admitted that he had realized the date was wrong, but Breen didn't ask him any further questions about the date.

Dan Fowler also testified. Again, he said that three months after the murder, Cruz had said he was present as the crime occurred.

On Thursday of the second week, Steven Pecoraro took the stand. As he had before, he testified that Cruz had said he was going to write a book titled *How to Kill a Little Girl, or Five Ways to Crush a Skull.*

Then prosecutor Christopher Wheaton asked Pecoraro if Cruz had ever told him anything else about the case. Pecoraro said, yes, Cruz had.

At the defense table, the lawyers swore under their breath. Pecoraro was flipping again. Who could have gotten to him this time?

Meanwhile, Pecoraro continued his answer. Cruz, he said, had claimed to have had nothing to do with the crime, that he was totally innocent.

It was a question that, from the prosecutors' viewpoint, never should have been asked.

By now, it seemed to the defense lawyers that the state's case was in disarray.

"On each successive day, we all walked out of there thinking that we are never going to have another day like this in a courtroom as long as we live," Kennelly said. "It was like carrying the other side out on a stretcher. And it got better and better each day."

The defense lawyers started preparing a robust motion for a directed verdict—a ruling in which a judge dismisses a case without even listening to the defense's side. They thought the state hadn't proven anything, but they didn't really expect to win a directed verdict.

"You bring it, but you don't expect to win it," Marshall said.

On Wednesday of the second week, the prosecutors had said Sheriff's Lieutenant James Montesano was going to testify. But he hadn't taken the stand.

On Thursday, Kinsella approached Tom Breen and told him that on Friday the prosecutors would have some "Brady" material—information that would favor Cruz and that under the Brady Rule would have to be given to the defense.

The defense team didn't know what the Brady material was, but the lawyers didn't let it affect their plans. They stayed up all night working on the motion for a directed verdict and some other evidentiary issues.

The next day—Friday, November 3, 1995—would be a long and important one. That morning, the prosecutors gave the defense a memorandum about Montesano. It said that Montesano had called Kinsella and told him that he could not truthfully say that he had received a call about the "vision" statement from Vosburgh or Kurzawa. Montesano said he now realized that on May 9, 1983, he was in Florida.

It was perhaps the biggest development in the history of the case. All these years, none of the defense lawyers had ever been able to crack the solid wall of prosecutors and sheriff's deputies who had steadfastly clung to their stories of what had happened during their investigation. Now a sheriff's lieutenant was finally saying that he didn't recall getting a phone call from Vosburgh and Kurzawa about the "vision" statement. He was saying he could not have received the call when it was supposedly made because he was out of the state. The wall had cracked.

Moreover, it suddenly appeared there was an explanation for why some witnesses had testified that May 9, 1983, was a Friday when actually it was a Monday. If the change in days of the week had gone unnoticed, it would have appeared possible for Montesano to have been in DuPage County to receive the phone call from Vosburgh and Kurzawa before he left.

Larry Marshall expected the state would drop charges immediately, and when Kinsella made it clear that wasn't going to happen, Marshall was furious.

"I had never before in my life known what it meant to be steaming, literally," Marshall said later. "I remember getting red in the face, and just breathing heavy, and literally feeling as if steam was coming out of me. I was so angry."

Meanwhile, the prosecutors said they were ready to rest their case. Tom Breen argued that the prosecutors had a duty to put Montesano on the stand first. The lawyers went back to Judge Mehling's chambers, and Mehling said that if the prosecution didn't put Montesano on the stand, he would do so himself as a court's witness.

It was time to break for lunch. Out in the courtroom, observers and reporters knew a court's witness was going to be called, but they didn't know who it was. Rumors started to spread.

After lunch, Montesano walked into the courtroom. He was pale and looked extremely nervous. To Randy Garrett, he looked as though he had not slept for days.

John Kinsella put him on the stand and took him through the direct examination. Montesano said that when he had claimed he had received a call about the "vision" statement, he'd believed it to be true at the time. He said that when he had testified at the suppression hearing in August, he had thought he remembered the conversation. Now, though, he realized that he was in Florida at the time and he now realized that he had no memory of that conversation taking place.

Something, he said, had jogged his memory on Monday night, and he looked up his credit card records. A May 9 MasterCard receipt from Treasure Island in Florida near Orlando and another receipt dated May 12 showed he had indeed been in Florida. Looking emotional and uncomfortable, Montesano also said he had no recollection of the conversation he had testified about in which Cruz supposedly had confirmed talking with Lieutenant Winkler.

What had seemed like a huge mistake in August—calling Montesano to the stand during a hearing—ended up being a huge victory in November, during the trial.

The state rested its case. Judge Mehling said he was ready to hear arguments for and against a directed verdict.

Matt Kennelly went first for the defense. Then Bob Huiner delivered the argument for the state. Larry Marshall presented the rebuttal argument. While preparing to do so, he had to make a complicated legal decision.

In a criminal jury trial, when a judge is considering a directed verdict, he or she must look at every piece of evidence in the light most favorable to the state. Every witness must be considered to have told the truth. Physical evidence must be interpreted as the state's experts interpret it. Only if the case still doesn't add up can a judge grant a directed verdict.

In a civil bench trial, the rules say a judge can decide—even at the directed verdict stage—whether a witness is telling the truth. The judge can say, in effect, I have heard your evidence, but I don't believe your witnesses, so we might as well end the case right now. In a criminal bench trial, there is no such specific rule.

The defense lawyers had to decide whether to ask Judge Mehling to adopt the civil rule in a criminal context. They decided not to. Judge Mehling probably did not want to issue a directed verdict in such a controversial case, they figured. Even if he intended to acquit Cruz, waiting until the defense had put on its case would make such a decision much easier.

But if the defense asked Judge Mehling to make credibility findings and he chose not to grant a directed verdict, he in effect would be saying that the prosecution's witnesses were believable.

Instead, the defense lawyers decided to argue that even if Judge Mehling believed the prosecution witnesses, the state still had not met its burden of proof. All the pieces of evidence didn't add up to anything.

Judge Mehling announced that he was taking a break. A half hour later, he called everyone back into the courtroom.

People throughout the courthouse, even around town, had heard that something big had happened, so the place was packed. A retractable transparent partition had been moved into place to separate the reporters and spectators from the judge and lawyers. Tension was already high, and the appearance of the partition intensified it.

When they saw the partition, some people interpreted that to mean Cruz would be freed. Matt Kennelly wasn't so sure.

"That didn't tell you anything," he said later. "That could go either way."

The defense lawyers knew they were finished for the day no matter what happened, so they cleaned off their table and put away their files. Once the table was cleared, they just sat there with their hands folded. Tom Breen went back into the part of the courtroom occupied by the spectators and gave a short speech. He said that the judge was about to rule and that it was very important that everyone maintain complete decorum. If the judge doesn't grant the motion, he said, all it means is that the trial will go forward as any other trial would.

If the judge does grant it, he said, then it would be very important to respect the dignity of the moment and the people who were present.

Judge Mehling returned, took his seat on the bench, and began to talk. He described a little of the case's background and then said that the break had been longer than expected "because the defense brought up something during their motion that the court frankly disagrees with."

Now Marshall was worried. "Oh, God," he said to himself.

"The court [cannot] ignore necessarily all of the evidence that was adduced, including any impeaching witnesses," Judge Mehling said. "And, two, the state has the burden to prove beyond a reasonable doubt that the defendant is guilty of the crimes that he's been charged with."

Suddenly Marshall was feeling better.

Judge Mehling asked that People's Exhibit Number 1, a picture of Jeanine Nicarico taken before the crime, be brought to the bench.

Holding the photograph, he reminded those in the courtroom that Jeanine Nicarico was the most important person in the case.

"This case wouldn't be here except for what occurred to this apparently very warm human being who obviously has a loving family."

However, Judge Mehling reminded the courtroom, the state has the burden of proving guilt beyond reasonable doubt.

"Let's look at what the evidence shows or does not show," he said. "And what troubles me in this case, ladies and gentlemen, is what the evidence does not show. . . . Is there any physical evidence in connection with this case, anything at all, that connects this hideous crime and connects Mr. Cruz? Anything? Fingerprints, blood spots, blood, DNA, hair, fibers, clothes, something left there, something taken from the home that he had? Anything? Anything at all? Any item? There is none. There is absolutely none.

"I as a judge, frankly . . . can't recall so many witnesses that have testified one way at one time and then now testified a different way. . . . I had some questions about the dream statement before today. After this afternoon at one-thirty, I have no questions anymore, because I have made up my mind. . . .

"I'm sure the defense and the state realize what actually occurred here today. It was devastating. It was unique in the annals of criminal justice. . . .

"Did Cruz ever make the dream statement? I don't think I need to answer that, because I'm going to enter a finding of not guilty and he will be discharged today. Case is closed."

Larry Marshall was momentarily stunned when Judge Mehling had announced the directed verdict on November 3, 1995. Marshall turned around to talk to Rolando Cruz, but Cruz was already gone, escorted quickly away by the bailiffs. On opposite sides of the courtroom, members of both the Cruz and Nicarico families were hugging one another and crying. The case was over, and it was time to leave. It was almost ten years to the day since Edward Cisowski of the state police had heard Brian Dugan confess that he alone had abducted and murdered Jeanine Nicarico.

Thomas and Patricia Nicarico left the courtroom in tears without commenting to reporters.

Outside the courtroom, the lawyers held an impromptu press conference. They made a point of emphasizing how brave and righteous they thought Judge Mehling's ruling had been. Then Larry Marshall went over to the county jail, but Cruz already had left with his mother, Dora, after an unpleasant moment with a television crew he thought had crowded too close. So Marshall went to a rental shop and picked up a tuxedo for his sister-in-law's wedding the next day in Michigan. It was an odd feeling. Here it was, the biggest professional moment of his life, and he was running an errand in a small rental shop.

Then Marshall went back to War Room West. Soon an unplanned party began. Ed Cisowski came. Mary Brigid Kenney arrived. Rolando Cruz showed up an hour or two later. The party went late into the night. Someone showed Cruz how to play games on the computers in the war room. It was something Cruz wasn't familiar with because he'd gone to jail in 1983, when personal computers were far less common and far more primitive. He wound up staying awake all night.

The next morning, Marshall took Cruz out to get a toothbrush, toothpaste, and the morning papers. They walked into a gas station near the border between Naperville and Aurora, and the attendants treated Cruz like a celebrity.

It was time for Cruz, who had acquired a high school equivalency degree while incarcerated, to start adult life at last. Later, when he went with Tom Breen to get a birth certificate, the only proof he had of his identity was his death warrant.

Jim Ryan, who had been elected Illinois attorney general in 1994, defended his decisions to keep prosecuting Cruz and Hernandez through the years.

"I did what I did, and I acted properly," Ryan told reporters. "Given the state of available, admissible evidence, I made the right decision as a prosecutor.

"I did what my predecessor did, I did what my successor did, and I did what [former Illinois attorney general Roland Burris] did. I went forward."

Ryan said he wasn't fretting about how the case might affect his political career.

"I can't worry about that. I'm human. Of course I feel the sting of criticism. But you have to put that aside and do what's right. And that's what I did in this case," Ryan said.

Anthony M. Peccarelli, the new DuPage County state's attorney, said Cruz's acquittal would have "no impact whatsoever" on Alex Hernandez.

An angry Sheriff Doria told the *Chicago Tribune,* "My department and my officers have been damaged, and they don't deserve it. I intend to do everything I can to clear my men, and I am sure they will be vindicated."

On Monday, Rolando Cruz went for a walk with Marshall along Lake Michigan from Northwestern University School of Law to Chicago's Navy Pier and back. He was fascinated by the birds. Along the way, Marshall noticed him stopping and just staring at an ordinary seagull, watching it and listening to it, absorbed in its beauty.

Suddenly, Cruz was a media celebrity. Reporters and television cameras followed him. An Italian media conglomerate flew him to Rome and put him up in a luxury hotel. He appeared on *Nightline*. Five days after his release, Cruz showed up with his defense lawyers at a forum at Northwestern University School of Law. He apologized for the lies he had told in the early days of the investigation.

"I'm real sorry I ever lied," he said. "I was just a smart-ass kid off the streets. That's the honest-to-God truth.

"It's hard to sit up here and admit this, but it's true. I didn't have respect for the law because they didn't have respect for me or my people when I was out there. I'm sorry to the Nicaricos that I ever lied and allowed myself to get caught up. I'm sorry the police did it to them, too."

Cruz called on Jim Ryan to give up his law license and resign. Later, in an interview with Bill Kurtis on his cable TV show *American Justice*, Cruz suggested that those involved in his prosecution should be charged with attempted murder.

On November 21, 1995, DuPage Judge Thomas Callum reduced Alex Hernandez's bond to $400,000. Relatives posted equity in their homes to come up with the $40,000, or 10 percent of the bond, to free Alex. After eleven years in prison, he walked out of jail. He hugged his mother so hard that he cracked his glasses.

On November 30, Illinois attorney general Jim Ryan wrote a letter to the *Chicago Tribune* in response to a critical editorial. In defense of his decisions, Ryan cited Justice Heiple's opinion upholding Cruz's conviction.

"Following Mr. Cruz's second jury conviction in Rockford,

the Illinois Supreme Court affirmed the conviction and death sentence, characterizing the evidence as 'overwhelming,' " Ryan wrote.

On December 8, 1995, prosecutors dropped charges against Alex Hernandez and DuPage County Judge Thomas Callum dismissed the case.

"I've always been innocent of my charges," a teary-eyed Hernandez told reporters. "I want to say that I just want to go home and be with my family now. I knew that God would not leave me behind. . . .

"You know, we're going to celebrate Christmas together like a family should."

State's Attorney Peccarelli released a five-page statement that was strikingly reminiscent of the statement Jim Ryan had read when he'd dropped charges against Stephen Buckley. As did Ryan, Peccarelli implied that a solid case had fallen apart because so much time had elapsed. The statement read, in part, "The case against the defendant is different than it was five years ago or 10 years ago. The passage of time takes its toll. Decisions such as this are very difficult, but I must be pragmatic in evaluating the case as it exists today."

Technically, the charges could be resurrected against Hernandez if new evidence surfaced. But former U.S. attorney Dan Webb, the leader of the team that was ready to represent Hernandez, had he had a fourth trial, said that the charges were dropped for good.

"This man happens to be innocent of the crime," Webb told the *Chicago Sun-Times,* "so this is a final judgment today. Alex Hernandez will never be back in the criminal justice system again."

Alex went to work for a while installing drywall with his

father, but had difficulty establishing a new life for himself. Rolando Cruz worked at a social service agency for about a year and a half and then at other jobs, but he, too, struggled with financial concerns and anger over his years in prison. He never got back together with Nicole after leaving prison, and their marriage fell apart. Later, he remarried, but that relationship ended, too.

"People say put it behind you, but that's impossible," he said.

22

WILLIAM J. KUNKLE JR.

---

*I would feel much, much better if more states would really
consider whether they think the benefits [of the death
penalty] outweigh the very serious potential injustice,
because in these cases the emotions are very, very high on
both sides and to have stakes as high as you do in these
cases, there is the special potential for error.*

John Paul Stevens, U.S. Supreme Court justice, to the
Seventh Circuit Bar Association, May 10, 2004

WILLIAM J. KUNKLE JR. had a tough assignment:
find out if there was any obstruction of justice in
the murder trial of Rolando Cruz and, if there was,
prove it to a DuPage County jury.

Kunkle, age fifty-four, had acquired a reputation as a hard-
nosed prosecutor when he held various supervisory positions in
the Cook County state's attorney's office, including the job of first
assistant state's attorney, and he was an outspoken advocate of the
death penalty. He was best known for prosecuting serial killer John
Wayne Gacy, who, coincidentally, had once given Brian Dugan a
lift when Dugan was hitchhiking. At one point in 1994, Jim Ryan
had approached Kunkle about leading the prosecution against
Cruz as a special state's attorney, but the two men never had
reached an agreement. After going into private practice, Kunkle
had represented Chicago Police Lieutenant Jon Burge, who had

been accused of torturing suspects during interrogations. Lieutenant Burge retired to Florida after hearings in front of a Chicago police board, but he prevailed in two federal civil proceedings and never was charged criminally.

Kunkle had political connections to the state Republican Party. He had appeared before the Republican slate-making committee as a potential party nominee for Cook County state's attorney in 1990, and from 1990 to 1993, he'd served as the first chairman of the Illinois Gaming Board in a Republican administration. Twice, he'd been among the three or four finalists for the job of U.S. attorney for the northern district of Illinois. He'd also run unsuccessfully as a GOP candidate for judge and had contributed to Jim Ryan's campaigns for attorney general. Now he was a partner in the Chicago firm of Pope, Cahill & Devine.

Kunkle had been called into the case by Edward Kowal, who now was chief judge of DuPage County. Kowal had acted in response to Judge Ronald Mehling's comments when he'd acquitted Cruz.

"He [James Montesano] told us that he lied," Mehling had said in court. "Lied to me on August 31, 1995, when he told me that he received a call from Vosburgh."

Mehling had said he thought the changes in testimony during Cruz's trial should be investigated. "When Montesano testified that he did not receive the call, that he was in Florida, that called into question the other testimony," Mehling recalled later. "It was a domino effect. There was a question of the veracity of the witnesses." Two days after Mehling's ruling, Anthony M. Peccarelli, who had replaced Jim Ryan as state's attorney when Ryan was elected Illinois attorney general, asked Kowal to look into Mehling's complaint. Two weeks after Cruz was freed,

Kowal—the judge who had presided over the first three trials in the Nicarico murder case—appointed Kunkle as a special state's attorney with the power to bring witnesses in front of a grand jury and to grant immunity. Judge Kowal said that Kunkle would have the freedom to investigate others besides Montesano.

"He can go in any direction he feels is just," Judge Kowal said.

Some of the people who had worked on behalf of Stephen Buckley, Rolando Cruz, and Alejandro Hernandez thought Kunkle was too sympathetic to prosecutors and would take a lenient view of DuPage County authorities' actions. They thought Kunkle, while a prosecutor, had tended to be dismissive of defendants, and they didn't like the way he'd handled the controversial Burge case.

Kunkle, though, promised the investigation wouldn't be a whitewash.

Shortly after his appointment, the law firm of Pope, Cahill & Devine had dissolved, and Kunkle joined with nine other partners of the old firm to form Cahill, Christian & Kunkle. He recruited Michael Bartosz, another partner in the new firm, to help him. Kunkle met with county officials to work out financial details—how much he would be paid and to whom he would send his bills. And he and Bartosz started educating themselves about the case itself, trying to learn what exactly had happened over the years.

By now, it was a long, convoluted case. But there was an underlying mystery. Over the years, witnesses' testimony and expert findings had repeatedly changed, and the changes had followed a pattern.

For example, Joann Johannville's original description of the person she saw on Clover Court somewhat resembled Brian Dugan, although nobody knew about him then. Suddenly, though, she changed her story to say she saw Steve Buckley, who did not fit her description. How did that happen?

The shoeprint on the Nicaricos' front door was the right size for Brian Dugan, and the pattern matched the kind of hiking shoe a friend said Dugan owned. But two experts—Robert Olson and Ed German—said the shoeprint probably was Buckley's. A third expert, Louise Robbins, testified it was Buckley's, even though a later FBI test determined it wasn't. Who could explain the conflicts in the shoeprint testimony?

At first, when prosecutors argued that Jeanine was killed on the Prairie Path, coroner Frank Cleveland and others testified in support of that theory. Later, though, when officials were trying to debunk Dugan's story, Cleveland and others said that evidence showed Jeanine was killed elsewhere. What explained those changes in testimony?

Why did the "vision" statement not emerge until just before the first trial? Why did police come forward so many times with admissions they said they'd heard months—or years—earlier but for which there were no reports? Why did witnesses tell stories they later recanted to implicate Buckley, Cruz, and Hernandez?

People familiar with the case wondered if Kunkle ever would be able to explain how all those changes occurred.

Meanwhile, one of the early snags Kunkle encountered was that DuPage County authorities wouldn't give him access to the official records of the case, just as they had withheld them from Ed Cisowski as he led the state police investigation. By now, the records filled an entire room with files of police reports, grand jury proceedings, trial transcripts, court rulings, affidavits, records of the state police investigation into Brian Dugan, and other documents. Kunkle went before a judge and secured an order allowing him access to the records. But whenever Kunkle's team went into the room that held the records, a county investigator was sent in to keep an eye on them.

On January 8, 1996—two months after Cruz's acquittal—U.S. district judge David Coar ruled that Jim Ryan and four other prosecutors were not shielded by prosecutorial immunity against malicious-prosecution claims by Stephen Buckley, who had filed a lawsuit in 1988 that had gone all the way up to the U.S. Supreme Court. The other prosecutors named were J. Michael Fitzsimmons, Tom Knight, Patrick King, and Robert Kilander. Later, Rolando Cruz and Alex Hernandez also filed suits alleging wrongful prosecution. Fifteen others also were named as defendants. All those named in the lawsuits denied liability.

On June 27, 1996, Sheriff Richard Doria released a summary of an internal six-month investigation into alleged improprieties in the probe of the Jeanine Nicarico murder case. The investigation had been supervised by Sheriff's Lieutenant Robert Winkler, who had testified in all of the trials against Cruz and Hernandez. A press release issued by Doria said there was "no legal basis to charge any of the detectives with a violation of any criminal statute."

Meanwhile, Kunkle started bringing witnesses before a grand jury. One of the witnesses was Rolando Cruz, who had testified so many years before as a young street punk who thought he was in line for some easy money. Now he was recounting his legal nightmare as part of a probe into the people who had investigated and prosecuted him. Former DuPage County prosecutors Tom Knight, Patrick King, and Robert Kilander also testified. So did many of the sheriff's deputies, including Dennis Kurzawa, Paul Sahs, John Sam, Thomas Vosburgh, Warren Wilkosz, and Robert Winkler. But Lieutenant James Montesano—whose startling testimony had ended the Cruz case and triggered the Kunkle investigation—did not testify.

Kunkle also hired an investigator, Steve Kirby. One of the things Kirby learned was the possible identity of the "screwdriver lady" for whom the state police had searched. Brian Dugan had said he stopped to borrow a screwdriver before driving to Clover Court, but the police never found anyone who could corroborate that. Now, a woman who lived on a busy street near the Nicaricos said her mother, who was in the early stages of Alzheimer's disease, had said someone had come to their house at about the time of Jeanine's murder and asked to borrow a screwdriver. Moreover, the woman's mother frequently wore a dress similar to the one Brian Dugan described.

As Kunkle had learned more about the case, he'd realized that many of what he considered improper actions by authorities had taken place during the trials of Stephen Buckley and Alejandro Hernandez. But the charter he'd been given by Judge Kowal had only mentioned Rolando Cruz, and it was too late to go back to Kowal for a different charter that included Buckley and Hernandez because Kowal had retired shortly after Cruz was acquitted. The helpful chairman of the DuPage County Board, Gayle Franzen, also had left office. By the time Kunkle realized he needed a broader mandate, it was too late. He sensed there was no way to obtain one under DuPage County's realigned political structure. The people running things now, Kunkle thought, were opposed to his investigation.

"If I'd been smarter at the time, I would have asked Kowal to change [the mandate]," Kunkle said later. "A great deal of the most serious misconduct dealt with the prosecution of Buckley—the [shoeprint] and some other things—and Hernandez in particular.

It would have been a very different trial if the scope had been phrased to look at the investigation and prosecution of the Nicarico homicide or look at any misconduct relevant to the investigation and prosecution of Cruz, Hernandez, and Buckley."

The three-year statute of limitations on official misconduct was another problem. Anyone who had testified at Cruz's 1995 trial could be charged, but the prosecutors who had directed the earlier cases wouldn't have to answer for any misdeeds. Kunkle decided to structure the case as a conspiracy charge, in which all acts furthering the conspiracy can be part of the case as long as the most recent falls within the statute of limitations. Conspiracy cases—which are rare in state courts—are not easy to win without a cooperating insider who tells the jury how everything worked. But of the various options, Kunkle thought a conspiracy charge was the best way to proceed.

By December 1996, the results of Kunkle's investigation were in. They were virtually unprecedented. At a press conference on December 12, Kunkle announced the indictments of the men who would soon become known as the DuPage Seven—former assistant state's attorneys Tom Knight, Robert Kilander, and Patrick King; Sheriff's Lieutenants James Montesano and Robert Winkler; and Detectives Dennis Kurzawa and Thomas Vosburgh—on charges of conspiracy to commit obstruction of justice and conspiracy to commit official misconduct.

The four investigators faced additional charges. Vosburgh's other charges were six counts of perjury and of obstructing justice and twelve counts of official misconduct. Kurzawa's were four counts of perjury and obstructing justice and eight counts of official misconduct. Winkler's were one count each of official misconduct, obstructing justice, and perjury. Montesano's were one count each of official misconduct and perjury. (On January 21, 1988, a northwestern Illinois judge brought in to handle the case, William A. Kelly, threw out the perjury charge, saying Montesano corrected his inaccurate statement in what technically was the same legal proceeding. On April 1, 1988, Judge Kelly reinstated the charge.)

Knight and King were charged with knowingly presenting perjured evidence to a jury. Kilander was accused of withholding notes of his interview with Brian Dugan's public defender, George Mueller. The indictment alleged that Vosburgh and Kurzawa had committed perjury when they'd said Cruz had made the "vision" statement. Montesano was charged with falsely corroborating their account.

Warren Wilkosz, the chief agent on the case, was not charged and remains a sheriff's detective.

The seven indicted men all entered pleas of "not guilty."

"The indictments . . . [are the] latest sordid chapter in the long and sorry saga that began with the death of a child and nearly ended with the execution of a man who did not commit the murder," a *Chicago Sun-Times* editorial stated.

At the December 12 press conference, Kunkle said there was no evidence of criminal conduct by former DuPage County state's attorney Jim Ryan or by DuPage County sheriff Richard Doria.

"Every elected public official is rightly subjected to public or political criticism based on the acts or failures of his subordinates," Kunkle said. "However, the criminal law requires personal knowledge and intent, as well as personal involvement."

The indictments focused on the "vision" statement, Winkler's changing testimony, and the withheld notes of the November 13, 1985, meeting among Kilander, King, and George Mueller.

"There must always be a line between vigorous prosecution and official misconduct, between advocacy and unfairness, and between justice and injustice," Kunkle said. "That line was crossed."

23

THE DUPAGE SEVEN

Asked what had gone wrong in the case, Creswell put it succinctly: "Everything."

David Protess and Rob Warden, *A Promise of Justice*

ILLIAM J. KUNKLE JR. admitted his evidence for the DuPage Seven indictments didn't include a smoking gun. Unfortunately, though, his case did include a big target for the opposition: Rolando Cruz's credibility. The court records were littered with one outrageous statement after another. Cruz had made up the "Donatlan" statement, which early in the investigation supposedly linked Emilio Donatlan, Ray Ortega, and Alejandro Hernandez to Jeanine Nicarico's murder. He'd told investigators he was in the Marines and lied about his birthday to keep it consistent with a phony ID he used to buy liquor. He'd told a girlfriend he was an Apache descended from Geronimo. In the original 1983–84 grand jury proceedings, he'd fabricated stories about burglaries he committed, saying that he threw TVs through walls and jumped up and kicked chandeliers off of ceilings.

Cruz was ready to admit he had lied to authorities during their original investigation, but he would have to persuade the judge and jury that he now was telling the truth. Yet even since his 1995 acquittal, he'd had trouble keeping his facts straight. He'd given two different versions about what he had really said on May 9, the date of the alleged "vision" statement, telling the FBI one thing and Kunkle's grand jury another. Of course, what he said that night wasn't considered significant until twenty months later, so it was understandable if he couldn't remember. But if Cruz was to persuade the judge and jury to believe that he now was a model of truth-telling, he couldn't be vague or adjust his testimony. The minute that Cruz took the stand, defense lawyers would accuse him of serving up more whoppers than had the Burger King chain in its entire history. Far from being a star witness, Cruz was more like a meteor that might crash and burn at any moment.

Kunkle's grand jury in December 1996 had indicted the DuPage Seven partly because of their conflicting stories. But Cruz also had conflicting stories. Kunkle would have to do a good job of explaining why Cruz's discrepancies were inconsequential while those of authorities were unlawful.

For Kunkle, that was a problem central to the case. If Cruz took the stand and denied making the "vision" statement, he would be confronted with his fuzzy narratives as well as the many lies he'd told in the past. Look, the defense lawyers would say, how can you send law enforcement officers to prison on the word of someone who has told so many lies to authorities? Very possibly, we can't, the jurors would say. Of course, Cruz didn't have to testify for the prosecution, but Kunkle thought Cruz was essential. Cruz had to take the stand both to deny the "vision" statement and to show the jury that a real, live individual had suffered immensely because of misdeeds by authorities.

"I would have loved not to have had to put him on, but I don't know how you try that case without a victim," Kunkle said later.

Kunkle's partner Michael Bartosz agreed.

"I didn't see how in the world a jury could ever bring a conviction upon law enforcement officers for concocting evidence without hearing the alleged declarant come in and say, 'No, I didn't say this,'" Bartosz said later. "And if we didn't put him up on the stand, the defense was going to subpoena him anyway."

Cruz's vulnerability wasn't the only problem. The case had other weaknesses, too. In a key pretrial ruling, Judge William A. Kelly—whom the Illinois Supreme Court had appointed on January 17, 1997, to preside over the case—had said Kunkle could tell the jury only about parts of the case that affected Rolando Cruz. Anything that affected only Stephen Buckley or Alejandro Hernandez was out. Kunkle had wanted to paint a complete panorama for the judge and jury. He thought the recurring patterns against all three defendants would illustrate indicia of intent, showing that what happened to Cruz was not just a series of mistakes. Judge Kelly, though, was not going to allow it.

Now Kunkle was in the same position as Jed Stone had been at the second Cruz trial. Stone had wanted to tell jurors about Brian Dugan's criminal history of acting alone to help show that Dugan was the only murderer, but Judge Edward Kowal wouldn't let him. Now Kunkle wouldn't be able to tell the jury, for example, that Robert Winkler's testimony had changed not only about Cruz but also about Hernandez. He wouldn't be able to show that, just as the "vision" statement emerged with no report many months after the fact, the jailers' story about Hernandez saying he went to the Nicarico home to commit a burglary also suddenly appeared long after the incident allegedly occurred, and in that instance, too, no report had been written at the time. He would not be able to show that, just as the "Kilander notes" had not been turned over to the defense when they should have been, Ed German's notes on the shoeprint analysis had not been turned over, nor the information that the shoeprints outside the Nicaricos' window were made by teenage girls' shoes, nor any report on the search of Buckley's car, nor the information confirming Dugan's story about where he bought the tape used as part of the blindfold. Nor, for that matter, could he say anything about the receipt Haydee Hernandez said she turned over to authorities to document that the family had indeed purchased gravel on the day they said Alex was helping to spread it. Haydee said that when she asked about it later because it would support Alex's alibi, authorities said they didn't remember receiving it.

In another pretrial ruling, Judge Kelly also had said Kunkle couldn't point out that DuPage authorities had let Edward Cisowski be accused of feeding information to Brian Dugan even when they knew they had in their possession the so-called Kilander notes that could have vindicated Cisowski.

Kunkle needed to prove intent, but Judge Kelly's rulings would make it easier for the DuPage Seven defendants to argue that their actions really were just understandable mistakes in a huge, complicated case.

Also before the trial, Judge Kelly accepted the DuPage County Board's decision to pay the legal bills of the DuPage Seven defendants without waiting for a verdict. In effect, that placed a huge financial burden on any defendant considering a plea bargain. Pleading guilty would take away the free legal defense provided by the county, because the county would expect to be reimbursed by anyone who was convicted. And the county's deep pockets meant the defendants would be able to mount a much more vigorous defense with far more pretrial preparation than they could have afforded on their own.

Gayle Franzen, then the president of the DuPage County

Board, thought paying for the criminal defense of the DuPage Seven was illegal. Franzen's earlier job as head of the Illinois Department of Corrections had made him a defendant in numerous lawsuits; some 700 that were still pending when he left the department took ten years to clear up. In each case, the Illinois attorney general's office sent him a form letter reminding him that, if criminal allegations surfaced, the state would not defend him and he would have to hire his own lawyer.

Franzen issued a challenge: find a state law or a precedent supporting payment of legal bills up front. No one met that challenge, he said later.

Instead, Joseph Birkett, the new DuPage County state's attorney, called for paying the fees partly because a strong legal defense in the criminal trial would help protect the county in the civil lawsuit that Cruz, Buckley, and Hernandez had filed. Franzen thought that was improper because Terry Ekl, who stood to earn a large fee as Tom Knight's lawyer, had helped to run Birkett's political campaign.

"To this day, I would still stand up and argue as loudly as possible that this was illegal, that it was not proper, and that the only reason that it was done was because the lawyers representing these defendants wanted to be paid up front," Franzen said later.

During the debate over whether to pay for the DuPage Seven defense, Ekl wrote a letter to DuPage authorities that said, in part, "In the event the DuPage County Board authorizes the advancement of legal fees . . . [the defendants] will do no act which adversely affects the defense of the civil case . . . [and] will not testify on behalf of the prosecution [in the criminal case]."

The letter drew criticism from *Tribune* columnist Eric Zorn, who wrote, "By offering for money to foreclose the option that any one or more members of the DuPage Seven will break ranks or cop a plea, the lawyers appeared to attempt to engineer a new conspiracy—one in which, Musketeer-like, the defendants would guarantee they'd stand one for all and all for one."

In the end, the county spent more than $3.2 million for some of the better-known Chicago area defense lawyers to represent the DuPage Seven, including expenses for two private investigators.

On top of all those challenges for Kunkle was another, unspoken one: jurors would want to know who really killed Jeanine Nicarico. Kunkle knew he couldn't show them a smoking gun, but they still would want to know who pulled the trigger. Judge Kelly had ruled that the case was to be about the investigation into Cruz, not Cruz's own guilt or innocence. Kunkle wasn't going to be allowed to introduce evidence just to show Cruz was innocent. But the jurors would be picked because they didn't know much about the case. In fact, one juror said during jury selection that she thought Rolando Cruz was a professional baseball player. The jurors would wonder: Was Cruz really guilty? No jury would convict police officers for crossing the line if their target was in fact guilty of a brutal child murder. The question about Cruz's actual innocence was the elephant in the courtroom that Kunkle would have to pretend wasn't there even as the defense lawyers kept parading it past the jury box.

By now, some people with ties to the DuPage Seven thought Kunkle's case was so weakened that he should just drop it. Not only, they thought, was there no smoking gun, but even the whiff of gunpowder had practically disappeared. They felt there was just no evidence that a crime had been committed. For example, one federal prosecutor who was not part of the case, but who had studied the evidence against Patrick King, said he didn't think there was a basis to prosecute.

"You look through the discovery, and it's just not there," he said before the trial began.

Joseph Birkett, who succeeded Anthony M. Peccarelli as DuPage County state's attorney, was especially critical of the indictment of Robert Kilander for not turning over the so-called Kilander notes.

"It does definitely have a chilling effect when prosecutors are now subject to being investigated and prosecuted for what basically amounts to an allegation of a discovery violation," Birkett said on a WBBM-AM radio program. "I was deeply saddened by these indictments."

James Sotos, a DuPage County lawyer who was representing the county and several of the DuPage Seven defendants in the civil suits filed by Buckley, Cruz, and Hernandez, said Kunkle was pushing ahead without a strong enough case, just as DuPage prosecutors had been accused of doing earlier.

"It's the prosecution complex," Sotos said.

But in one of his pretrial rulings, Judge Kelly found there was indeed enough evidence to allege a conspiracy. And Kunkle was certain his case was sound. "The evidence is there," he said. On April 6, 1999, he stepped in front of the judge and jury to give his opening statement.

The jury had taken three weeks to select. Four of the defendants—Vosburgh, Kurzawa, Montesano, and King—had tried to move the trial to another county because they thought they couldn't get a fair trial in DuPage, but Judge Kelly had turned them down. A fifth defendant—Robert Winkler—decided to have the judge, not the jury, decide his case. When the final twelve jurors and four alternates had been empaneled, the defense lawyers had been pleased with the jury's composition. DuPage County juries often are much more likely to side instinctively with law officers than juries do in Cook County, which includes the city of Chicago, and these jurors seemed to fit the DuPage mold. Some reporters who sat through jury selection thought Kunkle would have a hard time getting twelve guilty votes at the end of the trial.

"There is no way this jury is going to convict police officers," *Chicago Sun-Times* reporter Dan Rozek privately predicted.

Later, Rozek said he was surprised Kunkle didn't fight harder over jury selection.

"I've seen lawyers fight and fight over every single jury spot," Rozek said. "But Kunkle just seemed to be tiptoeing through the tulips."

Kunkle, though, thought the jury was as good as any that could be reasonably expected in DuPage County. After all, he pointed out, the new jury had been drawn from the same pool of people as the earlier DuPage Seven grand jury, and the grand jurors hadn't had any trouble understanding the case. The questions they'd asked of the defendants who'd testified had been very much to the point, he thought.

The courtroom—the biggest one in the new DuPage Justice Center—was the same one where Judge Ronald Mehling had acquitted Rolando Cruz three and a half years earlier. The seven defendants and their ten lawyers sat to Judge Kelly's right. The jury of eleven whites and one Latino was on his left, and the four prosecutors sat in between. Besides Bartosz, Kunkle had added Daniel Collins, a young associate at his law firm, and William

Hedrick, a private practitioner with some experience in conspiracy cases. Reporters, relatives of the defendants, and others packed the seats. As potential witnesses, the Nicaricos were barred because they no longer qualified for an exemption as members of the victim's family, as they had in earlier trials. The decision was routine, but Patricia Nicarico hadn't been expecting it, and she left the courthouse in tears.

"Why isn't the special prosecutor anxious to prove his case to us first-hand in court with the facts he is prepared to present?" the Nicaricos wrote in a letter printed in the *Chicago Sun-Times*. "Or is it possible that Kunkle's case revolves around errors or lies that we possibly could dispel?"

Similar accusations—claims that Kunkle was pursuing the case only to make money for his new law firm or because he had once prosecuted cases with Tom Breen (as he had with several of the defense lawyers)—swirled around the case. But in his opening statement, Kunkle knew, he would have to focus on persuading the judge and jury that the defendants' actions were not simply mistakes and—most important—that the case did not turn on whether Cruz was believable.

"What the evidence will show you, ladies and gentlemen," Kunkle said in his opening, "is that this is a history of obstruction of justice, official misconduct, and perjury committed by these seven defendants who had sworn duties to uphold the law of Illinois. Much of this evidence will come to you from court records. . . . You heard during [jury selection] about Rolando Cruz and this is a bad guy and this is a guy you shouldn't be believing. Well, ninety-nine and nine-tenths of our evidence in this case that the People will present to you is going to come from sworn court transcripts."

To help the jurors understand the history of the case, Kunkle recounted how Jeanine had been abducted and killed and how authorities had investigated the case. So much of it was the same information that had been told to past juries that Tom Knight, as he left the courtroom for the lunch break, complained to those around him that Kunkle was giving the same opening as Knight had back in 1985.

After lunch, Kunkle resumed his opening. Using an overhead screen, he projected a time line showing the arrest of Brian Dugan, the date that Patrick King and Robert Kilander met with Dugan's lawyer, the Illinois State Police investigation into Dugan, the evidentiary hearing on the Dugan evidence, the second Cruz trial, and how Robert Winkler's testimony at the second trial about Cruz's statement was different—and more incriminating—than Winkler's testimony at the first trial. Kunkle then explained what happened at Cruz's third trial. Finally, he summarized what the conspiracy charge was all about.

"I will show you," Kunkle told the judge and jury, "that if the oral ["vision"] statement of May 9, 1983, did not happen as Kurzawa and Vosburgh have testified and as Knight and Montesano and King have corroborated, indeed if it didn't happen at all, Vosburgh and Kurzawa had to agree on that story and on those details. Knight had to actually or implicitly agree to corroborate it, as did King. The evidence I have described will show Winkler invented or improved on another unreported oral statement and improved on it again. Knight again provided the excuse for the absence of a report and Kilander put the new and improved version before a jury. King and Kilander secreted and withheld the important Dugan notes. . . .

"The evidence we will present will show that they did it in

concert. They did it with criminal intent. They got away with it twice. Maybe three is a charm. Maybe the tangled web finally gave way of its own nasty weight.

"At the close of final arguments in this case after you've heard all the evidence for both sides, heard the instructions of the court and everyone's argument, I'll come back here, and I will ask you to return guilty verdicts."

Some listeners in the courtroom thought Kunkle's opening statement wasn't strong enough to overcome the lack of a smoking gun. Kunkle delivered it in a straightforward manner without much passion. In fact, the only time Kunkle seemed outraged was when he quoted Steven Miller, a law student who had overheard Sheriff's Detective Dennis Kurzawa in the hallway outside the courtroom where Sheriff's Lieutenant James Montesano was about to testify about the "vision" statement before Cruz's third trial.

"Are you going to back me up?" Miller had said he'd heard Kurzawa say to Montesano. Kunkle repeated that twice for the jury.

Kunkle, though, had to pack so much information and so many issues into his presentation that it was possible the jury just couldn't grasp it.

In fact, one juror, a sales representative for an industrial company, later said that much of Kunkle's opening statement went right over her head.

"I was flustered," the juror said. "I couldn't ask questions. I didn't know what he was talking about."

On the defense side of the courtroom, Terry Gillespie, lawyer for Dennis Kurzawa, had known it would be difficult for Kunkle to lay out the entire case in an easy-to-grasp way.

"I think it was as difficult a factual presentation to keep straight and organized as I have run across," Gillespie said later.

Because Kunkle finished his statement in the early afternoon, he didn't have the advantage of letting his words sink in with the jury overnight. Instead, Gillespie stepped in front of the jury to give an opening statement on behalf of Dennis Kurzawa.

Gillespie, a veteran defense lawyer who had honed his courtroom techniques as a Cook County prosecutor and who had prosecuted cases with Tom Breen, gave a folksy, passionate opening that portrayed Kurzawa and the other detectives as unsophisticated, error-prone officers in a placid county who hardly knew the prosecutors with whom they allegedly had conspired and who were victimized by a lying Rolando Cruz.

"They needed a break . . . not to have someone come in and try to make [their investigation] go haywire," Gillespie told the jury.

Gillespie also disputed Kunkle's assertion that all the important statements were in court records. Gillespie wanted the jury to focus on Cruz's lies instead.

"Make no mistake about it," Gillespie said. "[Cruz] isn't one-tenth of one percent of this case. He is ninety-nine and ninety-nine hundredths of this case."

The next morning, Brian Telander, the former chief DuPage County criminal prosecutor, gave his opening statement on behalf of Thomas Vosburgh. Telander designed his opening to help the jury identify with the law officers, who came from their own county, rather than a young Hispanic man with a checkered past who lived in the next county.

"While Tom was working his second job to put his children through college, Rolando Cruz was unemployed, sniffing paint, doing dope, dropping acid," Telander said. "While Tom was working long hours away from his family on Christmas, on Easter, at nights, on weekends, whatever they made him do so that you and I could have safe homes, Rolando Cruz was out breaking into people's homes, destroying their homes, taking whatever he wanted."

Implying that the case was so feeble it should never have been allowed in a courtroom, Telander asked the jury a question that other defense lawyers would repeat as a recurring motif:

"What are we doing here?"

To bolster the defense argument that the conflicting statements by law officers could simply be mistakes, Telander cited a dozen errors Kunkle had made in his opening statement. Kunkle had said the first report on an April 19, 1983, meeting with Cruz was done by Kurzawa when he meant Vosburgh. He'd given the Nicarico's address as 622 Clover Court instead of 620. He'd incorrectly set an encounter between Cruz and Hernandez at the courthouse in DuPage County instead of Kane County. Twice, he'd given the date of the "vision" statement as February 9, 1983, instead of May 9. He'd been off a day in pegging the date Cruz first was brought in to talk to Tom Knight. He'd said Sam and Kurzawa, instead of Sam and Wilkosz, asked Cruz about Chesty Puller. He'd incorrectly said Cruz was asked no questions at a January 26, 1984, grand jury session, and he'd described a May 13, 1984, conversation between Cruz and Wilkosz when he meant Cruz and Winkler. He'd confused Wilkosz with Winkler at another point, too, and had said Ray Ortega's name when he meant Emilio Donatlan.

"Everybody makes mistakes," Telander said, driving the point home, "even superstar accomplished lawyers."

Telander also argued that Cruz—because he had given detectives and the grand jury misleading information—was responsible for whatever harm he suffered.

"He should be on trial here," Telander said. "Rolando Cruz is not a victim in this case. Whatever happened to him, he did to himself."

After Telander, Terry Ekl gave his opening statement on behalf of Tom Knight. Ekl, a former Cook County prosecutor who once had prosecuted cases with Tom Breen, now was a defense lawyer in DuPage County with strong ties to the Republican organization.

As Gillespie and Telander had, Ekl talked about his client's accomplishments, both as a lawyer and a family man. He ridiculed Kunkle's argument.

"Where's the evidence of conspiracy? . . . You don't infer a conspiracy from the normal everyday acts of a prosecutor," Ekl said.

Ekl also introduced an argument Gillespie and Telander hadn't used. He suggested that Cruz might have known Brian Dugan, implying they could have committed the murder together.

"I believe Cruz will come in here and tell you he does not know Brian Dugan," Ekl said. "I think you're going to hear evidence from which you may very well conclude—you guessed it— that it is a lie."

Ekl was followed by Ronald Menaker, lawyer for Robert Kilander, who was accused of concealing notes from the meeting at which DuPage County authorities first learned of Brian Dugan's admissions. Menaker said Cruz's defense lawyers received reams of information about Dugan from the Illinois State Police and didn't need the "Kilander notes." Moreover, he argued, Kilander never tried to hide them.

"Bob Kilander didn't rip them up like a conspirator," Menaker said. "He didn't burn them."

Next, Daniel Reidy, lawyer for former DuPage County prosecutor Patrick King, called absence of a report on the "vision" statement nothing more than an "embarrassing miscommunication."

Ernie DiBenedetto, lawyer for Sheriff's Lieutenant Robert Winkler, said Winkler was not a trained detective and never had testified in a murder trial before. DiBenedetto argued that Winkler's testimony sounded different from trial to trial only because he was asked different questions. For example, he said, Winkler didn't withhold the fact about Cruz arranging to crush the green Lincoln until the third trial; Winkler had told prosecutors that before the second trial, but they just hadn't used it.

Finally, Joseph Laraia, lawyer for Sheriff's Lieutenant James Montesano, gave his opening statement. He maintained that Montesano hadn't changed his story at all; all along he'd said he didn't really remember a call from Vosburgh and Kurzawa. He just didn't know for certain there was no call until he remembered he could check his receipts from Florida.

When Laraia finished, prosecutor Michael Bartosz worried that the combined effect of all those impassioned appeals might have overwhelmed Kunkle's opening in the judge and jury's minds.

"I didn't appreciate before the trial as much as I did right after it happened what the impact would be of seven defense opening statements back to back to back to back from seasoned, well-prepared, excellent legal orators," Bartosz said later. "In terms of conditioning the atmosphere of the courtroom before we called a witness, I think it was more powerful than I might have foreseen before we started the case."

Terry Gillespie, defense lawyer for Dennis Kurzawa, said later that the defense openings were effective partly because the ten attorneys on the defense team worked so well together. Sometimes, lawyers in trials with codefendants undercut each other as they pursue the strategies they each think are best for their clients, but the DuPage Seven defense team was "the closest-knit group of lawyers that I ever worked with," Gillespie said.

"The lawyers worked together every night, and we met every morning and on weekends," Gillespie said "There were some pretty strenuous discussions about the best way to go and everyone had a great deal to say, but it was the most experienced group of defense lawyers I've ever worked with, and everyone liked each other."

By the time the lawyers gave their opening statements, the group had decided that "the issue was the credibility of Rolando Cruz," Gillespie said.

"I thought from the beginning that the prosecution's case rested solely on the back of Rolando Cruz," he said. ". . . I think Kunkle did everything he could to take Rolando Cruz out of the equation, and I think the defense team did everything they could to put him in."

After the opening statements, it was time for the case in chief. And immediately, from the point of view of Kunkle's team, things began to get even worse.

Kunkle wanted to introduce as evidence the huge number of police reports that had been filed in the original investigation. He wanted to show how Cruz's statements before and after the alleged "vision" statement were all documented in police reports. He wanted to show that the DuPage County sheriff's officers had grilled John Ruiz when he said he'd had a dream. They'd taken blood and hair samples, given him a polygraph test, and interrogated him extensively. But when Cruz supposedly gave his "vision" statement to police, it just disappeared until it was time for the trial. A big stack of police reports about the other events would vividly illustrate how mysterious it was that the sheriff's officers hadn't written a single report about the "vision" statement, Kunkle thought.

"We never anticipated any problem in just introducing them wholesale," Kunkle said later. "And that was going to be the first day. I mean it was going to take a while to do that, because there were a lot of them—and we wanted to bring out very specific high points about that, with respect to Ruiz, blood and hair—but in any event, as soon as we started to do this, somebody objected and cited the statute that says police reports aren't admissible."

Normally, police reports aren't admissible against a defendant because they might contain damaging information and the defense can't cross-examine a report. Instead, the police officer who filed the report is expected to testify. But these reports were being introduced to illustrate police procedures, not to use the information in them against Cruz. Kunkle thought the defense objection was offered almost as a joke, and he was amazed when Judge Kelly took it seriously and ruled the reports could not be admitted.

Terry Ekl, Tom Knight's lawyer, didn't miss the opportunity to take a jab at Kunkle.

"Two-and-a-half years [of trial preparation], and he can't put on admissible evidence," Ekl said outside of court.

Kunkle had chosen the police-report tactic instead of another option: bringing in an expert witness. He could have used a top Chicago homicide detective or a national figure who trained investigators to explain to a jury that no state's attorney would ever instruct detectives to stop questioning a suspect who had just made a significant oral admission.

"This is a guy who's breaking down supposedly," Kunkle said later. "He is giving you exactly what you want. So that now that you've got it—oh, let's quit. Let's not write it down. And let's not record it. And let's not even remember it tomorrow morning. I mean, it was just totally absurd."

Kunkle had decided not to bring in an expert witness because the defense lawyers would procure their own, and it would become a battle of expert witnesses. Instead, he thought he could make his point more effectively by introducing the huge stack of police reports as the trial opened. Now, he wouldn't be able to do that.

"That really knocked our socks off at the beginning of the trial," Kunkle said later.

Kunkle had to delay the testimony of his first witness, Tom Laz, who had represented Cruz at the first trial, while Kunkle restructured his case to take Judge Kelly's ruling about the police reports into account. It was the last day of testimony for the week. Over the weekend, Kunkle and the other prosecutors worked to get reorganized.

The trial resumed the following Tuesday, and Laz finished his testimony, saying he first heard of what turned out to be the "vision" statement only four days before the 1985 trial began. Then it was time for Kunkle to put on Rolando Cruz. Kunkle had hoped to build up momentum with his opening statement and the police reports before Cruz took the stand, but the case was off to a slow start. It was going to be up to Cruz to get it back on track. And up to now, no jury ever had sided with Rolando Cruz.

The courtroom was filled to capacity on the third day of testimony. Everyone knew Rolando Cruz was scheduled to take the stand. Cruz arrived nicely attired in a white shirt and a tie with his new wife, Dora. The lawyers and jury took their place, and Kunkle was ready to begin.

First, Kunkle asked Cruz questions about his background. Cruz said that his father, Robert Roger Medina, was a body-and-fender man who also was an Aurora city councilman and his mother, Dora, had been a factory worker all her life. He said he had three sisters and attended a number of different schools because he moved frequently after his parents divorced in about 1978 while he was in junior high.

Cruz then said he left school in the tenth grade. At that point, he entered the army reserves and went for basic training at Fort Dix in Kentucky. He admitted, though, that he stopped showing up later for weekend duties and eventually was dishonorably discharged. He also admitted committing three burglaries of drug dealers with Arthur Burrell in 1982 as well as serving twenty-six days in jail on an attempted burglary charge that was reduced to criminal damage to property.

Kunkle knew he would have to explain to the jury about Cruz's history of lies. He had Cruz describe his falsehoods and why he told them. Cruz said it was because he didn't like the people he told lies about and didn't like the police because he blamed them for his cousin's drowning death. He had seen them beat people up, and he thought they had lied to him. Cruz's most emotional moment was when he described how his cousin, Rico, drowned while running from police. Cruz said Rico's death was one of the reasons he didn't like police and lied to them.

Then Kunkle got to the heart of the "vision" statement.

"Did you tell them anything about having a dream or a vision?" Kunkle asked.

"No, sir," Cruz said.

"Did you tell him you had imagined something about the crime or how it might have happened?"

"No, sir," Cruz repeated. "I never said anything like that."

"Did you tell them that in this dream or vision that you saw the girl being hit in the head so hard that it left an impression in the ground or in the mud?"

"I never mentioned anything about any dream or vision or anybody being hit in the head that left any kind of marks in the mud or anything like that," Cruz testified.

The direct examination took a full day and part of the next. Then it was time for the cross-examination. For months, defense lawyers had been talking about how eager they were to get Cruz on the witness stand. Now was their chance.

Terry Gillespie, Dennis Kurzawa's lawyer, stormed up before the witness stand, looking angry. He grilled Cruz about why he had left his various jobs and whether Cruz, who said he was a Muslim, knew lying was a violation of the Ten Commandments. He asked about his association with Latin Kings gang members and his history as a burglar. Striding around the well of the courtroom, he took Cruz over and over the incident with Arthur Burrell that resulted in Cruz's conviction for criminal damage to property.

At one point, when Gillespie challenged Cruz over his description of the distance between him and Burrell, Cruz said, "He didn't have to be next to me to talk to me."

"Were you screaming ahead?" Gillespie asked. "Hey, Arthur, are you going to burglarize that house up there?"

"Well," Cruz replied, "you haven't been standing right next to me, sir, but you've been talking to me, also."

"And you haven't been answering my questions," Gillespie snapped.

"Yes, I have," Cruz said. "You just don't like my answers."

"That I don't," Gillespie said.

As Gillespie went on, he kept hammering Cruz about his lies, misstating Cruz's answers to keep him off balance and asking some questions apparently more to keep the jury thinking about lies than to get information.

"You lied so much you don't even know how you did it, is that what it is?" he asked at one point.

For the most part, though, Cruz held his own, and he even drew sympathetic laughter several times from the courtroom.

That changed dramatically, though, when Brian Telander, Thomas Vosburgh's lawyer, took his turn to cross-examine Cruz. Telander followed Gillespie's pattern, grilling Cruz about his statements over the years and asking about his lies and the discrepancies in his testimony.

Then came a moment that might have been the turning point of the trial.

Continuing to interrogate Cruz about his fabrications, Telander asked: "I take it you're trying to tell these ladies and gentlemen by 1996 your lying days are over, isn't that right?"

"Yeah," Cruz said. "I see a psychiatrist now, and I work real hard on stopping lying, sir."

The minute Cruz said that, almost everyone in the courtroom knew they had just witnessed one of those key moments that can define a trial. Cruz—whom Kunkle had put on the stand to deny making the "vision" statement—was implying that he couldn't stop lying, even in 1999. Although he was working with a psychiatrist, Cruz implied, sticking to the truth was still a challenge for him.

Everyone in the courtroom was stunned. It was huge. It was like O. J. Simpson trying on the glove that didn't fit. The reporters started working out the leads of the stories they would write or broadcast, all focusing on Cruz and his psychological struggle with lying. William Kunkle sank down into his chair, wishing he was somewhere else far, far away. Telander, making sure the judge and jury didn't miss the significance of Cruz's answer, turned toward Cruz and threw up his hands in surprise. Savoring the moment, Ernie DiBenedetto, lawyer for Robert Winkler, asked Cruz to repeat what he'd said.

"Judge, I didn't hear well," DiBenedetto said. "I need to hear that again, sir."

It would turn out later that, ironically, Cruz's admission wasn't even accurate. True, he had seen a psychiatrist, but that was to help him adjust to life after twelve years in prison. The psychiatric help was a fact that, had Kunkle known it, he could have brought out on direct examination, helping to portray Cruz as a sympathetic figure. But it was too late now. The DuPage Seven case, a huge challenge from the start, probably was close to beyond salvaging.

"It was just horrible," Kunkle recalled later. "It wasn't even responsive to a question. He just volunteered it. You know those airline ads where you have just ruined the company's computer system and you want to get away? I wanted to be in Disney World."

Instead of being whisked away to Disney World, Kunkle had to watch, objecting when he could, as the defense lawyers did their best to pin down Cruz in contradictions.

At one point, Terry Ekl, lawyer for Tom Knight, asked Cruz, "Did you tell [probation officer] Jody Blair when she did her probation report in early December of 1983 that you had lived at 128 South Fourth Street, Aurora, Illinois, with your mother and aunt from April of '78 to November of '83?"

Cruz answered, "That's a lie. . . . My mother didn't live there in '78, sir."

Ekl showed Cruz an adult social history form Cruz had filled out listing his previous address as 128 South Fourth Street, naming the occupants as his mother and aunt and listing the dates as April 1978 to November 1983.

"This is what you told Jody Blair, right?" Ekl said.

"No, that is what I wrote but that is not what I told her," Cruz replied.

The cross-examination lasted two days. When it was over, Kunkle asked only a few questions on redirect. He hoped to patch up some of the holes the defense lawyers had torn in Cruz's story, but he didn't want to ask anything that could lead to a re-cross by the defense lawyers. He wanted to get Cruz off the stand.

But the damage was done. As the blistering cross-examination had worn Cruz down, he'd become more hostile and defensive. Patrick Tuite, one of Robert Kilander's two defense lawyers, later called Cruz one of the worst courtroom witnesses he'd seen in his career. Cruz wound up looking so bad that even one of the reporters who had covered the case extensively muttered bitterly, "I don't care. He's guilty of something."

The jurors were affected, too. Many of them didn't find Cruz credible and thought his testimony undermined the whole case, juror Richard W. Besler said later.

Calling Cruz's testimony a "pivotal moment," one of the alternate jurors later said, "It was hard to take his word when we knew he was sitting in front of us not telling us the truth."

The juror who was a sales representative later said, "When Cruz testified, that did it for me."

When it was over, Terry Ekl said the DuPage Seven lawyers were pleased with the results of the cross-examination for which they prepared such a long time.

"He was worth the wait," Ekl said outside the courtroom.

Things didn't get any better for Kunkle's team over the next three weeks. Kunkle hoped he might get some dramatic testimony from the witnesses he called, among them John Sam, Gary Johnson, Bill Clutter, and Robert Mull, who was an investigator for the DuPage County public defender's office. But none of them turned out to be a bombshell. That was partly because Kunkle was limited in the questions he could ask them. But there were missed opportunities as well, Kunkle thought. To him, Gary Johnson seemed careful to the point of being stilted. John Sam acted so chummy toward his former colleagues that the judge and jury might have interpreted that as support for them, and he waffled, Kunkle thought, in his testimony. Laz had been a disappointment at the start of the trial, and Mull came across as confused.

The prosecutors had hoped to use the testimony of Michael Metnick, who had represented Hernandez, to make it clear to the jury why the defense needed the "Kilander notes" even though so much other information had been turned over. Metnick was ready to explain how the notes would have reshaped the pretrial hearings into the Dugan evidence, but Judge Kelly wouldn't let the prosecutors ask Metnick about it.

"We weren't able to have Metnick tell the story," Bartosz said later. "We were hamstrung in trying to get that out in a way where people would [understand it]. Metnick was going to explain how it mattered [but] we weren't able to put it in the way we wanted to."

Warren Wilkosz, though, turned out to be surprisingly helpful. Wilkosz said that he always filed reports on important statements made by suspects, thus helping to show how unlikely it was that detectives would not write a report on something as important as the "vision" statement. He said he never had heard of the "vision" statement, even though he was the lead detective on the case, until it turned up at the first trial. And he described his original investigation into Brian Dugan, saying he stopped when he was told to take no more action until he received further orders, which never came.

Jed Stone, Cruz's lawyer at the second trial, was another bright spot for Kunkle, although he was on the stand only briefly. Stone was prepared, if the right questions were asked on cross-examination, to say that Kilander had denied there was anything of evidentiary value from the Prairie Path when in fact there were tire castings that were very important. Stone also was eager to testify that Kilander had withheld the so-called Kilander notes that documented Brian Dugan's early statements. But Kunkle couldn't ask about those issues on direct examination, and the defense lawyers wisely decided against an extensive cross-examination.

"You don't cross swords with Darth Vader," Brian Telander told Stone after he left the stand. Stone took that to be a compliment.

The witness who spent the most time on the stand was Ed Cisowski, who led the Illinois State Police investigation. Kunkle wanted Cisowski to explain the importance of the Kilander notes, the heart of the case against Robert Kilander and Patrick King.

Up until now, Daniel Reidy, King's lawyer, had followed an effective strategy: because King's alleged role in the conspiracy was so small, Reidy had kept him out of the jury's eye as much as possible. Before the trial, King's photo had been the hardest for the local newspapers to get; in some cases they'd gone days before running a picture of him with the other defendants. In the courtroom, Reidy and King sat farthest from the jury, behind other defendants, where they could hardly be seen.

When Cisowski took the stand, though, Reidy started a long cross-examination. By the time he and other lawyers had finished, trying to pin Cisowski down in contradictions, Cisowski had testified for four days. In the end, the jury felt sorry for him.

Tim Gabrielsen and John Hanlon, the appellate defenders for Cruz after the first trial, drove up from Springfield to testify briefly that they never received the Kilander notes. Hanlon was amazed at how crowded the well of the courtroom was; he had never seen that many defendants and lawyers in a courtroom before. Things were running behind schedule, though, so they drove several hours home and then came back the next day.

When Gabrielsen finished testifying, he walked out of the courtroom into the wide, empty hallway. Thomas and Patricia Nicarico were seated by themselves on one of the benches along the walls. They weren't allowed inside the courtroom during testimony, so they sat outside to keep track of developments and to show their support for the defendants.

Gabrielsen went over to the Nicaricos to tell them how sorry he felt for what had happened to Jeanine. It was an emotional encounter. Thomas Nicarico shook Gabrielsen's hand, and then Patricia held it gently the entire time they spoke.

"I just told them that I had young daughters, and I was sorry for what happened to their daughter," Gabrielsen said later. "We stood there and talked for maybe ten minutes."

Gabrielsen, who had grown up in the DuPage County town of Elmhurst, thought Jeanine's murder had affected families throughout the area.

"I grew up in DuPage County, too, and I don't think anybody when I was a kid thought you couldn't leave your kids home from school," he said. "You would have felt completely secure in that, and I think that the Nicarico case kind of shattered that for a lot of people."

Some mornings and afternoons of the prosecution's case were devoted to reading aloud portions of transcripts from earlier trials. Court reporters, taking the roles of various witnesses in earlier trials, read large sections to the judge and jury for hours at a stretch. The transcripts contained nuggets of significant testimony, but there was no way to highlight the important parts as the reading droned on. Whenever it was time to introduce more transcripts, the pace of the trial seemed to slow to a quantum state in which even the clocks didn't see any point in trying to watch the time. Kunkle needed to make the statements from the earlier trials part of the evidence, but the jury found it very dull.

On a Saturday morning midway through the trial, some of the reporters covering the case discussed it on a program titled *At Issue* on WBBM-AM, a Chicago news radio station. The reporters on the show, which was hosted by radio journalist Craig Dellimore, agreed that the defense lawyers' strategy seemed to be working. *Chicago Tribune* reporter Ted Gregory said he didn't think any of the reporters covering the case thought it was going well for the prosecution.

From Kunkle's point of view, though, things were about to get much worse.

After Kunkle rested his case, the defense lawyers filed a

motion for a directed verdict, just as Cruz's lawyers had done after the state rested its case at his third trial. Outside the courtroom, they told reporters they didn't expect to win it, just as Cruz's lawyer's hadn't expected to win the one they filed with Judge Ronald Mehling. But just as Judge Mehling decided in 1995 that there was not enough evidence to proceed with the case against Cruz, Judge Kelly on May 13, 1999, ruled that there was not enough evidence against Robert Kilander or Patrick King. Even before the defense called its first witness, the case against those two men was over. Kilander and King were free to go, and the DuPage Seven had become the DuPage Five.

Down in the temporary pressroom set up for the trial, Robert Kilander told reporters he was elated.

"I am truly delighted to be able to go back to my regular duties as a judge," he said. "I intend to renew those as soon as my wife and I have a couple of days to come to be reacquainted in a normal world. I'm proud of my lawyers and the case they presented on my behalf, proud of the judge for doing what he should do."

Pat Tuite, one of Kilander's two lawyers, said Kunkle simply had not proved that Kilander had intended to obstruct justice for Cruz.

"The fact that two pages of notes were not turned over to Cruz's lawyers in 1989 was of no consequence when 800 to 900 pages of much more valuable evidence was being turned over on a regular basis," Tuite said.

Kunkle hadn't expected directed verdicts, but he knew the effect it would have on the jury. Although no one would say it directly, it would be clear the judge thought the prosecution's judgment was wrong about King and Kilander. Any doubts the jury had about the case—and by now there were sure to be plenty—

would just intensify. How strong could the conspiracy case against the remaining five men be if the judge thought the two others had nothing to do with it?

"Throwing out Kilander and King just killed us," Kunkle said later. "I don't care how you instruct [the jury], that is just deadly."

24

THE DUPAGE FIVE

*It's a lot easier to find someone guilty than it is later to
prove him innocent.*

Scott Christianson, in *Innocent: Inside
Wrongful Conviction Cases*

ROSECUTOR WILLIAM J. KUNKLE JR. had said he didn't
have a smoking gun. The lawyers for the remaining five
defendants knew they didn't need a smoking gun of
their own. Just the smoke would be enough if it clouded the case
sufficiently to make it impossible for the judge and jury to reach
guilty verdicts.

By now, the defense lawyers had reached an agreement: none
of the defendants would testify. Robert Kilander, perhaps the most
personable of the defendants and therefore a likely candidate to
get on the stand if any did, was gone from the case. Thomas
Knight wanted to testify, and his lawyer Terry Ekl had said he
would, but the other lawyers prevailed on him not to. They felt the
case was right where they wanted it, and they didn't want Kunkle
grilling any of the defendants about discrepancies in their stories.
If Knight testified about his side of the "vision" statement,
Vosburgh and Kurzawa might feel compelled to tell their sides of
the story. The defense case might sink into a sea of pointing fingers
that could turn into convictions for one or more of the defendants.

Also, a pretrial ruling had kept all grand jury testimony out of the case, but if the defendants testified, the prosecutors could use the grand jury testimony to challenge their stories. The grand jurors had heard the testimony of six of the seven defendants, and the prosecutors felt that the grand jury just didn't believe the defendants' explanations of what had happened. Prosecutor Michael Bartosz thought the grand jury testimony contained a land mine that could blow up the defense case: the "vision" story had changed again. Instead of taking place on May 9 as had always been testified to, the "vision" statement now could have happened over a span of several days in May. That, Bartosz thought, would be the smoking gun Kunkle needed.

Instead of having their clients testify, the defense team decided to limit its witnesses mostly to people who would say they heard Cruz talk about dreams. The more times the jurors heard about Cruz and dreams, the less likely they were to believe authorities fabricated a "vision" statement. In an answer to one of Kunkle's questions, Rolando Cruz had testified that he had never said anything about a dream or a vision. Now the defense lawyers wanted to make it look like he talked about nothing else.

Jean Tuzik, who had transported Cruz around the county as part of the witness protection program, testified she heard Cruz talk about a dream. A letter from one of Cruz's old girlfriends was introduced that included a description of Cruz dreaming about a motorcycle. Statements from two Naperville police officers were presented to the jury in which the officers said they had heard discussion about a Cruz dream in which he included details he shouldn't have known. Kevin Buchholtz, a former DuPage County sheriff's officer, testified he heard Vosburgh and Kurzawa telling Patrick King about the "vision" statement at the Christmas party before the first trial but didn't pay much attention because it was old news. (Buchholtz's story had not come up at the earlier trials, and outside of court, Kunkle scoffed: "Nobody believes him. I don't.") Two employees of the police department in the DuPage County town of West Chicago said they heard Cruz talking in a bar about a dream.

Perhaps most surprising was testimony of some members of the 1984 grand jury—the panel of twenty-three people that, Frank Wesolowski had said, thought it was up to them to solve the crime. Now, five of those people said Cruz had mentioned a dream when he was present to testify before the grand jury, even though no such statement showed up in the transcripts. One of the former grand jurors even said he discussed Cruz's dream with prosecutor Thomas Knight outside of the courtroom. Terry Ekl, Knight's lawyer, said Knight did not remember that. Moreover, Knight had signed a stipulation at the first trial that if the grand jury court reporters were to testify, they would say they had heard nothing from Cruz about a vision.

A sixth grand juror who didn't testify had taken detailed notes that mentioned no dream, and at first she told investigators that she hadn't heard Cruz say anything about a dream. Later, she said she remembered Cruz mentioning a dream, but she said it happened much later during the proceedings than the other grand jurors thought.

By now, the "vision" statement scenario had become one of the strangest stories ever heard in a DuPage courtroom. Just as it once had seemed to 1985 juror Michael Callahan that half of East Aurora was testifying against Cruz and Hernandez, many people in DuPage County now seemed to have heard about Cruz's dream or vision. Yet the people closest to the investigation never had picked up the slightest hint of it until Detective Thomas Vosburgh brought it up just before the 1985 trial. John Sam had never heard of it. Warren Wilkosz—the lead detective on the case—knew nothing about it. Patrick King, the assistant prosecutor on the case, was unaware of it until Vosburgh mentioned it. And Tom Knight, the lead prosecutor in the case, maintained he hadn't known about it, either, even though others said they had talked about it with him.

Detectives Vosburgh and Kurzawa said they told Knight about the vision statement before Cruz testified at the grand jury. Several grand jurors said Cruz mentioned the vision during the grand jury sessions. One grand juror testified he had a detailed discussion with Knight about the vision after one of the grand jury sessions.

The statement was such common knowledge around the county that two Naperville police officers said they had heard of it, and former DuPage sheriff's officer Kevin Buchholtz called it old news. Yet Knight—the man running the investigation—didn't know anything about it. And none of the people who said they knew about the vision statement at the time—and therefore arguably should have considered Cruz a suspect—put Cruz under surveillance or objected to the county housing him among the families of Glen Ellyn and Wheaton and near the students of Wheaton College.

Detective Vosburgh testified that Kurzawa had been present when Cruz made the vision statement and at the December 20, 1984, Christmas party conversation with assistant prosecutor Patrick King. Vosburgh also said that he and Kurzawa then had gone to Knight to tell him about the vision statement. Yet according to Robert Mull, the defense investigator, when Mull subsequently talked to Vosburgh in January, 1985, Vosburgh said he was alone with Cruz when Cruz made the vision statement. And at the 1996 grand jury, King said he didn't remember Kurzawa talking about the vision statement at the Christmas party.

There was also something odd about the vision statement itself. Some of the key information—the things Cruz wasn't supposed to have known—resembled details that a law officer might be more likely to notice than a perpetrator. It was true that there was an indentation in the ground under Jeanine's head, but that would have been visible only after the body had been moved or rolled away. A perpetrator would have been less likely to see it than someone who came to the scene later. Moreover, a perpetrator would have been more likely to describe the area where the body was found as a nature trail. It was the law officers who trudged across a farmer's field to get to the scene so they wouldn't disturb evidence, and therefore would be more likely to think of the location as near a field. And the statement that Jeanine was dragged from her house was consistent with the police theory at the time because they believed they saw marks of her fingers along the wall near the door and they thought the bloodhounds followed her scent along the ground from the house to the street. It was only later that the State Police concluded those were not Jeanine's finger marks and that Brian Dugan's description of what happened provided an alternate explanation for the dogs' behavior.

The fourth key fact in the vision statement—that Jeanine had been assaulted anally—was a piece of information deliberately withheld from the public so that police could test the veracity of someone making statements about the case. It was something police were listening for. Yet Kurzawa didn't ask Cruz about it the next morning in the tape-recorded interview.

Questions about the "vision" statement, though, didn't stop Terry Ekl, Tom Knight's lawyer, from introducing a separate line of defense.

"[Ekl] set out to prove, once again, that Cruz had, in fact, killed Jeanine Nicarico," defense lawyer Patrick Tuite later wrote in an analysis of the trial that appeared in a legal publication. "The rest of the attorneys thought he was taking on an unnecessary burden, and that it was potentially dangerous. If he was unsuccessful in convincing the jury that Cruz was the killer, it might somehow affect our ability to obtain acquittals for our clients."

Ekl, though, hoped to make the jury think that Dugan and Cruz were involved in the crime together. Earlier in the trial, when Ekl had cross-examined Cruz, he had asked him about a number of witnesses whom Ekl planned to call. Ekl wanted Cruz to deny those witnesses' stories.

"I asked him those questions because we intend to put witnesses on who will then impeach what he said when he says he never did burglaries with Brian Dugan or with Alex Hernandez," Ekl said outside of court.

Ekl never did call many of those witnesses, but he did put others on the stand to try to link Cruz to Dugan.

"I think the big lie in this case is that Brian Dugan and Rolando Cruz did not know each other back in 1983 on the streets of Aurora," Ekl said outside of court during the trial. "We are going to put on witnesses who will establish that those two did in fact know each other on the streets of Aurora, both committing burglaries together, fencing property together, and hanging out together."

In the end, though, Ekl couldn't support that argument.

Many of the witnesses he mentioned never were called. Others offered only sketchy testimony. One said he'd seen a Hispanic man on crutches with Dugan at a time when Cruz had a broken leg, but the witness didn't know if the man he'd seen was in fact Cruz.

A private investigator testified about Cruz's and Dugan's addresses, showing that at various times they lived near each other in East Aurora. At one point, for example, Cruz lived at 245 S. Lincoln Avenue while Dugan lived 150 yards away in a boarding house at 306 S. LaSalle Street. The most significant claim was that Dugan and Cruz lived on the same block on the east side of Aurora in buildings separated only by a vacant lot. One building was a rooming house where Dugan was known to have stayed, and the other was a converted duplex where Cruz's family lived on the second floor.

Ekl used an undated car insurance application to suggest that they lived there at the same time. Later, though, it turned out that the form was filled out six months later than Ekl guessed and that Dugan had showed up at that address only after Cruz had moved out early in 1983. A friend of the person who rented the room told Randy Garrett that Dugan was at that address for just a short while in July 1983, sleeping on the sofa.

"They continued to suggest Cruz was guilty, which I found outrageous," said Hal Dardick, now a *Chicago Tribune* reporter.

Then, on a Friday, May 28, it was time for closing arguments. Kunkle went first, saying that the actions and statements of DuPage County authorities proved Cruz never gave a "vision" statement with incriminating details. The record of Cruz's visit to the sheriff's office on May 9, 1983—with no record of what he said—later gave DuPage County authorities the chance to insert their own story, Kunkle argued.

"When you don't have a police report, and when you don't have a tape recording, and when you don't have a court reported statement, and when you don't have a videotape, you have the opportunity to fabricate," Kunkle said.

"[DuPage County authorities] did not treat Cruz in the way that they treated John Ruiz when he made a dream statement," Kunkle pointed out. "They did not ask any other witness—think about this one for a minute—any other witness, Cruz's acquaintances, these other defendants, they didn't ask anybody whether Cruz talked about a dream until 1995 or 1996 when it became important for other reasons."

Before Kunkle could come close to finishing, though, the courthouse administrators learned they were going to lose much of their power and that the air-conditioning would have to be shut off. Judge Kelly knew the courtroom would heat up quickly with so many people in the room, so he sent everyone home for the weekend. It was just one more snag for Kunkle's case.

The following Tuesday, Kunkle resumed his closing argument, explaining why Cruz gave inconsistent statements on what he really said on May 9, 1983.

"If the dream statement didn't happen that night, he can't remember," Kunkle said. "For a good reason. Because it didn't happen."

The grand jurors from the first trial who said Cruz had talked about a vision or dream were simply confused after fifteen years, Kunkle said. Their descriptions of what they remembered actually corresponded with Ruiz's story about a dream and Cruz's Donatlan statement, both of which were known to have been presented to the grand jury, he said.

Kunkle also said the judge and jurors didn't see elaborate evidence of a conspiracy because the defendants knew not to leave a trail.

"These are some smart people you're dealing with here," Kunkle said. "A wink and a nod is all that's necessary. A look at the other guy's testimony is all that's necessary. 'Are you going to back us up?' is all that's necessary."

It was absurd for the defense to argue, Kunkle said, that Cruz deserved all those years on death row because he lied to authorities.

"This case," Kunkle said, "is about going too far even when you think you're right. . . . The issue is that—whether you think you're right or not—you can't embellish. You can't fabricate. You can't make up evidence, and you can't obstruct justice. It's against the law. And it is very important to our rights and liberties."

Steve Warmbir, then a reporter for the *Daily Herald* suburban newspaper who was assigned to the case late in the trial, was disappointed. Kunkle's closing in the John Wayne Gacy case was a legend, and Warmbir had been excited about the chance to hear Kunkle's summary of another big case. But the presentation was flat and dry, thought Warmbir, who later became a *Chicago Sun-Times* reporter.

Other reporters thought Kunkle simply didn't tell a clear, persuasive story that would help the jury make sense of a huge, complicated case. To them, he seemed rambling and dispirited. One writer called the closing soporific.

Next, the defense lawyers gave their closings. They restated the same arguments they had used earlier.

"Rolando Cruz was a lifelong immoral human being who wouldn't know the truth if it ran him over," argued Terry Ekl, Tom Knight's lawyer. "To say they don't have a smoking gun is a gross understatement of this case. They don't have a cap gun. They don't have a spitball."

After the defense lawyers spoke, Kunkle had one last chance

to talk to the judge and jury—his rebuttal. During the rebuttal, he read from an earlier Cruz grand jury statement in which Cruz said that on May 9, 1983, he told Vosburgh and Kurzawa the Donatlan story. That was consistent with Cruz's testimony during the DuPage Seven trial. Kunkle thought the transcript startled the defense lawyers; it supported what Cruz had been saying.

Then it was time for the case to go to the jury.

The time passed slowly the next day in the pressroom. Some of the reporters went upstairs to the hallway outside the courtrooms where some of the witnesses from the trial were milling about. One reporter who hadn't been covering the case for a long period said he thought there would be convictions; no one else did. Some of the reporters remembered the defense lawyers joking about what would happen if there was a hung jury. If the jury convicted Montesano, Vosburgh, Kurzawa, and Knight, the lawyers were sure the judge would convict Winkler. If the jury freed the other four, the lawyers thought Kelly would do the same for Winkler. "But what happens if there is a hung jury?" one of the defense lawyers asked. "You can't have a hung judge."

That evening, on June 4, 1999, word came down that the verdicts were in. The courtroom was filled to overflowing. The verdicts were handed to Judge Kelly, who looked at them. Then he started reading his verdict for Winkler.

The tone of his verdict was harsh. The defendants and their lawyers looked worried; if Winkler was convicted, they thought everyone would be. Then Kelly announced his decision: not guilty. Moments later he read the verdicts for the others. The jury had found them not guilty as well.

Lieutenant James Montesano stood up, waving his arms in triumph. Elated, Ekl and Knight hugged each other. The defendants were so excited, they walked over and started hugging the jurors, who hugged them back. The crowd in the courtroom stood in ovation.

Juror Nancy Suero said that when deliberations began, about half the jurors were ready to acquit the defendants immediately and half wanted to take time to discuss each charge, which the jury did. In the end, she said, the panel decided that the circumstantial evidence alone wasn't sufficient to support convictions and that Cruz's testimony wasn't believable. After the verdicts were announced, the jurors were surprised by the emotional outburst, but it was understandable because the defendants' lives had been in turmoil for so long as they wondered what would happen to their careers, she said.

"We were supposed to leave the box right away, and when we started leaving the box, all of a sudden it turned into a free-for-all," she said. "It kind of felt good because we kind of gave them their lives back."

Later, many of the jurors and the defendants went over to the Viking, where they had drinks together and danced with each other late into the night. But the jurors said that shouldn't be interpreted as bias in favor of the defendants.

"You've got these defendants who are so relieved and happy and all this emotion in the courtroom, and everyone got swept up in that," said an alternate juror who returned to the courtroom to hear the verdict. "When I look back, I would agree that was a little unusual."

Juror Richard Besler also called the postverdict drinks and dancing unusual, but said, "They were going to buy us free drinks, so why not go?"

Another juror, though, said at least some of the jurors went to the Viking only in hopes of learning answers about the confusing trial they had just witnessed. The juror said some members of the panel felt the evidence showed that some of the defendants might have been guilty, but the trial was too confusing for jurors to be sure of anything beyond reasonable doubt.

"You could not get an accurate story line on what took place," the juror said. "There were so many parts that weren't admissible—things would be thrown out and they would start on one part and then change it back to something else. It was too many people with too much time passed and too many things changing for all of us to keep any of it straight."

When Judge Kelly started reading the Winkler verdict, sounding as though he was going to convict Winkler, the jurors momentarily worried that they had made a mistake and voted the wrong way, the juror said.

For many people, the outcome of the DuPage Seven trial was like absolution for the investigation and prosecution of the Nicarico case.

"Everyone acted like: See, we were right all along," said one DuPage County defense lawyer, a former prosecutor. "At least, that was the impression around the courthouse, but I'm not sure the population as a whole saw it that way."

Chicago Tribune columnist Eric Zorn said in 2003 that he was still getting voice mail and e-mail messages from people, some of them belligerent, who "read into the verdict a de facto conviction of Cruz" for Jeanine's murder.

"The reasoning seems to be that if there was no conspiracy and the jury felt that Cruz was a liar, therefore he participated in the rape and murder of a little girl," Zorn said.

25

THE ILLINOIS SEVENTEEN

We haven't learned that ignoring the evils of our
society . . . will hurt us.

Barbara Tuchman, historian, in an interview with Bill Moyers

HE CASES OF ROLANDO Cruz and Alejandro Hernandez had brought new attention to a problem faced by every state with a death penalty: it was just too easy to convict innocent people of capital crimes.

Illinois had enacted a new death penalty law in 1977 after the U.S. Supreme Court nullified all death penalty laws around the country in 1972. By 2000, the state's death row was filling up rapidly.

But there was a problem. Thirteen of the people sent to death row—men whom the state had planned to execute—had been freed because they clearly were innocent or there was not enough evidence to justify even a guilty verdict, much less a sentence of death.

The first Illinois cases to be overturned were those of Darby Tillis and Perry Cobb, two men who had been sentenced to death for the murder of a restaurant owner and his customer on Chicago's North Side in 1977. After the chief witness against them confided to a law student that her boyfriend at the time was the real killer, Tillis and Cobb were acquitted in 1987, but the story generated relatively little coverage in the news media.

Then, in 1995, Rolando Cruz was acquitted, and Alejandro Hernandez was freed shortly afterward. Whether because of the large amount of news coverage surrounding their cases or for some other reason, authorities suddenly seemed to be more willing to examine claims of innocence. And as they took a more careful look at other cases, they saw substantial flaws.

Just six months after Cruz was acquitted in November 1995, two more men who had been sentenced to death—Dennis Williams and Verneal Jimerson—were freed. Williams and Jimerson were part of the so-called Ford Heights Four—four men who had been wrongfully convicted of murdering a young couple in 1978 in the south Chicago suburb of Ford Heights. Their two codefendants who had been sentenced only to prison terms, Willie Range and Kenneth Adams, were freed as well later on. All charges were dropped against the four men on July 2, 1996.

Later that month, prosecutors said they wouldn't retry the case of a downstate Illinois man named Joseph Burrows, whose conviction had been overturned on April 19, 1996, by the Illinois Supreme Court. The court ruled that Burrows never should have been found guilty of the murder of an eighty-eight-year-old farmer. The chief witness, a woman named Gayle Potter, had recanted her testimony that Burrows and another man, Ralph Frye, had fatally shot the victim. (Later, Potter pleaded guilty to committing the crime herself.)

Three months later, on October 4, 1996, Gary Gauger, age forty-four, a farmer living in McHenry County northwest of Chicago, walked out of prison after the Illinois Supreme Court upheld a lower court's decision to overturn his conviction for the murders of his elderly parents. A year later, federal prosecutors charged members of the Outlaws motorcycle gang with the murders.

Carl Lawson, convicted and sentenced to death in 1990 for the 1989 murder of an East St. Louis boy, was freed in December 1996, after a jury in Murphysboro, Illinois, acquitted him at his third trial.

A little more than two years later, Steven Smith, age thirty-six, was freed in February 1999 after the Illinois Supreme Court reversed his conviction and ordered him released. Smith had been sentenced to death for the 1985 fatal shooting of an assistant prison warden in a tavern on Chicago's South Side. The Illinois Supreme Court ruled there wasn't enough evidence to convict him.

Then, on May 17, 1999, charges were dropped against Ronald Jones, who had been convicted and sentenced to death for the 1985 rape and murder of Debra Smith in the Chicago neighborhood of Woodlawn. DNA tests showed Jones couldn't have raped Smith.

Perhaps the most dramatic case was that of Anthony Porter, who was within fifty hours of execution when the Illinois Supreme Court voted a reprieve so that the justices could decide whether he should not be executed because he was mentally impaired.

Porter had been convicted of murdering Marilyn Green, age nineteen, and Jerry Hillard, eighteen, who were shot to death on August 15, 1982, on Chicago's South Side. But five months after the court issued the reprieve, another man—Alstory Simon—confessed on videotape to investigator Paul Ciolino that he was the murderer. Two days later, on February 5, 1999, Porter was released from prison, and the murder charges were dropped in March.

About a year later, on January 19, 2000, prosecutors dropped charges against Steven Manning, a Chicago police officer who had been put on death row for the murder of James Pellegrino, a suburban trucker and a former partner of Manning's. Manning was sent to serve a term in a Missouri prison for unrelated kidnapping charges. He was freed in February 2004.

By now, thirteen men had been freed from death row in Illinois—more than the twelve who actually had been executed since the death penalty was reinstated. As each case was overturned, it triggered a willingness to consider flaws in other cases. And, too often, flaws turned up in those cases, too.

"Each of these cases, beginning with Cruz, has had an impact on everyone involved in the criminal justice system," said Locke Bowman, legal director of the University of Chicago's MacArthur Justice Center. "It has an impact on the way potential jurors think, on the way defense attorneys react to a client's protestations of innocence, and hopefully on prosecutors and judges as well."

Even Tom Breen said the Cruz case taught him things he hadn't known about the criminal justice system. After leading Cruz's defense, Breen pushed for the reopening of a case against two men he and Terry Ekl had prosecuted in 1977—Michael Evans and Paul Terry. Some elements of that case were similar to Cruz's, and—having been educated by the Cruz case—Breen now worried that they might not have been guilty after all. After the case was reopened, newly available DNA testing showed the men were innocent, and they were freed.

On January 31, 2000, Illinois governor George Ryan declared a moratorium on executions. Illinois became the first of the thirty-eight states with a death penalty to put the whole process on hold. (Nebraska's legislature had approved a moratorium in the previous year, but it was vetoed by the governor.)

Ryan (no relation to Jim Ryan, the DuPage County state's attorney who prosecuted the Cruz case) said he was troubled by the high number of capital cases in which the courts found serious errors.

"There is no margin for error when it comes to putting a person to death," Ryan said.

On March 9, 2000, Ryan set up a fourteen-member blue-ribbon panel called the Commission on Capital Punishment to study death penalty reforms in Illinois. The chairman was former U.S. Judge Frank McGarr. Cochairmen were former U.S. Senator Paul Simon and Thomas P. Sullivan, who was U.S. attorney for the Northern District of Illinois from 1977 to 1981. Lawyer-author Scott Turow, who had represented Alejandro Hernandez, also was on the panel.

On September 26, 2000, DuPage County state's attorney Joseph Birkett reluctantly agreed to settle wrongful conviction lawsuits filed by Stephen Buckley, Rolando Cruz, and Alejandro Hernandez for $3.5 million. The agreement also ended lawsuits by DuPage County detectives Thomas Vosburgh and Dennis Kurzawa, who alleged that Cruz and one of his lawyers had orchestrated the DuPage Seven indictments to boost Cruz's chances for a large civil settlement.

Public comments by DuPage County officials showed how the DuPage Seven acquittals had changed public perceptions from sympathy for Cruz to suspicion that the original Nicarico defendants were killers.

"I feel guilty for making this decision," Birkett told the *Chicago Tribune.* "It is morally repugnant to give money to someone we believe may have been involved in this crime."

DuPage County Board president Robert Schillerstrom, who could vote only to break ties, said he opposed the deal.

"I can't agree or go along with giving money to people who we believe were involved in the abduction, rape, and murder of one of our citizens," Schillerstrom told the *Tribune*.

DuPage County Board member William Maio said, "This is the most disgusting and disturbing motion I've had to make in 15 years on the board."

Michael McMahon, a Republican DuPage County Board member from Hinsdale and longtime political ally of Joseph Birkett, went further: "If it was up to me, we'd take these three guys into the basement and shoot them," McMahon said.

On April 15, 2002, the Commission on Capital Punishment recommended eighty-five reforms designed to reduce injustices in the death penalty.

Attention then turned to a clemency petition Lawrence Marshall had filed on behalf of Rolando Cruz on September 18, 2002. Marshall argued that Illinois governor George Ryan should pardon Cruz. DuPage County state's attorney Joseph Birkett, however, filed papers arguing that there still were questions about whether Cruz was, in fact, innocent.

Marshall objected to Birkett's filing.

"For ten years these prosecutors vehemently argued that Brian Dugan had nothing to do with this crime, that he was lying about any involvement," Marshall told the *Chicago Tribune*. "Now they acknowledge Dugan's involvement, yet they somehow refuse to acknowledge that not only were they profoundly mistaken as to Dugan but they were, of course, equally mistaken about Cruz . . . having been involved."

Birkett also said that the investigation into Brian Dugan was continuing. A new DNA test, even more precise than the one before Cruz's trial, had been conducted and again matched Brian

Dugan, and authorities said they expected to indict Dugan for the Nicarico murder in 2005.

During the election campaign in the fall of 2002, both Jim Ryan, who was running as the Republican candidate for Illinois governor (Republican incumbent George Ryan had decided not to seek reelection), and Joseph Birkett, who was the GOP candidate for state attorney general, were criticized for their handling of the Rolando Cruz case. Oddly, the issue was raised less in Jim Ryan's campaign than in Birkett's; Ryan was running far behind in the polls, and Democratic front-runner Rod Blagojevich saw no reason to introduce additional issues that might cloud the campaign.

Birkett, though he played only a small role in the case, was chided by Democratic opponent Lisa Madigan for the way he handled the interview with Stephen Schmitt, the witness who recanted his story that Cruz had admitted committing the Nicarico murder with Dugan as well as the other two original defendants.

"Joe Birkett needs to come clean and tell us about his involvement with the prosecution of Rolando Cruz," Madigan said at a September 23, 2002, news conference.

"Joe Birkett visited the home of a jailhouse snitch—actually a jailhouse acquaintance of Rolando Cruz—and threatened to arrest the man unless they secured a statement that Cruz confessed to the murder," Madigan said at the news conference. "It didn't matter that Birkett was told that the statement would be a lie. He provided details of the crime for the statement and knowingly submitted this false testimony for use in the prosecution. Mr. Birkett elicited this false testimony—again according to the petition—to discredit expected DNA evidence that would exclude Cruz."

Madigan also criticized Birkett for wearing a button reflecting support for the DuPage Seven during the trial.

"Joe Birkett proceeded to wear on his lapel a 'D7' sign. He wore it throughout the courthouse so that everyone who saw it, whether they be a juror or witness or judge, would know that he stood behind these men who had been indicted by a grand jury in his county for gross misconduct, perjury, obstruction of justice, conspiracy to kill, basically, Rolando Cruz. Wore it inside the courtroom during the trial, so that jurors who had elected him as their state's attorney would see he was not sitting with the prosecutors but with the defense. I can think of no more unethical behavior on the part of a prosecutor."

Birkett later told reporters that he had indeed secured the Schmitt statement but that he did not threaten Schmitt. Regarding Madigan's other allegations, he told *Chicago Sun-Times* reporter Abdon M. Pallasch, "There were obviously mistakes [but] I don't believe anyone acted unethically or improperly. I support the decisions that were made in our office because I was part of that office."

In November 2002, both Jim Ryan and Joe Birkett lost their races as part of a near-Democratic sweep of state offices that followed a driver's-licenses-for-bribes and corruption scandal under Governor George Ryan's Republican administration.

At a November 15, 2002, clemency hearing before the Prisoner Review Board at the Illinois Capitol, James Sotos, the lawyer who defended DuPage County in the civil lawsuits by Cruz and the other original defendants, told the panel that although authorities were taking no official stand on the clemency request, they should realize that Cruz was "conning them." Thomas and Patricia Nicarico, who were introduced to the panel by former prosecutor Tom Knight, said they still believed Cruz was guilty. They repeated their assertion that Cruz was involved in their daughter's murder. Cruz declined to address the board.

The Nicaricos still were bitter about the outcome of the case.

"Twenty years later, we're worse [off] than we were to begin with," Thomas Nicarico later told the *Daily Herald*.

On December 19, however, Governor George Ryan pardoned Cruz, along with Gary Gauger and Steven Linscott, whose twice-reversed conviction for the 1980 murder of an Oak Park nursing student was based on a dream Linscott said he'd had. Charges against him were dropped in 1992 after a DNA test showed no link to the murder.

"I always wanted to . . . have this expunged from the record because I didn't do anything," Cruz told an interviewer on WGN-TV, a Chicago television station.

Cruz's pardon, however, didn't clear the original three Nicarico defendants of all problems with the law. Stephen Buckley was convicted in 2001 of cocaine possession and sentenced to eight years in prison, with a scheduled parole date in September 2004. Alejandro Hernandez was ordered in August 2000 to pay $300 in fines on charges of drunken driving and speeding, and he was unable to apply for clemency at the time Cruz did because he had an outstanding warrant against him. Cruz also had new legal troubles: although charges were dropped against him for his part in a 1997 bar disturbance in west suburban Berwyn, he pleaded guilty in March 2004, to drunken driving in Livingston County in central Illinois. On August 23, 2004, he was sentenced to sixty days in jail for that offense, to run concurrently with a forty-day sentence in Cook County for driving with a suspended license.

Nor did Cruz's pardon erase the career setbacks of those who had worked to bring out what they considered the truth in the case.

John Sam, who was forty-six years old by the time Cruz was acquitted, had spent the previous ten years as the sales manager of a heating systems company. He had tried to get back into police work, but no one would hire him. To reporters, he had said of Cruz's acquittal, "It's about time."

Ed Cisowski, after being removed from his duties as commander of the State Police Zone 2 investigative division, had retired early from his police career and had taken a job as head of security for a riverboat casino. He'd put ten years of effort into trying to clear his name after being accused of bungling the investigation and feeding information to Brian Dugan. Cruz's dramatic acquittal had been vindication.

Mary Brigid Kenney never got her chance to argue cases in front of the Illinois Supreme Court or U.S. Court of Appeals. Instead, she went into private practice, representing drunken driving defendants and motorists contesting traffic tickets. One of her clients paid her with a bicycle. Later, she got a job working for the Cook County public guardian's office in Chicago.

Rob Warden found the *Chicago Lawyer*'s focus on innocent people on death row and prosecutorial misconduct attracted few advertisers. He was unable to keep publishing the investigative monthly, which had printed several articles and editorials about the Nicarico case, and in 1989 he sold it to the publishing company that prints the *Chicago Daily Law Bulletin*. Later, he became executive director of Northwestern University School of Law's Center on Wrongful Convictions.

Frank Wesolowski, criticized for being too strong an advocate for Hernandez and Cruz, was fired from his job as chief of the DuPage County public defender's office. Public defender Carol

Anfinson, who had faced contempt of court on behalf of Stephen Buckley and received two death threats, had her title as chief of the public defender's felony division taken away. She left the office, but could not get a job with any DuPage law firm, so she opened her own practice. At an annual irreverent amateur theatrical production, the DuPage Bar Association put on a skit with other lawyers playing Anfinson and Gary Johnson dancing in handcuffs.

Tom Laz, Cruz's lawyer at the 1985 trial, thought the case affected him when he applied for a judgeship in 2000. In rating Laz "not presently qualified," members of the DuPage Bar Association's judiciary committee cited a legal article he'd written criticizing the treatment Cruz had received compared with the treatment of the DuPage Seven. A "not presently qualified" rating virtually disqualifies a candidate from consideration. Before writing the article, Laz had received "highly recommended" and "recommended" ratings.

Judge Ronald Mehling was stripped of his post as chief of the court's felony division after his forthright ruling on the Cruz case. Later, Mehling said he was told the decision was made because the new chief judge needed to get along with the DuPage County Board and the sheriff's department. One top county official even kept in his office a dartboard with Mehling's picture on it. After the news media stirred up a furor, Mehling's title was restored for six months. He retired in July 2002.

When William J. Kunkle Jr., who led the DuPage Seven prosecution, ran in a primary election in 2004 for a judge's seat, DuPage County state's attorney Joseph Birkett and DuPage County Board chairman Robert Schillerstrom held a fund-raiser for Kunkle's opponent even though the race was in Cook County.

Naperville Police Chief Jim Teal, whose conclusions about

the case angered some local political leaders, grew tired of the friction his efforts had brought him and retired early, opening a small consulting business. He also noticed how the case had negatively affected others who had worked on behalf of Buckley, Cruz, and Hernandez.

"It's almost as if there was a demon spirit that came out of this case and affected all of us," Teal said.

Meanwhile, many of those who took part in the investigation and prosecutions of Buckley, Cruz, and Hernandez found their career paths were going in the opposite direction—up.

Jim Ryan was elected Illinois attorney general in 1994. In 1996, the National Conference of Christians and Jews awarded him the organization's "Defender of Justice" award. A 1997 survey showed his job-approval rating stood at a hefty 69 percent. He won reelection in 1998 and was the state GOP's candidate for governor in 2002, the race he lost to Democrat Rod Blagojevich.

Richard Stock, who helped prosecute Cruz's second trial and Hernandez's second and third trials, was named deputy Illinois attorney general, Ryan's top aide. On November 29, 1993, Judge Kowal was elected chief judge of the DuPage Circuit Court by the county's thirteen circuit judges. Robert Kilander, who had been appointed a DuPage County judge in 1991, was named chief judge after Kowal retired.

Sheriff Doria won five consecutive elections as sheriff, and in 1997, when he was ready to retire at age seventy, he was appointed to a $59,556-a-year part-time position on the Illinois Prisoner Review Board.

Tom Knight took a job with the U.S. Justice Department's Strike Force after the 1985 trial, although Knight later left the office and went into private practice. Patrick King, who assisted Knight in that trial and later aided Robert Kilander in proceedings on Buckley, got a job first with the Securities and Exchange Commission's enforcement branch in 1987 and then as an assistant U.S. attorney in the Chicago office in March 1989, a job he still holds.

Terence Madsen, who took over the Illinois attorney general's effort to uphold Cruz's conviction after Mary Brigid Kenney resigned, became a judge. Barbara Preiner, who sought to have Alex Hernandez's second conviction upheld, became Illinois's solicitor general.

John Kinsella, who led the prosecution at Cruz's third trial, became a DuPage County judge in 2003.

Justice James D. Heiple, who wrote the opinion upholding Cruz's second conviction, went on to become chief justice of the Illinois Supreme Court in 1997. Later, he relinquished that post amid charges of abusing his position in traffic incidents.

Mary Ann G. McMorrow, the Illinois Supreme Court justice who voted to uphold Cruz's second death penalty conviction, was named the court's chief justice in 2001.

Earlier, as part of the continuing Dugan investigation, DuPage County investigator David Hamm had gone to Florida to meet with Randy Garrett, who had moved there in 1996. The two men met in a conference room at the Holiday Inn in Titusville.

Hamm chatted about the investigation and asked Garrett why anyone should believe that Brian Dugan alone committed the Nicarico murder. Garrett made a list that, when he looked it over, seemed very persuasive. Every eyewitness saw just one person in a car. Aside from the unidentified hair in the blindfold, which might have had nothing to do with the crime, there was no evidence of multiple perpetrators. John Sam had always said it was the type of crime that is committed by one person. In all of Brian Dugan's other known sex crimes, he acted alone. Dugan said he acted alone, and he passed a polygraph test. The DNA test results matched Dugan; there was no sign of anyone else. No one ever had found a clear, credible connection between Dugan and the original defendants, even after years of trying (although Hamm had names of new witnesses who had come forward to claim they could connect them). All the physical evidence—the tire tracks on the Prairie Path, the size of the shoeprint on the Nicaricos' door, the color and body style of the car seen on the Prairie Path—matched Dugan's story but had no link to anyone else. Eloise Suk had seen Dugan by himself in Naperville on the day of the crime. Of all the people Garrett had talked to, none had linked Dugan to any of the original defendants. Perhaps most telling, when Cruz and Hernandez were naming other people, they never mentioned Dugan, not even to save themselves from execution. When Dugan wanted a plea deal—a deal he probably could have received by naming Buckley, Cruz, and Hernandez— he never did.

Garrett told Hamm that if authorities had had Dugan's name at the beginning of the investigation and all the Dugan evidence that later emerged, they would have focused on him alone. No one ever would have heard of the other defendants.

Then, on January 11, 2003, in a dramatic move that made headlines around the world, Governor Ryan commuted the death sentences of all 163 men and four women on death row to life in prison. A day earlier, he had given pardons to four other men on death row who had confessed to crimes after alleged police torture: Madison Hobley, Stanley Howard, Leroy Orange, and Aaron

Paterson. Their releases brought to seventeen the total number of men who had been freed from death row.

"Like it or not, the decision I make about our criminal justice system is felt not only here, but the world over," Ryan told students and anti–death penalty activists at Northwestern University School of Law, where he made the announcement.

Nancy Bothne, Midwest regional director for Amnesty International, told the *Chicago Sun-Times,* "This will be a defining moment in the abolition of the death penalty in the United States."

In September 2003, Rolando Cruz dropped in with some family members to visit John Hanlon in Springfield. Just two days before, Hanlon had returned from visiting another client at the Menard prison, where Cruz had been on death row. The old death unit, which sat atop a bluff overlooking the Mississippi River apart from the rest of the prison, had just been razed. Watching Cruz interact with his children, Hanlon was struck by the notion that the man who once had been condemned by the State of Illinois had outlived the seemingly impregnable structure where he had spent so many gloomy days. Hanlon described the tearing down of the old death row, and Cruz said he wished he had been there to see it.

"It really struck me as having some cosmic meaning," Hanlon said later. "It was a kind of satisfying feeling to see that he had outlived that unit."

On November 19, 2003, the Illinois House of Representatives voted, 115 to 0, in the final legal step to enact death penalty reforms that included giving the Illinois Supreme Court more power to toss out unjust verdicts, granting defendants more access to evidence, and allowing judges to rule out the death penalty in cases based on the testimony of a single witness. On January 20, 2004, Illinois's new governor, Rod Blagojevich, signed the remaining part of the death penalty package into law.

For the defense lawyers who had poured so many years and so much money into the Nicarico case and for the journalists who covered it, there were many lessons to be learned about the prosecution complex.

"Police officers often feel by instinct that they have the right person," said Cruz defense lawyer Matt Kennelly, who later became a federal judge. "They've got the guy. But they are not quite sure they have enough evidence. They don't trust judges. A lot of them don't even trust prosecutors. So they always want to make sure they have got enough evidence.

"They also express frustration about all these rules about what they can ask people, what they have to say to them. In most cases, we're not talking about people cooking up cases. We are talking about just nudging the evidence a little bit. Pushing it. They know the judges or juries are not going to believe this mope up on the witness stand—he's got three prior convictions. They're going to believe the guy in the uniform.

"There's sort of a basic distrust, I think, of the legal system. And you know, it's like a kid who shoplifts. Once you do it a few times, it becomes easy. It becomes second nature. You don't think about it as something wrong."

Cruz defense lawyer Jed Stone also said the abuses he saw in the Nicarico case were part of a larger pattern.

"Police perjury goes on every day in every criminal court-house in the United States," he said. "Every day. Prosecutors know it, and judges know it, and they either participate in it or turn a blind eye and deaf ear to it.

"And partly it's because we've ended up in a jihad [holy war] mentality, where it's the good guys against the bad guys, and in a jihad, anything is okay. So it's okay to tell a white lie if a bad guy goes to prison. It's okay to pretend that there was probable cause, if a bad guy is going to get caught."

That jihad mentality is especially likely to kick in when a case acquires must-win status, just as the Jeanine Nicarico murder case did, Cruz defense lawyer Tom Breen said. "You don't have to go to the police and say, 'Okay, I am going to need an oral statement, you guys. You, Mr. Prosecutor, I need you to try the three guys together. Judge, I need you to overrule the defense objections to this and that.'

"You don't need that kind of direction. It just happens. Everybody knew it was a must-win case. We prosecutors used to call these the governor's mansion cases. If you win a case like this, the voters will send you to the governor's mansion."

Chicago Tribune columnist Eric Zorn thought Cruz and Hernandez were freed partly because of the close attention that those in the news media finally paid to the case.

"I think what we did, all of us, was we created a climate within the courthouse in DuPage County and within the Illinois attorney general's office and perhaps even in the Supreme Court of Illinois in which it was thinkable for the justices or judges to take a look at this case in a really rational way," Zorn said later. "The justices and judges could feel they could make the decision that they believed was justified solely by the facts because they knew that the public would accept it, that there would not be a riot."

Hernandez defense lawyer Michael Metnick thought the case illustrated how important it is for citizens to monitor their criminal justice system.

"The government has the potential to do bad, and by that I am not saying that it does bad," Metnick said. "It has the potential to do bad. I believe that the citizenry has to be vigilant in making certain that the government does not abuse its power."

Part of that vigilance means requiring more of prosecutors than that they be aggressive, said Ronald Sadowski, a former DuPage County prosecutor whom lawyer-author Scott Turow recruited for Hernandez's defense team after the appellate court granted a new trial. Too often, prosecutors can do anything they want without fear of public criticism. In fact, Sadowski said, the only time they are criticized is when they take an action that is seen as too lenient.

"When I was hired as a prosecutor, I was told that I was the last line of justice for a defendant," Sadowski said. "If you're asking for the death penalty, you'd better believe the guy deserves it."

That last line of justice failed Rolando Cruz, defense lawyer Larry Marshall said.

"The idea that Cruz's conviction could have been affirmed was a major wake-up call to me," Marshall said. "People want to say this case proves that [the system] works. If it hadn't been for the fortuity of an election, Cruz would probably be close to dead right now."

To public defender John Hanlon, the lesson was that too often authorities "twist this and prop up that" to strengthen a case against someone they believe to be guilty.

"They think they are doing a greater good," Hanlon said. "Too many law enforcement people, when there is a horrible case and a horrible crime, have the attitude: Let's do what we can. I think that's the real conspiracy."

Breen said his experiences defending Rolando Cruz taught him that authorities cross the line too often, creating too many victims of justice.

"I am still not a cause lawyer, but I am awful close to it, because this really opened up my eyes to a lot of things," Breen said. "There is in our justice system a real evil streak. It probably always has been there and probably always will be there. That narrow streak has got to be watched and pointed to when you see it."

CHRONOLOGY

1982

AUGUST 13: Brian Dugan is paroled from prison.

AUGUST 23: Brian Dugan attacks a young woman who is a service station employee. She struggles and escapes.

1983

FEBRUARY 25: Ten-year-old Jeanine Nicarico is kidnapped from her Naperville, Illinois, home. Her body will be found two days later.

MARCH 14: An anonymous tipster tells authorities Alejandro "Alex" Hernandez (age twenty) "has information about the murder of Jeanine Nicarico." When detectives interview him, Hernandez will tell them a story about a young man named "Ricky" who says he killed the girl because she wouldn't stop screaming.

MAY 9: Rolando Cruz, age twenty, is interviewed by DuPage County detectives. Later, they will say he told of a "vision" that included details about the crime he shouldn't have known.

MAY 12: Prosecutor Tom Knight starts calling witnesses to testify before a special grand jury investigating the crime.

1984

JANUARY 26: DuPage County state's attorney J. Michael Fitzsimmons issues a public plea for information about the Nicarico murder.

MARCH 8: Three Aurora men—Cruz, Alejandro Hernandez, and Stephen Buckley (age twenty-one)—are charged with the Nicarico murder.

MARCH 20: Fitzsimmons is defeated for renomination, losing to Jim Ryan.

MAY 2: Brian Dugan, age twenty-eight, is arrested on burglary charges in Addison, Illinois, and jailed.

MAY 24: Dugan is released from jail.

JULY 15: Donna Schnorr of Geneva is raped and murdered.

DECEMBER 1: DuPage County sheriff's detective John Sam resigns.

DECEMBER 20: A Christmas party is held at which DuPage County sheriff's detective Thomas Vosburgh later testifies he told prosecutor Patrick King about what is later called the "vision" statement.

1985

JANUARY 3: Defense lawyers get a pretrial supplemental disclosure that for the first time indicates the existence of the "vision" statement.

FEBRUARY 22: Hernandez and Cruz are convicted of the Nicarico slaying. Three weeks later, they'll be sentenced to death. The jury deadlocks on Buckley.

MAY 6: Dugan abducts, rapes, and releases a twenty-one-year-old woman in North Aurora.

MAY 28: Dugan attempts to abduct a nineteen-year-old woman in Geneva, but she escapes. She sees his license plate number as he is driving away and immediately reports the incident to the Geneva Police Department, but authorities do not follow up on it until later.

MAY 29: Dugan abducts, rapes, and releases a sixteen-year-old woman in Aurora. He tells her his name, of which the victim can remember only the first name and last initial. The victim is too frightened to report the incident to police until later.

JUNE 2: Seven-year-old Melissa Ackerman of Somonauk is raped and murdered. Dugan will be arrested and charged with the killing later in the month.

NOVEMBER 8: Dugan's lawyer says his client claims he is Jeanine Nicarico's lone killer.

NOVEMBER 13: Via hypothetical statements, Dugan provides DuPage County prosecutors Robert Kilander and Patrick King with fifty-one facts about the Nicarico murder.

NOVEMBER 19: As part of a plea agreement, Dugan is sentenced to life in prison for the rapes and murders of Melissa Ackerman and Donna Schnorr.

DECEMBER 2: A lie detector supports Dugan's account of the Nicarico death.

DECEMBER 19: Dugan demands immunity from a death sentence in exchange for a formal confession to Jeanine Nicarico's murder.

1986

MAY 5: The Illinois Supreme Court upholds a gag order imposed on the Buckley retrial by DuPage County Circuit Judge Robert A. Nolan.

SEPTEMBER 5: Judge Nolan calls Dugan's story "totally unreliable" and bans it from the pending Buckley retrial.

1987

FEBRUARY 22: A panel of forensic scientists concludes that the shoeprint identification method used by physical anthropologist Louise Robbins in the 1985 trial was unsound. Robbins had used the method to link Buckley to a shoeprint on the Nicaricos' front door, which had been kicked in.

MARCH 5: The charges against Buckley are dropped.

APRIL 13: Jeanine Nicarico's parents say that Dugan's story about killing their daughter was riddled with inconsistencies never made public.

JULY 30: Dugan is stabbed nine times by a fellow inmate at the Pontiac Correction Center.

SEPTEMBER 4: Taking the stand, Dugan refuses for the second

time to testify without immunity about his claims that he murdered Jeanine Nicarico.

DECEMBER 8: Jackie Estremera, age nineteen, says he concocted an account that linked Hernandez to the Nicarico killing because of threats from a sheriff's investigator.

1988

JANUARY 19: The Illinois Supreme Court overturns the Hernandez and Cruz convictions.

OCTOBER 3: The U.S. Supreme Court refuses to hear an appeal by the state of Illinois on the conviction reversal. The DuPage County state's attorney's office decides to retry Cruz and Hernandez.

1989

APRIL 17: At a pretrial hearing for Cruz, lawyers for both sides agree to get blood samples from Dugan, Buckley, Cruz, and Hernandez to see if any of their DNA matches the semen sample from Jeanine Nicarico. Tests subsequently performed using limited DNA technology of the time rule out Buckley and Hernandez but allow both Cruz and Dugan as possible matches.

1990

FEBRUARY 1: Cruz is convicted a second time and later will once again be sentenced to death.

MAY 11: The second trial charging Hernandez with the murder ends in a hung jury.

1991

MAY 16: Hernandez is convicted at his third trial. This time he will be sentenced to eighty years in prison.

1992

MARCH 6: Illinois assistant attorney general Mary Brigid Kenney, who was assigned to defend Cruz's conviction, resigns.

Kenney says she doesn't want to help execute an innocent man.

DECEMBER 4: The Illinois Supreme Court upholds Cruz's second conviction.

1993

MAY 28: The Illinois Supreme Court agrees to reconsider its decision to uphold Cruz's second conviction.

1994

JULY 14: The Illinois Supreme Court overturns Cruz's second conviction and orders a new trial.

1995

JANUARY 30: The Illinois Appellate Court overturns Hernandez's second conviction and orders a new trial, which would be his fourth.

SEPTEMBER 21: DNA results exclude Cruz as the source of semen found in Jeanine's body and implicate Dugan in her rape.

OCTOBER 24: Cruz's third trial for the Nicarico murder begins.

NOVEMBER 3: DuPage County circuit judge Ronald Mehling acquits Cruz.

DECEMBER 8: Prosecutors drop all charges and DuPage County circuit judge Thomas Callum dismisses the case against Hernandez.

1996

DECEMBER 12: Prosecutor William J. Kunkle Jr. announces the indictments of the DuPage Seven, seven law officers and lawyers accused of conspiring to deny Cruz a fair trial.

1997

JANUARY 17: The Illinois Supreme Court appoints Judge William Kelly to preside over the DuPage Seven case.

1998

APRIL 28: The DuPage County Board votes to pay legal expenses for the DuPage Seven.

1999

APRIL 6: Opening statements begin in the DuPage Seven trial.

MAY 13: Judge Kelly acquits two of the DuPage Seven defendants.

JUNE 4: Judge Kelly and the jury acquit the remaining five DuPage Seven defendants.

2000

JANUARY 31: Illinois governor George Ryan declares a moratorium on executions.

SEPTEMBER 26: DuPage County state's attorney Joseph Birkett agrees to settle wrongful conviction lawsuits filed by Buckley, Cruz, and Hernandez for $3.5 million.

2002

APRIL 15: Commission on Capital Punishment recommends eighty-five reforms designed to reduce injustices in the death penalty.

NOVEMBER 15: DuPage authorities disclose a new, even more accurate DNA test has again matched Brian Dugan to the rape and murder of Jeanine Nicarico.

DECEMBER 19: Governor George Ryan pardons Cruz.

2003

JANUARY 11: Governor George Ryan commutes the death sentences of all 163 men and four women on death row to life in prison, a day after he pardons four other men on death row who had confessed to crimes after alleged police torture.

NOVEMBER 19: The Illinois House of Representatives votes, 115 to 0, in the final legal step to enact a package of death penalty reforms.

2004

MAY 28: Gordon Randall "Randy" Steidl is the eighteenth man freed from death row since Illinois reinstated the death penalty in 1977. Accused of taking part in the murders of Dyke and Karen Rhoads of Paris, Illinois, Steidl spent seventeen years in prison, twelve of them on death row.

INDEX